The Gospel of Power

Egoist Essays
by
Dora Marsden

Trevor Blake, editor

Union of Egoists
Columbus / Baltimore 2021

The Gospel of Power: Egoist Essays by Dora Marsden
by Dora Marsden
Edited by Trevor Blake
Introduction, Index, Glossary, original elements
Copyright © 2021 Trevor Blake. All rights reserved.

This original work includes elements in the public domain in the United States, including *The Egoist* (Dora Marsden, editor). The symbol "≠" indicates a footnote original to *The Gospel of Power*.

Cover Design by Kevin I. Slaughter.
Proofreading by Teresa Bergen.

First Impression: 2021
Stand Alone SA1185
Union of Egoists, Columbus IN / Baltimore MD

Marsden, Dora
[English]
The Gospel of Power: Egoist Essays by Dora Marsden
ISBN 978-1-944651-20-6
1. Philosophy
2. Women's Studies
Dora Marsden (1882 - 1960); Trevor Blake (b. 1966)

The Union of Egoists publishes original research and rare reprints concerning the philosophy of egoism as published between the years 1845 and 1945. For more information, see...

UnionOfEgoists.com

127 House: At every turn in its thought society will find us waiting.

Contents

4

Advertisement for *The Ego and His Own* by Max Stirner.
The Egoist Volume I Number 1 (January 1st, 1914).

Introduction

Salvation is amusing to saviours, and we would
not remonstrate with them, having no desire to
spoil fun: and few things provide as much sport
as a good cause! We merely endeavour to give
the tip to the quarry: to the people who are
in danger of being saved, and it is "DON'T."
Refuse to be dealt with! It is a matter we
cannot enlarge upon here, but it is the gist of
the gospel of power to those who would be free
men.

Dora Marsden
The Egoist
Vol. I No. 16

I. The World of Dora Marsden

DORA Marsden's life was a series of bursting free from the chains that confined her. The first was the confine of being born in Marsden Village in 1882, growing up with the small town opportunities it afforded. As soon as she was able she left Marsden for Manchester.

Only eighteen years old, she began teaching in Manchester at Owen's College in 1900. From that position she became a headmistress. While in the bohemian Manchester Colony she met suffragette Christabel Pankhurst and joined the Women's Social and Political Union (WSPU). By 1908 she was among their leaders. The confines of a career were the second chain she burst, and in 1909 she became a full-time suffragette.

Dora marched for the vote and disrupted political meetings, including a speech by a Winston Churchill. She was arrested and imprisoned for street fighting several times. Questioned at her trial, she said she would not adhere to the the policy of the WSPU of committing violence only against property and never against persons. She insisted on being tried as a prisoner of war. When she was sent to jail she refused to wear prison garb and served her sentence nude. She also broke out the windows of her jail cell with her fists.

When Dora was first to the fight the WSPU benefited from her militancy and unwillingness to compromise. But when Dora turned that wrath to the WSPU and accused them of half-measures in militancy, she was as withering to them as she had been to their mutual critics and they suffered for it. To neutralize Dora as a street-fighter (and in-fighter) in London, the WSPU 'promoted' her to a desk job in Southport. Dora Marsden joined the suffrage movement because it advocated militancy to free each individual woman. When Dora learned the WSPU advocated militancy but played politics, the WSPU became the third confining chain that Dora burst free from. Dora removed herself from what she called the "skirt movement" and returned to London.

In 1911 Dora Marsden began an inquiry into the nature of individual freedom that consumed the rest of her life. Dora founded a journal called *The Freewoman* (1911 – 1912). Dora considered the term "feminist" to have been compromised by reduction to mere suffrage. Freewomen was her term for women who would use their individual freedoms to expand their individual freedoms. These individual freedoms were not based on chimeras such as rights, but on demonstrable abilities such as power and ownership. Dora demanded all of her printer, and her printed responded with his power to refuse her business. The periodical was re-launched as *The New Freewoman* (1914) and (after similar difficulties with a second printer) re-launched again as *The Egoist* (1914 – 1919).

Her journals were the first to publish significant work by James Joyce, Ezra Pound, H. D., Margaret Storm Jameson and T. S. Eliot. Freewomen Discussion Circles were founded in London, the first public and documented gatherings of individualists in history. Essays on suffrage and current events are found in the early issues of her journals, but over time philosophy and literature predominated. Her journals were a success in generating more words, but not more deeds or more individual freedom. In the first issue of *The Freewoman*, Dora wrote: "She has pinioned herself with words–words–words, and these, not her own[1]." The responsibilities of editing and budgeting her own journals were the fourth chain that Dora burst asunder. The leadership of The Egoist Press was passed to Harriet Weaver Shaw. The essays gathered here as *The*

---

[1] *The Freewoman*, Vol. 1 No 1 (June 15th 1913).

Gospel of Power were first published in *The Egoist* in 1914, when Dora's writing had turned entirely to philosophy.

The Egoist published essays by Dora Marsden for the remainder of its existence. The audience for Dora's work diminished, due to the difficulty of Dora's inquiries combined with her continually combative character. Life in London and writing to a schedule were Dora's fifth confining chain, another to be burst asunder. In 1919 Dora Marsden, her mother Hannah and her cat Sara moved to an abandoned mining town named Seldom Seen, where she could write books on her own schedule.

She wrote two books, *The Definition of the Godhead* (1928) and *The Mysteries of Christianity* (1930). Both were published by The Egoist Press. Her books were not well received as measured in sales or in reviews. Her mother died. Her cat died. Dora, her isolation now infinite, committed herself completely to individualist inquiries into the chains that bind us all: the nature of time, space and language.

The few friends and family she had not yet alienated grew concerned about Dora's health. In 1935 Dora Marsden was committed to Crichton Royal Hospital in Dumfries. While in Dumfries she knitted, re-read her own books, continued writing, and produced her final book *The Philosophy of Time* (1955). She broke free from all confining chains in 1960.

The Jerusalem that is above is the freewoman;
she is the mother of us all.

Galatians 4:26
Quoted in *The Ego and His Own*
by Max Stirner

TO THE GREAT NAME HIDDEN AMONG
US FOR SO LONG OF HER, HEAVEN, THE
MIGHTY MOTHER OF ALL.

Dedication, *The Definition of the Godhead*
by Dora Marsden

II. Dora Marsden Vs. The World

In the early Twenty-First Century, nearly every nation
on Earth has women suffrage. Many know there were times
and places where there was no women suffrage, but not as
many know the arguments–defeated and discredited–against
women suffrage. The argument against women suffrage as
presented by one outside the movement can be found in *The
Unexpurgated Case Against Woman Suffrage* by Sir Almroth E.
Wright[1]. The argument against women suffrage as presented
by one outside the movement can be found in *The Militant
Suffrage Movement: Emancipation in a Hurry* by Teresa
Billington-Grieg[2]. The later author, as with Dora Marsden,
was a woman who was not mute when she saw women betrayed
by the women's movement. In the essays published here as
The Gospel of Power, Dora Marsden advances three arguments
against women's suffrage.

In *The Egoist* Vol. I No. 3 (February 2nd, 1914), Dora
mocked the idea of prophylactic suffrage. "The entreaty

---

[1] London: Constable and Company Ltd., 1913.
[2] London: Frank Palmer, [1911].

of the cry 'Virginity for men' coming from so favoured a class as those of the 'pure' women has a comical sound, and Miss Pankhurst's disease-story is overdone[1]." Christabel Pankhurst, the woman who recruited Dora Marsden to the suffrage movement, claimed in her book *The Great Scourge and How to End It* that women needed the vote to enforce male chastity:

> The sexual diseases are the great cause of physical, mental, and moral degeneracy, and of race suicide. As they are very widespread (from 75 to 80 per cent of men being infected by gonorrhoea, and a considerable percentage, difficult to ascertain precisely, being infected with syphilis), the problem is one of appalling magnitude.
>
> To discuss an evil, and then to run away from it without suggesting how it may be cured, is not the way of Suffragettes, and in the following pages will be found a proposed cure for the great evil in question. That cure, briefly stated, is Votes for Women and Chastity for Men[2].

Dora opposed women suffrage because it was ridiculous. The reader may distinguish whether votes for women has engendered chastity for men, or whether Dora's derision of this argument for women's suffrage is more enduring.

In *The Egoist* Vol. I No. 12 (June 15th, 1914), Dora wrote of the First Mother and First Daughter of the suffragettes using a centuries-old slur: "Mrs. Pankhurst was and is a politician. All her interests are political as are Miss Pankhurst's[3]."

---

[1] p. 69.
[2] London: E. Pankhurst, 1913, pp. vi-vii.
[3] p. 159.

How long has it been since "politician" was anything other than an insult, the author does not know.

The Women's Suffrage Political Union was a political party. Membership in the WSPU was exclusive, in that a member could not be a member of any other political party. The WSPU initially had a constitution and its members could vote for their own policies and leaders. After suffrage within the WSPU was established, Emmeline and Christebel Pankhurst held a meeting that was unscheduled, closed and not documented. After this meeting they announced the WSPU constitution was no longer in effect, that Emmeline and Christebel Pankhurst were the perpetual leaders of the WSPU, and that members did not have a vote. As Emmeline Pankhurst wrote in her autobiography:

> [If] at any time a member, or a group of members, loses faith in our policy; if any one begins to suggest, that some other policy ought to be substituted, or if she tries to confuse the issue by adding other policies, she ceases at once to be a member. Autocratic? Quite so. But, you may object, a suffrage organisation ought to be democratic. Well the members of the WSPU do not agree with you[1].

And as Christabel Pankhurst told one member at her expulsion hearing: "You have a democratic constitution for your federation, we do not want that."

Supporters and critics of women suffrage differentiated adult suffrage and equal suffrage. Under adult suffrage, every adult may vote. Under equal suffrage, only the minority of women who met the same criteria as the minority of men men

---

[1]Pankhurst, Emmeline: *Suffragette: My Own Story* (London: Eveleigh Nash, 1914).

who could vote may vote. The WSPU favored equal suffrage and opposed adult suffrage, listing the criteria without which women must not be given the vote:

> The Women's Suffrage and Political Union are NOT asking for a vote for every woman, but simply that sex shall cease to be a disqualification for the franchise. At present men who pay rates and taxes, who are owners, occupiers, lodgers or have the service or university franchise possess the Parliamentary vote. The Women's Suffrage and Political Union claim that women who fulfil the same conditions shall also enjoy the franchise[1].

Women who pay rates and taxes, who are owners, occupiers, lodgers or have the service or university franchise—an accurate description of Emmeline and Christebel Pankhurst, less so of most women in England. The Labour Party and the WSPU worked together as friendly parties until 1907, when the Labour Party announced their support for adult suffrage. In opposition to giving women the vote, preserving its advocacy of only giving some women the vote, the WSPU broke ties with the Labour Party. The politician is for suffrage until he or she is against it.

The WSPU held that equal woman suffrage was a necessary step toward the end of war. In a circular letter dated August 13, 1914, Emmeline Pankhurst wrote: "We believe that under the joint rule of enfranchised women and men the nations of the world will, owing to women's influence and authority, find a way of reconciling the claims of peace and honour and of regulating international relations without bloodshed."

---

[1] *Votes for Women*, Vol. II No. 77 (August 27, 1909, p. 1108).

In this same circular letter, she wrote that the WSPU was suspending all suffrage activities until "the right time comes." The resources of the WSPU would instead be devoted to the support of Great Britain in what would be come to be called World War I, the war to end all wars. By January 1915 the WSPU newspaper carried the subtitle "The War Paper for Women." After the announcement of the suspension of all suffrage activities, a general amnesty to suffragette militants was granted by the government. In June Emmeline Pankhurst offered women's war services at a speech in London that was reported in the *Times*. His Highness King George V directed Minister of Munitions Lloyd George to take Pankhurst up on her offer. George met with Pankhurst and offered her a stipend of £4,000.00 a year, without any oversight. For the remainder of her life, Emmeline Pankhurst never again found the time "right" to advocate for women's suffrage. The politician is against war until he or she is for it.

In 1927, Emmeline Pankhurst openly become the politician Dora Marsden claimed she was thirteen years earlier. Members of the Conservative Party withdrew their candidacy so that Emmeline Pankhurst could run for office as their representative. She was not the only former suffragette to find political expression after the WSPU dissolved in 1917. Other leading suffragettes continued their activism, nearly never on the left and nearly always on the right. Former suffragettes became members of the Conservative Party, worked as strike breakers or stood with Sir Oswald Mosley as part of the British Union of Fascists. In spiritual matters, the suffragettes turned not to atheism or paganism but the Roman Catholic Church, Rosicrucianism and Theosophy. Among the few suffragettes who opposed the war and favored the political left was Sylvia Pankhurst, Emmeline's daughter and

Christabel's sister. It was Sylvia Pankhurst who was expelled from the WSPU–expelled on her own mother's orders, orders carried out by her own sister–for wanting votes for women within the WSPU.

The reader should know that not every accusation, such as "politician," is made true by being an insult. Turn away from words of the wspu and consider their deeds. The WSPU spoke of Votes for Women. Their actions were for votes for *some* women, those fitting the description of the leaders of the WSPU and no others. The vote was the greatest issue of the age, until war came and it was not. No amount of money would substitute for the vote, but quiet payments to leading suffragettes led to a swift silence in suffragette activities. Most women were not given the vote, and most women were decidedly not paid to become inactive activists. Adult suffrage came to the United Kingdom in 1973, nearly sixty years after Dora Marsden accused the Pankhursts of playing politics. There remains no women's suffrage to elect British Royalty nor the House of Lords. There is no women's suffrage for some women who have served time in prison, nor for some women who have been out of the United Kingdom past a certain period of time, nor for some women in the National Heath Service system.

Dora opposed women suffrage because it was a ruse. The reader may consider whether "votes for women" or political power for the Pankhursts was the function of the WSPU.

In *The Egoist* Vol. I No. 7 (April 1st, 1914), Dora wrote in favor of war. "There is much to be said in favour of a gala performance of Civil War[1]." This was not a statement in favor of the looming war of England against Germany, although she did favor that war. This was a statement in favor of *war*. War

---

[1]p. 119.

between nations, war within nations, war of women against men, war of the individual against the universe.

In the early Twenty-First Century, British suffragettes are considered to come in two varieties. Some suffragettes are thought of as those who conducted lectures, wrote essays and perhaps carried signs in marches, while others, the "militants," did the same thing while shouting. Dora Marsden had a different understanding of militancy.

Dora Marsden, Teresa Billington-Grieg and other women were accomodating, even enthusiastic, about the undemocractic structure of the WSPU. An autocracy is the most appropriate structure for what Emmeline Pankhurst called a "standing army." A standing army marches lockstep not for the sake of the march: it marches to war. When Dora wrote: "If Englishwomen elected to, there exists nothing in themselves to prevent them from being as good a fighting force as the Japanese, for instance: and that would do to be getting along with[1]," her contemporary readers would have understood this as a reference to Japan's defeat of the Russian Empire ten years earlier. Japan had fewer soldiers, less and more primitive armaments, a weaker industrial infrastructure and every other disadvantage. And yet Japan sent the Russian bear home, howling. Dora did not write about carrying a banner and raising her voice. Dora wrote about armed women killing as many human beings as necessary to get what they want. This is what the suffragettes meant by "militancy." Militants like Dora Marsden and Teresa Billington-Grieg learned that the Pankrhursts were not militants, that they were instead politicians, and ties were severed accordingly. The WSPU only played soldier.

Militant suffragettes were not at play. On July 18th 1912,

---

[1] *The Egoist* Vol. I No. 19 (October 1st, 1914).

militant suffragette Mary Leigh spread petrol and set off a bomb in a theater crowded with women and men. On January 29th 1913, a letter bomb sent by militant suffragettes detonated in the sorting office, wounding the postal clerks. The letter was addressed to Lloyd George, who later gave Emmily Pankhurst a stipend of £4,000.00 a year. On February 5th 1913, another letter bomb sent by militant suffragettes detonated in the sorting office of Dundee, wounding five postal clerks. That evening a letter bomb went off in a postal box in London. On February 22nd 1913, another letter bomb sent by militant suffragettes detonated in the hands of a postal clerk in London. On April 3rd 1913, a bomb set by militant suffragettes detonated in a train car in Stockport. On June 8th 1913, militant suffragette Emily Davison died while attacking a working-class man whose injuries were such that he later committed suicide. On July 7th 1913, another bomb set by militant suffragettes detonated in a train car in Manchester. On July 16nd 1913, another letter bomb sent by militant suffragettes detonated in the hands of a postal clerk in Dublin. On July 19nd 1913, another letter bomb sent by militant suffragettes detonated in the hands of a postal clerk in Birmingham. This time instead of a phosphor bomb the militant suffragettes used sulphuric acid. In August 1913, militant suffragettes set fire to a building occupied by the caretakers of the Abergavenney cricket pavilion in Nottinghamshire. In September 1913, militant suffragettes set fire to a building occupied by the caretakers of Penshurst Place in Dundee. On December 18th 1913, two sticks of dynamite were detonated against the wall of Holloway Prison, then housing militant suffragette prisoners. The explosion did not bring down the prison walls, but it did rain down debris and broken glass into the beds of the children sleeping in a building next door. That night a firebomb fitting the description found in a WSPU letter seized by police in April 1913 went off in the Portsmouth Dockyard. Two men were burned alive. On December 22nd 1913, another letter bomb sent by militant suffragettes detonated in a postal sorting station in Nottingham, injuring several clerks. On January 23rd 1914, a nightwatchman saw two women fleeing Kibble Palace in Glasgow. He found a woman's veil, an empty champagne bottle, cake and a lit pipe bomb. He defused the pipe bomb, but not the other pipe bomb next to him he had not seen. Militant suffragette Marion Crawford went to trial for that action. In February 1914, militant suffragettes set fire to a building occupied by the servants of Aberuchill Castle in Perth. On April 10th 1914, militant suffragettes set fire to a building occupied by the caretakers of home in Belfast. On June 11th and 14th 1914, millitant suffragette bombs went off in Westminster Abbey and St. George's Church. On July 11th 1914, another letter bomb sent by militant suffragettes detonated in a postal van near Manchester. Postal clerks and a passer by were injured.

The tedium of reading such a repetitive list might be relieved with the knowledge it is much abbreviated. These are only some of similar militant suffragist actions. This is what "militant" meant to Dora Marsden. These are the deeds that inform Dora Marsden's essays published here as *The Gospel of Power*. Dora Marsden opposed suffrage as a distraction, a weak half-measure that delayed her power. "Authority shattered, the only right is might—right to what one can get, that is: one's just dues[1]."

Armed women willing to kill as many human beings as necessary to get what they want did not end with the expulsion

---

[1] p. 41.

of militants from the WSPU. As one example among many, see Nikki Craft's Women Armed for Self Protection (WASP) from 1975. Women betrayed by the women's movement did not end with the dissolution of the WSPU. As one example among many, see "Trashing: The Dark Side of Sisterhood" by Joreen[1].

Dora opposed women suffrage because it was not enough. The reader is invited to conduct a thought experiment. Consider two groups of women. In one group are women who speak. In another group are women who act. Which group of women will have their way?

Dora was familiar with authors in the egoist canon. She cited Niccolò Machiavelli and Friedrich Nietzsche as well as Max Stirner, author of *Der Einzige und sein Eigentum*. Contemporary egoists including Benjamin R. Tucker, Clarence Lee Swartz and Steven T. Byington sent her friendly letters, which she published with barbed replies. She wrote of Max Stirner that "creative genius folded its wings when Stirner laid down his pen." However, I do not wish to overstate the case that Dora Marsden was an egoist. In the same breath as the preceding quote, she wrote that "Stirnerian" was "not the adjective fittingly to be applied to the egoism of *The Egoist*. What the appropriate term would be we can omit to state[2]."

Refuse to be dealt with! Read *The Gospel of Power*. Those seeking emancipation in a hurry may consult "The Gospel of Power Concentrated" on page 363.

Trevor Blake
Columbus, Indiana
March 2021

---

[1] *Ms. Magazine* (April 1976).
[2] p. 45.

Dora Marsden. December 1909.

22

1. Liberty, Law and Democracy

"Life is feasting and conflict: that is its zest."

THE concepts with which one age will preoccupy itself, and in which it will invest its surplus emotional heat have shown themselves to be so essentially casual as to be now a matter for mirth rather than wonder with its successors. The subject of an age's Master Passion round which its interest rages will be anything accidental and contingent which will serve: stand the heat, that is, and last out until enthusiasm tires. The amount of genuine enthusiasm which Athanasius, Arius and their followers were able to cull from the numerical problems in the concept of the Trinity was—incredible though it may seem—equal to that which this age culls from the figures of the football scores. The Crusaders who were so concerned about the possession of the Tomb of Christ looked forward to finding as much diversion and profit as a Home Ruler expects to get from the possession of a Parliament on Dublin Green. It is only from a distance that these dead dogs look so determinedly dead. Nearer to, one would swear the body had stirred; and we who are so near to an age when the mere mention of "Universal Law" would produce lyrical intoxication, "All's love, All's law[1]," a very swoon of security, do not purpose here to break in upon the belated obsequies of that dead or dying concept. As the sport of the ribald and the mockers "Universal law" is the perquisite of the youth of 1950, not of 1915. And we will not here trespass on the future.

The reference in the title of this article is limited to statutory law, a prosaic and earth-bound branch which not even

---

[1] ≠ "I report, as a man may of God's work—all's love, yet all's law!" *David Singing before Saul* by Robert Browning.

Apollo himself could have strung to the lyrical note, and it
must be allowed that however excellent a run "Universal Law"
as a symbol and idealised concept may have been accorded
by a generation now settled in obesity, its society representative, so to speak, with which we are here concerned, has
never been held in any too high esteem. The increase in its
bulk and scope of application, which oddly enough, grows
rapidly alongside something called the "Liberty of the people"
have proved matters for complexity even when they have not
created indignation and alarm. Visions of those not the least
penetrating, have seen in the steady advance of the statutory law a devastating plague in which the parchment of the
politicies has seemed as capable of devouring the spirit of the
people as a swarm of locusts devouring green grass. Proudhon
writing in 1850 on the subject says:

> Laws and ordinances fall like hail on the poor
> populace. After a while the political soil will
> be covered with a layer of paper, and all the
> geologists will base to do will be to list it, under
> the name of *papyraceous formation*, among the
> epochs of the earth's history. The Convention,
> in three years one month and four days, issued
> eleven thousand six hundred laws and decrees;
> the Constituent and Legislative Assemblies had
> produced hardly less; the empire and the later
> governments have wrought as industriously. At
> present the *Bulletin des Lois* contains, they say,
> more than fifty thousand; if our representatives
> did their duly this enormous figure would soon
> be doubled. Do you believe that the populace,

or the government itself, can keep its sanity in
this labyrinth[1]?

And yet, while no one would care to dispute these facts or
deny they had significance, it is the libertarian interpretation
of them which provides the clue to the mystery why the gospel
of liberty carries with it so little conviction. The Libertarian
creed has no "bite" in it; "Liberty" remains the "beautiful and
ineffectual angel[2]." In its devouter moments common speech
will accept the gospel, but common sense invariably slips past
it. While not wishing to hurt its feelings, so to speak, it
refuses to have any serious dealings with it. Now common
sense is quite prepared to be serious about statutory law, even
where it is suspicious of it. It is willing to hear law described
as a threatening power and will think out ways and means
of cutting its claws: but "liberty" it does not discuss. The
discussion for and against the "principle of liberty" appears
similar to a discussion on the ultimate and eternal implications
involved in the "principle" in which one wins or loses a game
of patience: or the principle of that popular child's game
where one "arranges" either to tread on every chink in the
pavement or to avoid treading on every chink. "You do, if you
do, and don't if you don't." It is however only when one gets
at the temper behind law and realises its permanent nature
that it becomes apparent why discussions concerning liberty
are more or less frivolous diversions, and nothing makes law
more clear than considering it under that form of "government"
which has promoted its luxuriant growth—democracy.

A law means that "state" support is guaranteed on behalf

---

[1] ≠ Quoted in *Anarchism* by Paul Eltzbacher, translated by Steven T. Byington
(New York: Benjamin R. Tucker 1908).

[2] ≠ Matthew Arnold called Percy Bysshe Shelley a "beautiful and ineffectual angel,
beating in the void his luminous wings in vain" in *Essays in Criticism* (London:
Macmillan & Co., 1888).

of an interest which has obviously already sufficient power to command it. This law has a reverse side to it which implies a "state" guarantee to repress another interest or interests, too weak to command its support. Democracy, putting aside its alliterative and rhetorical jargon, means just the quickening of the pace at which these alliances of the State with owners of "interests" are put through. Representation of people is an impossibility. It is intended for platform purposes only, but representation of interests is a very real thing, one which can be judged with precision as to its efficacy or no. An "interest" is the particularised line of fulfilment which the accomplishment of a willed purpose takes. At points it breaks into and clashes with other interests: and at these points it becomes necessary for their owners to fight the situation out.

These are the precise points where rhetoricians and moralists try to work in their spoof. The people have "a right to" protection from invasion of their interests, and owners of "interests" should "respect" each other's interests. The "liberty" of each and all "should" be "respected." One "should" repress one's interest when likely to interfere with another's.

The fact to be borne in mind is that whether one "should" or "should not," the strong natures never do. The powerful allow "respect for others' interests" to remain the exclusive foible of the weak. The tolerance they have for others' "interests" is not "respect" but indifference. The importance of furthering one's own interests does not leave sufficient energy really to accord much attention to those of others. It is only when others' interests thrust themselves intrudingly across one's own that indifference vanishes: because they have become possible allies or obstacles. If the latter, the fundamental lack of respect swiftly defines itself. In face of opposition to a genuine interest, its owner respects neither "his neighbour's ox, his ass, his wife, his manservant, his maidservant, nor anything that is his[1]." Not even his opinions. One has only to think what jolly old proselytisers the world's "great" men have been to realise what "respect" they have for their neighbour's interests. What each has been concerned for has been to see his will worked upon any soul or body upon which his whim or purpose has seen lit to direct it. Their success has been proportional to the unformedness of the characters with which they have had immediately to deal.

If it is borne in mind that genuine "interests" are things which are never abandoned: that smaller interests are sacrificed ("sacrifice" being a word which has no meaning apart from an audience: it means a virtue, i.e. something likely to win the applause of an audience, for an act which did no audience look on we should do as a matter of course) for a bigger interest as we should "sacrifice" small change of, say, eight half-crowns for a guinea, we can clear "democracy" of its bluff and remove the complexity which the multiplicity of statutory laws creates. They are seen to be two names for one phenomenon. Democracy is government, i.e. persuasion by compulsion exercised from a largely increased number of centres. Multiplicity of laws indicates the detailed channels through which it is effected. It is too vague to say that democracy represents the liberty of the people: rather one would say democracy represented the increase in the number of people who are prepared to take liberties (i.e. persuade by personal violence), with the people who refuse assistance in the furthering of the audacious ones' interests. It is the increase in the number of those who have the courage and ingenuity to become in an open and unequivocal fashion the tyrants we all are subtly and by instinct. It is part of the human trend

---

[1] ≠ Exodus 21-23.

towards explicitness. If "democracy" had no "believers"–no followers whose voices break with lyric intoxication at mention of it, its clean swashbuckling character would be in no danger of being misunderstood. As it is, we are seldom permitted to view it, save through the veil of brotherhood, love and what not, as it steps forward like a mincing lady with a Clergyman on the one hand and a Wizard on the other: Liberty and the State, companions not chosen in stupidity.

It is not by accident for instance that Democracy and Liberty preach in pairs. Liberty is as necessary to Democracy as the second blade is to a pair of shears. Democracy boldly affirms government: Liberty whispers "Don't govern." Liberty plays "Conscience with a task to't." It is the ghostly spirit the moralists would have the meek always carry inside their waistcoats: it plays the policeman inside the man. Unfortunately for the meek, it is only on them that Liberty is able to impose. Those who *can* govern, *i.e.* forward their own interest to the detriment of those who let them, *will* govern. Those who feel no stomach for "governing" will espouse, the gospel of liberty. That is why to those who already have, shall be given and from those which have not shall be taken away that which they have. The cry for "liberty" is the plea for the substitution of melodrama for drama in life: the life according to concept in place of life according to power. It is the hoisting of the white flag followed by an attempt to claim victory in virtue of it. It is the request that the powerful should refrain from taking liberties with the weak because they are afraid to take liberties with the powerful. That is what Libertarians have in mind when they speak of conduct which "should" be "non-invasive," not minding that it is scarcely possible to live a day in a community of two without being "invasive." We are one another's daily food. We take what we can get of what we want. We can be kept out of "territory" but not because we have any compunction about invading. Where the limiting line falls is decided in the event, turning on the will, whim and power of those who are devoured and devourers at one and the same time. Life is feasting and conflict: that is its zest. The cry for peace is the weariness of those who are too faint-hearted to live.

So Liberty remains the foible of the poor in spirit, who monopolise most of the virtues. The plain man (a rarer person alas! than is imagined) does not trouble to stretch the irregular canvas of his life to fit into the framework of the moralists' concepts. When Liberty whispers "Do not be so unbrotherly, so rude, so wicked as even to desire to govern," it is in a deaf ear, and it is this plain person whom Democracy's other companion, the State, must deal with. The State is the National Repository for Firearms and Batons Company Ltd. It is owned, directed and exploited by State's men whose main qualification is to preserve the State's charter granted to it by the people, the chief terms of which are: The State cannot be dissolved; it can do no injury sufficiently serious to justify retaliation or attack; it can get as much money as it thinks safe out of the people; and use it to defend such "interests" as it seems "good" to the State's men to make an alliance with. The charter was no doubt granted when the "people" were being put by dexterous directors of the State under the hypnotic influence of "law and order": and in this state of trance they have been lying—in the main—ever since. Occasionally there seems to be a hint that common intelligence might return to the people when they will waken up: whereupon a "great" statesman will arise and with a few skilful passes of the hand bring them back under the influence of "law and order"—other people's law and order: he will pacify the unrest.

It is the existence of this chartered state which makes "democracy" into a bludgeoning menace. It is the existence of the State which makes the rapid increase of "democratic" law a danger where French leave would be a sport. The difference between the two is the difference between the lists in a tournament and a slaughter-house. To empower a state after the fashion of a modern "civilised" state, and then leave it free to ally itself with interests already powerful is not merely for the lamb to lift its neck to the blade: it is to fashion the knife and drop it ostentatiously at the butcher's feet. A modern "poor" citizen appears so unmitigatedly a fool in his attitude towards the "state" that he suggests he is not merely a fool but is a knave in addition. One of an awestruck crowd of toilers, who when they are not licking their wounds in gaol for not minding their manners, are performing forced labour to feed and fatten—their governors, he fashions elaborated weapons of offence in quantities and allows them to be handed over—to those who dare govern: use them, to wit. They dream of heaven, toil, starve and are penalised: then lisp of liberty. All the same, they seem able to stand it. If these things have a lesson to teach, the meek at any rate have not learnt it.

However, the "flux of things" is in no way concerned to "teach." It defines itself more often than not before our intelligence can claim to have deserved it, and the modern democratic state is making its nature very clear indeed. Already it begins to look like the effigy of a stout and stupid old lady, twitching and lurching as though badly taken with hysteria and St. Vitus' dance. Without any organic living principle in itself it is at the mercy of every interest which cares to tweak at it. It is part of the jargon of "democracy" that the "state" is run in the interests of all: that before it, all interests are "equal," and though obviously they are not, every "interest" is quite ready to make what little it can out of the possibility. We all pay the piper so we all call a tune, and the chorus which results becomes so mixed in the long run that skilled "readers" are unable to decipher the score. The multiplicity of interests "protected" defeats its own ends. The very swelling in the volume prevents the guarantee of state protection from proving effective. A state which protects too many interests becomes like an army which fights on both sides: no use to either, and no credit to itself, and the falling into discredit of the "State" is tantamount to the change of statutory law into French leave; individual will and whim.

Moreover, nature will out, life is too short to spend over-much attention on an institution which will serve a "states-man's" immediate purposes more if he practises a certain fine carelessness. Even successful politicians can have so much straightforward honesty in their natures as to be unmoved by the fierce necessity to practise hypocrisy which the mock-heroic pose of the "State" demands. They cannot be diverted from their genuine interests: so we get a defalcating "reform" governor, the achievements of Tammany Hall, a Chancellor who accepts tips from the Stock Exchange, and a speculating Lord Chief Justice. It gives one a warmer respect for one's kind, but it is the death-knell of the State. To be sure the State dies piecemeal: for the spectators a tedious way of dying. To die—for the State—is to be found out: for its mouthpieces and component parts, individuals all, so to act as to be understood. The "noble democrats" who stand for "clean government" are wretched spoil-sports. They point to the parts from which the cover has slipped and say: it is corrupt: it must be washed: we are the men to do it. Except that they are serious, they are like the funny man in the pantomime who requests the plain-visaged female to take off her mask. They imagine that with Mr. Hilaire Belloc for instance as Prime Minister, we should feel happier in our insides. One would just as lief have Sidney Webb or Herbert Samuel, or Mr. Asquith. For choice, it would fall out to be the kind which would exist between Mrs. Webb sending a blue paper ordering us to take our food in lozenge form and demanding statistics how many times a day we washed: and Mr. Chesterton hesitating before granting us a dog-licence uncertain whether our secret imaginings were such as could be described as sound and British, such as the virgin Mary could whole-heartedly endorse. Of the two most people would prefer to swallow the Webb lozenge.

The growth of an interest in *clean* government would be the overcasting of a brightening sky. The will to govern is beginning to reveal itself as the inborn ineradicable force: and welcome or unwelcome is the form in which power inevitably makes itself manifest. Its trappings slip from it and it is seen stark for what it is. Of its ephemeral attendants, "Liberty" and the "State," Liberty is feeble and faded and the hypnotic passes upon which the State depends for its privileged position as failing to work. Respect is gone from it, and without it democracy becomes individual caprice: the first and final basis of the will to govern. When all these veils are being rent what unsportiveness to reintroduce, confusion as *clean* government! A mystery-play where life offers high drama!

2. Sky-scapes and Goodwill

"The only right is might—right to what one can get."

IF the skill of a doctor were bespoken to effect the cure of a madman, and he proceeded to attempt the systematising of the insane ravings while giving no heed to the existence of the madness one would say there was little to choose from in soundness of mind between doctor and patient. Yet no one marvels when from all those who have a nostrum to offer as a cure for the disease of civilisation and its complications no voice is heard drawing attention to the species of sickness which is its antecedent cause. It remains nameless and unsuspected, to be indicated only by a description of its symptoms.

It begins with the failure of the self-assertive principle of the vital power: a Failure of courage Tolerated, it acts on the power of the heart and thins it out to a degree at which it is too light to retain its seat there, and forthwith mounts to the head where transmutation begins. The power of the heart, already grown virtueless and thin, distills poisonous clammy vapours which emerge from the head. As they grow denser they settle, a heavy cloud of mist about the herd. Descending, they breathe a film upon the eyes and dim the senses. Within, the heart left tenantless of power is contracted by ghostly hands—the hands of fear. The face becomes pallid under the Thought-wreaths with the chilliness of fear. The vapours become the breath of his nostrils and are breathed in as Duty and Circumspection. They penetrate each limb and fibre, inoculate with obedience and virtue. The hands fold meekly: the man walks with circumspection. He is already civilised: he awaits merely the idiosyncracy of the particular civilisation.

❦

A civilisation is the attempted working out of a Scheme of Salvation: a plan of escape. It is the imperfect form built up from the perfected plan which the religious philosophies of the "great" "constructive" "thinkers" of its age have projected. For it is not merely that a race of men bleached white with the failure of courage would do well with a prelaid scheme of action: they refuse to move on without one. They bleat for a Deliverer—a great constructive thinker—as sheep for a shepherd. Being without prescience, without inner compelling desire, they wail to be told. The great world of audiences puts out its distracted agitated tentacles, swaying about aimlessly, dumb appeals to be told how to expend themselves, and where. Culture, training in the art of spending oneself, is the imperious necessity of the bleached race, whether lettered or simple. Life without the courage for it, is so bad a business that they must needs approach it with caution. Earth is so little to their taste that they demand the construction of a Heaven. To construct the "New Jerusalem," work to the plan of the Deliverer, and make a Heaven on earth is a task they can put their hands to. But to live for themselves—to lose "faith?" They would as soon not live at all.

So the heads steam with fresh purpose, and the thought-wreaths mount apace: until there is enough and to spare to build Heavens without end, Hells to match and Attacking and Delivering Hosts of Thoughts to storm and defend. What the battalions shall be named and how they shall be drawn up is nobody's concern save that of the "constructive" thinker who outlines the vaporous sketch. He maps out a bold sky-scape in smoke, and the civilised group themselves under whatever concept taste or convenience dictates. They follow out the scheme as a whole as they would the colour-scheme and revelries on the floor of some great hall in imitation of its painted ceiling. So are they safe: linked up with Heaven. If their earthly concerns get neglected and somewhat mixed on account of conducting their affairs on a pattern pertaining strictly to a Heaven of thought who is to say they would not have been more hopelessly confused had they turned their feeble temper upon them: and whatever befalls, have they not Faith—in Heaven? And does not their bemusedness give the earthly sort their chance to use them, for what they are worth?

It is the flexibility with apparently unlimited power to make adjustments according to order in human nature which the Thought-weavers work upon when rigging out their canvases. Human nature can be accorded a summary treatment quite other from that which is given to inert matter. If the Thames flows east and the Severn west "thinkers" will acknowledge and respect the stubborn tendency; but human nature must set itself to all the points of the compass if the Plan of Salvation demands it. As it can if it works to it with Goodwill. The Goodwill can in fact accomplish all things. It is therefore the base of every "constructive" scheme of thought. It is the one factor indeed which makes them thinkable. That is why it is so extolled. What system is there which does not give the palm to the Goodwill: the set intention to work to pattern. If the weavers of shadows can count on this set intention, it is enough. The result they can safely leave to the slow wearing down of habit and constant repetition. In time, with Goodwill, the "plan" will be plotted out in conduct as quantities are on squared paper to give a curve. This "plan" plotted out by Goodwill into conduct will similarly "reveal itself in our lives." The plans differ, and the "curves" of civilisations differ in consequence, but Goodwill is the same in them all. It is the amenable teachable will: the fluttering tentacle, beating about uncertainly, charged with energy but without direction. It stands for the intention to follow if only directions are given to it—if the canvas is stretched across its sky.

The humanitarian sky-scape under which we walk nowadays and which we are all expected to be "revealing in our lives" is the residue of rubbish left over after the Revolution had enabled what there was in it of egoistic temper to obtain the desired spoil under exceptionally favourable circumstances. This vapourous design is the maleficent legacy which has been bequeathed to succeeding centuries after the French *bourgeoisie* had acquired the sole benefits of the insurrection. The legatees have done handsomely by it, spreading it out and patching it up like old property, until now it is both neat and compact. It could be sketched out on half a sheet of notepaper and leave plenty of available space.

It demands first of course the Goodwill which is taken for granted but encouraged in well-doing by an apothesis of a sort. Goodwill is so essential that the fluttering little tentacle is elevated to the rank of the sacred, and as fraternity takes its place in the humanitarian Olympus. In the deification ceremony Goodwill unequivocally asserts its intentions, and proves itself so completely at the service of the Scheme of Things and above the level of suspicion, by divorcing itself completely from its own selfish interests, cutting itself off at the very outset from the Plan's only serious rival, the natural bent of the Self. As the hymn puts it, it plumps for "None of

Self and all of—the Plan[1]." (There is no form of literature
so profoundly informing as a hymn-book.) The ceremony is
the formal abandonment of the Self-will by which Goodwill
becomes Goodwill in earnest as fraternity, in which role it will
reappear later in the sketch as the divine parent of Humanity.
From this point all is plain sailing. To love one's neighbour as
oneself: to love the Public Good, *i.e.*, all one's neighbours put
together, better than ourselves: that is the fruitful spirit in
which is begotten the "more than Brotherhood," the Oneness
of Humanity and the Race, when we shall "all one body be[2]."
Then shall each little one be as a limb to the great body, each
well-pleased that he pleases not himself but serves the Whole.
The design grows. Dimension has entered into it, and with
it a greater and a less: a standard of measurement therefore
and a seat of authority: a scale of values which indicates automatically when a "member" offends. If the smaller frets the
greater: perish the smaller or let it amend its ways. What is
the greater? What can it be but Humanity, the Type, the generalisation, the thing with capitals, high conception and lofty
thought. How the heads steam, and thoughts mount—rise
to the "All," the "each and every" pounded out of recognition into sameness, bound together by the fraternal cement
into—Man: the master-achievement to accomplish which we
sink our mean differences and forget our inequalities. Has not
each become equal in willingness to serve—Man. Equal then,
we are: with equal "rights" to protection of our "freedom"
to perform our "duties" towards—Man; receiving equal dues
from a blindfolded "Justice" with even scales. The tableau

---

[1] ≠ "None of the Self and All of Thee." Rev. Theodore Monod (1878).

[2] ≠ "Supremely blessed! to God thy Spouse / So linked in chaste and constant vows;
/ O may we all one body be, / One spirit with The Lord like thee!" from *Laude
Syon: Ancient Latin Hymns of the English and Other Churches* Part II by John
David Chambers (London: J. Masters, 1866).

grows complete: Goodwill: fraternity: Humanity: Peace: Order: Law: Rights: Justice: Liberty: Man—the Humanitarian Heaven, so balanced and symmetrical that it requires an unregarding egoism to break into it. Unfortunately for the picture's stability, the power of Goodwill is not equal to its intentions. It is like the God of Arnold's *Empedocles* who "would do all things well, but some times fails in strength[1]." When it abandons self-will to enter the empyrean of the gods, it does not annihilate it, and the "obtuse unreason of the she-intelligence" which is the temper of men whose intelligence has had strength to resist the torturings of intellectual feebleness, breaks regardless into the pretty thought tight systems, only to leave them lying in the path of history broken and awry like shattered mechanical toys[2]. The spikes and burrs on the garment of the selfish man rip into the gossamer thought meshes which stretch like cobwebs across the field of action. It is the selfish man who reduces all the systems to inoperation: who is the despair of the "constructive" thinkers. The power to annul any and every thought-system is founded in the absence of Goodwill. The streak of self-determination cuts the selfish man off from the well-intentioned from the outset. Unless the docile temper is available to work it on to the warp of reality, the "Plan" is futile. Its beginning and end rest on the Goodwill, which will plod along like an industrious mole to "realise" the "philosophic" scheme fashionable to its day and generation. Temper, which is energy self-conscious of its direction, has plans and insight of its own: it is not amenable to direction, or to moral suasion. Instead of an intention to serve Man, its Intention is to serve itself and its own soul as suits itself: it has no "standard" save its

---

[1] ≠ *Empedocles on Etna, and Other Poems* by Matthew Arnold (London: Ballantyne Press, 1896).

[2] ≠ *Numpholeptos* by Robert Browning (London: Smith, Elder & Co. 1876).

own satisfaction. It saves its soul alive by respecting it; by preventing it from being merged with blunted characteristics into anything else—the whole or anything other. It holds by the instinct that emergence from the herd is the proof positive that it is not of the herd; that to be conscious of its emergence is its distinction and master achievement, and to maintain and accentuate it is its supreme business; to make it more and more of its "own" kind, unique; to weed out that which is alien to itself; to be "sincere" through and through; to free itself from all elements non-selfish: this is the work to which it finds it has a natural bent, and by it, it makes itself impregnable; incapable of being broken into or broken down. It is the instinct for its own permanence, its immortality may be, which, without regard, eats up or casts out every particle of Goodwill. Hence the futility for all save the herd, of all schemes of salvation based on Goodwill, and the value which temper sets upon its antagonisms equally with its attractions. The one is as essential as the other for that light and shade in which individual differentiation finds itself clear. To be incapable of being repelled by any of the brethren is at least as much death in life as to be incapable of being attracted. Antagonism, not for what is bad for the fancy picture—the community and the race—but for that which repels the something within oneself, independent of its relation to the scheme of values, is as valuable—more exciting if not as comfortable—as attraction. Oh universal brotherhood, universal love, sameness, monotony, extinction! Mankind pressing onward to Unity, swept forward as by one impulse to the bosom of the Type! Like those swine which it says somewhere, were swept into the Gadarene Sea[1]!

---

[1] $\neq$ Mark 5:1-20

❧

Happily the nightmare lives mainly only in the picture: in reality, individuals pair off in twos and threes or scrap among themselves. Universal brotherhood is mainly subscribed to by people very capable of giving the salutary cut to the simple brother foolish enough to assume that they mean it. The fact which misleads, and encourages the notion that Goodwill is more than a thought-mist for any not of the herd is the extension of the imaginative area by the wide sweep of the senses, whereby things which one sees, hears or hears of, become part of the mental landscape; and as such are subjected to efforts which would change them to our liking. One makes effort to remove unsightly features which disaffect us in those about us from a motive like that which would impel us to remove an unsightly structure which faced one's window. Not for the sake of the structure, but for the sake of our personal comfort. But with more than that no one has truck with. Anything beyond that must be left to be indicated on the "Plan": as n is left to indicate the power of a number increased to infinity.

With the breaking of the thread of Goodwill, the humanitarian philosophy would unravel at a single pull, like a chain-stitched seam would if the right thread were seized. Humanity is robbed of its "principle" and dissolves soulless when egoists break in upon fraternity. It falls apart into its component individuals like the sand from mortar, if the cohering lime were removed. Its "progress," become the progress of a non-entity, vanishes and with it the source of authority which in its name advised and admonished individuals. What "progress" there may be, becomes a progression in the individuals themselves, which follows individual laws, each being a law to himself. Authority gone, "protection" goes, and "rights" go with it. There are no rights without protection. Anything of "rights" which is not might is "bestowed," "permitted," and only with the protection of Authority can there be adequate bestowal and permission. Authority shattered, the only right is might—right to what one can get, that is: one's just dues. The easy assumption that one has a right to anything, livelihood, "equitable returns," comfort, liberty, or life itself shrink like phantoms in daylight. When Goodwill is gone rights can be had for the commanding—for the power to enforce them—and no cheaper.

Liberty too is impossible without protection. Liberty is nine parts coercion, and the coercion of the weak—the only ones who make appeal for liberty—is exercised through authority. Liberty, the plaint of the feeble, is the "assumption" that the strong must stay the strength of their arm: if they refuse, authority must compel them. Of course authority and the powerful run together, as like to like; but that does not enlighten the libertarians. They still appeal that the right hand shall shackle the left: it is their trustfulness.

The tenth part of liberty is the claim to be "free." All claims are easy, but the claim to be free is easy of enforcement: which not all claims are. By the simple process of abandonment, one can be free of most things. Relatively very few persons are held captive in prisons or beleagured cities. Most can have as much freedom as they want: the truth is that they do not want it. Freedom even as a concept is negative, and the things one truly wants are positive. People are not greatly agitated by that which they desire to be rid of; it is the desire to have possession which makes their problem, and those who call out for freedom desire, not freedom, but property, and property is won and held only in virtue of the possession of power. The plaintive appeals of those who say they want liberty but who mean that they want to be presented with property and to be supported in its possession can be met only when the pathetic pleaders decide to increase their power to get and hold; or to support in power a strong authority to which they can make appeal for appropriation and protection; or to persuade the powerful already in possession to a voluntary act of grace towards the weak and non-possessing.

The second method has been tried, is being and is likely to be for some time to come; the third is the method which by common consent of all orators and clergy sounds the best: on all occasions sacred or profane: it is the method firmly believed in by all the feeble and none of the strong. It is the millennium arrived at by way of Liberty, Love and Humanity.

The first is the one the poor in spirit and pocket have no heart for; it has no friends; it dismays the rich as much as it sickens the poor, and in the long interval which is likely to elapse before it is put on its trial, the ravelling thread of the humanitarian canvas will be caught up and the array of vaporous combatants in the army of Humanity, the entire assemblage of the Delivering Hosts of Thought will wreathe themselves out like a painted battle until the real flesh and blood combat is ready to begin. The poor will continue to lay claim to rights—to look for the advent of a liberty they can never see; they will "claim" an equality with those with whom they are not equal; claim the "justice" which assumes a non-existing equality: a justice which is not just. And as they assume their possession of "rights" in these claims, they will—being in truth a humble and indoctrinated people—assume the duties to correspond, and perform the services. Their services will be accepted: the claims rejected. The *quid pro quo* they will obtain will be a clear title to the virtues, the reward for which is laid up in Heaven, high and away behind the Sky-scape and the stout form of Humanity. Of the property which they want when they ask for liberty—not one jot. To get that they would require to seize and thieve, and thieving is not prescribed on the Sky-scape. Nor is it compatible with virtue when exercised on a humble scale, and who can hope they will ever rob on the noble one, generously and like gentlemen? If one of them were caught red-handed, he would be found to be smuggling away a can of milk: which is hopeless as thieving. Scarcely in our time will they need to take in and pack away the humanitarian canvas—unless indeed there is force and a sting in irony.

.

3. Hedonism

*"We take what we can, and our
capacity is not measured by thimblefuls."*

THIS time it is hedonism. It was nominalism, and has been
realism, intuitionism, individualism, Socialism. Given
time, and the catholicity of these pages, we shall in the opinion
of one or other of our readers rehearse the entire procession
of isms and schisms, whether ancient, mediæval or modern.
The compliment paid to the wealth of our erudition would
no doubt be pleasant—and wholly undeserved—did it not
clash with our egoistic temper, which compels us to protest
as to our status. Our modesty notwithstanding, we protest
that we brew our own malt: we are not bottlers and retailers:
we are in the wholesale and producing line of business. If
our beer bears a resemblance in flavour to other brands, it
is due to the similarity of taste in the makers. "Stirnerian"
therefore is not the adjective fittingly to be applied to the
egoism of *The Egoist*. What the appropriate term would be
we can omit to state. Having said this, we do not seek to
minimise the amount of Stirner which may be traced herein.
The contrary rather, since having no fear that creative genius
folded its wings when Stirner laid down his pen, we would
gladly credit to him—unlike so many of the individualists
who have enriched themselves somewhat at his hands—the
full measure of his astounding creativeness. For it is not the
smallness in measure of what one takes away from genius
one admires which is creditable. It is a very old story—the
comedy of discipleship—that though the banquet of wisdom
is spread and open to all-comers the number of the foolish
abroad does not materially diminish. We may take from where

we please, but "how much" depends on how much we can. The wealth of the feast is the affair of the hosts: capacity to take from it concerns only the guest. Since then we recognise his value, why protest that we have drawn at the stream of his creation into thimbles? We take what we can, and our capacity is not measured by thimblefuls. And because it is not, "Stirnerian egoism" has not as Mr. Meulen suggests in the correspondence columns "taken such a firm hold" of us[1]. If that appears a paradox to our correspondent we ask him to work it out. It is really very simple and straightforward if he will bear in mind that we are very great pots and can therefore afford to be honest. So few people can. [...]

---

[1] ≠ "A Criticism of the Philosophy of Egoism" by Henry Meulen. *The Egoist* Volume I Number 1 (January 15th, 1914).

4. Men, Machines and Progress

*"Individual human temper is the standard
against which all tools are measured."*

IT is the distinguishing mark of the "Verbal Age" that when
the vogue of any of its shibboleths is at its zenith and
exerting its strongest influence it is the least open to the
questioning of sense. The hypnotism of sound lulls sense
into accepting a "thought," *i.e.* an error born of ineffectual
thinking, into its categories of existent things, and giving
to it a "local habitation and a name." The name is all-
important since over and above the name there is nothing of
reality connected with it. Men cling to the names of thoughts
because they are dimly aware that in abandoning the names
they abandon all. The name of a spade can be abandoned
and beyond a little hesitancy, a greater circumlocution in
speech, nothing is changed; the spade remains: but abandon
the names of thoughts and you have nothing left. Hence the
device of making "sacred" names—the sacred names of "Duty,"
"Right," "Obedience," "Liberty" and the entire "moral" outfit,
whereby it becomes sinful to question names. The sole purpose
in fact in making a concept sacred is to ensure its immunity
from being questioned.

It is therefore because this has been the "Age of Progress"
that those who believe in "Progress" have regarded it as blasphemous to attempt its definition. Differing things may have
been for or against progress, but as for "progress" itself—it
is just "progress." That has not prevented assumptions in
regard to "progress" being made. It is in fact under cover

of the sacred ægis that the largest assumptions always contrive to pass muster, and as far as "progress" is concerned it has been tacitly assumed that progress and an easing of the struggle with external environment are one. If the powers inherent in Nature can be set in such relation that one will overcome the other, and this with decreasing human effort so to set them: that, it is assumed, is progress. It happens that two pronouncements, one being an Individualist manifesto (which its author Mr. Heinrich Charles describes as "The Anti-Thesis to the Communistic Manifesto by Karl Marx and Friedrich Engels and the Synthesis of Social-Individualism") and the other that of a journal which believes itself to be the intellectual organ of English Socialism, both making this same assumption in regard to "progress" come to our hands together. Upon that on which individualist and socialist agree it is worth while to pause to consider. Thus the manifesto:

> What has been the world's greatest curse? Physical labour! Manual work! Mechanical drudgery! Toil oppressive to mind and body! Compulsory service! Who shall hew the wood? Who shall draw the water? Who shall do the dirty work? This has been the bone of contention... the immediate sole cause of all wars: of all the bloodshed and struggles between man and man; of all the land-hunger and the great migratory movements... of all the revolts, rebellions, and revolutions, the division of classes, of slavery, of serfdom, and the modern system of exploitation... Man's main mental work has been how to escape physical work. All the social systems and organisations of the past, all the mighty empires and republics, all the nations and states

were based on one proposition: that there must
be one class which does the work. To escape
from this class was the ruling ambition[1].

It is the writer's contention that that which distinguishes
developed man from the savage is the possession of knowledge
relating to inventions which relieve men from the necessity
of physical toil; that the genius of the few will never rest
until it has discovered a power upon which can be thrown
the performance of the labouring work of the world. All tools
he maintains are efforts in this direction. Harnessed to the
energy of the human hand and arms, a tool will lighten labour;
tools harnessed to the tremendous power in steam will turn
the world into a hive of industry where the man's task is that
of mere minder of the tool; progress is due to the men who
are possessed of unusual faculties, which provided them with
the inspiration and intuitive sense to see relations between
things which the ordinary man would never think of relating.
The pioneers of science are the true forces of progress. Not
the world's fifteen or sixteen great battles—but the fifteen or
sixteen decisive discoveries and inventions, from those of fire
and missiles onwards. It is not surprising therefore, holding
such views, that in judging the calibre of the thinkers of the
nineteenth century Mr. Charles should award the palm to
Marx and Engels!

> Great men were Karl Marx and Friedrich En-
> gels! There is no doubt that they were the most
> scientific and deepest thinkers, economists and
> sociologists of the Nineteenth Century. But
> with all their genius in seeing and relating

[1] ≠ The Electro-Individualistic Manifesto: the Anti-Thesis of the Communistic Manifesto by Karl Marx and Friedrich Engels, and the Synthesis of Socio-Individualism.
New York: Heinrich Charles, 1913.

things as Others in their day did not, they were
still hampered by human limitations. They
could not foresee what subsequent revolutionary changes, new inventions entirely beyond the
vision of even the loftiest imagination, would
make[1].

Marx and Engels (inevitably Mr. Charles thinks) faced with
the advent of steam-machinery came to the conclusion that
men must of necessity supply themselves with a new philosophy of living, to wit, one which would fit them—men—to the
increased dimensions of the tool. The desire to own things
individually must give way and adjust itself to Collective
ownership. Hence Socialism in all its varieties: Communism,
Collectivism, Guildism, which is Syndicalism without its soul;
and Syndicalism itself, of which the soul is anarchistic temper
and the body of a heavy-footed communism.

All these in his opinion were "moulds of thought" to which
the minds of thinkers of the 19th century, no matter how virile, penetrative and original, must accommodate themselves,
because forsooth the day of the steam engine was here. It
will not be necessary for us to say that we disagree entirely
with the dictum that a thinker, however great, is unable to
think around or away from the mechanistic appliances of his
age, but it is worth pointing out that the 19th century thinker
who preceded Marx provides a direct refutation of it. Max
Stirner was not hypnotised by the steam-engine. Nor would
any thinker who knew his own temper sufficiently well be
capable of exercising a selection among the services which his
time and age were able to offer him. *Das Kapital* was refuted
before it was written. Its theories based on word-values had
already been proved empty of relevance. Once it is recognised

---

[1] $\neq$ Heinrich.

that individual human temper is the standard against which all tools are measured, a proposal to adjust temper to fit the mechanism reveals itself as the flimsy excuse to cover the feebleness of those who are so spiritless as to allow even their tools to become their masters. Steam even with the machinery, enormous and cumbersome which its nature seems to demand, is not too big to be the tool of those who have the audacity to use it so. It is the tool of the capitalists, and there is no preordained class of capitalists. All may be capitalists who can be. Men who know their own minds know that they need tools, *i.e.* instruments subjected and amenable to their own wills, and by hook or crook they will get them. They cannot be bluffed by the mere size of a machine into accepting a master and calling it a tool; they leave that sort of thing to the philosophers. But, unless that which has been the desideratum of all who since the history of the world began have looked in pity at the hard lot of their fellows be achieved—a change of heart—there will always be those who are born tools, those who to relieve themselves of the burden of being responsible for themselves are more than willing to become not merely the appendages and tools of others but the tools of any instrument which should yield itself to their service. It is not the kind of tool which is the decisive factor: it is the lack of temper in the man who uses it. It is not the steam-engine which has created slaves and slaves will not be abolished by its supersession. Before its advent, when tools were of a maniable size, the slaves existed, hounded, beaten, branded and manacled.

So it seems worth while to get behind the generality "Progress" since obviously there exists no such thing. A person or thing can progress: that is, advance in any number of ways. He or it can "progress" downwards, upwards or onwards. But "Progress" as a generality is the instrument of the rhetorician and the professional exploiter of the brainless. In relation to the human kingdom, especially since the rise to popularity among the word-stunned of its related conceptual spook, "evolution[1]," human progress has been regarded as an inevitable transmutation of this planet into a human world where men can live without hardship, toil, danger and difficulty.

The "progress of civilisation" has been the softening of the rigours of the external world, the dwindling of harshness and asperity in the struggle with "nature." "Progress," so it is held, has proceeded *pari passu* with inventive energy expended to subject the power of nature into the service of men, relieving them of toil. That this is true to a large extent of "progress" in the development of tools cannot be denied. That it is true, explains why civilisation has become synonymous with decay, a blight eating into the individual lives which make up the human kingdom.

The notion that the condition of slavery and submission among men fluctuates about the type of tool which is prevalent in any age has arisen from thinking that the "progress of civilisation" need have any antecedent causal relation to the "progress of men": that the easy submissiveness of matter to handling by men has of necessity direct beneficial results for the advancement of men.

Increase in the amenities of a progressively softened environment, and the growth of men's sensitive power are two totally different things: they are almost opposites; in fact the greater part of the development wherein men have become more sensitive, aware and able has been achieved by rough

---

[1] ≠ see Bergson p. 79.

and harsh experience, which has accentuated their consciousness of the difference which exists between them and their
environment. It has broken the hypnotic spell which made
them at one with it. They have veritably cut their teeth
on the sharp edge of difficulties. The difficult task has been
the anvil on which human strength has been forged, and if
history is allowed to speak in the matter, life on a "press the
button" basis will be none too friendly to the growth of men.
"To increase the penetrative power of the senses" is the pe-
riphrasis which should oust "progress" as a term applicable to
living development from language. Reference to environment
is excessive because unnecessary. The "environment" is what
it is. Its potential powers and uses are given quantities: pos-
tulates to be learned in order to be accepted, and thereafter
used. Matter is not altered when it is used. It is accepted
for what it is. What alters is the intelligence which is increasingly able to recognise the existent character of environment.
To stand on the sea-shore and hold communion as power to
power with a jelly-fish for instance will make it all plain. Any
ordinary human intelligence regarding it is aware that the
inert mass of substance is surrounded by what the intellect
calls the "wonders" of the universe. Yet if the choicest of
such wonders were gathered from all the corners of the world
into its immediate vicinity it would make no difference to the
jelly-fish. The "discoveries" are there; what is behind time
is the fish. Everything awaits its awareness, and to intensify
this by even so much as a tremor means more for it than the
whole world beside. "What doth it profit a man if he gain
the whole world and lose his own soul[1]?" No more than it
profits the fish. Environment is a wholly secondary matter—a
result and not a cause. It will be acted upon readily enough

---

[1] ≠ Mark 8:6

when the intelligence becomes alive to it. To reverse the order of the relation between intelligence and its environment is not a matter of more or less: it is rather one of truth and its opposite. All thinkers of any value have risen superior to the environmental conditions accidental to their age. It is a sufficient condemnation of the Socialist thinkers merely to state that they have not, and their Nemesis is already treading at their heel. While yet the filthy spectacle of the industrial towns which an easy acceptance of steam machinery made possible still befouls the countryside, the hollowness of Marxian economics with their theories of value can be made demonstrable to the mind of a child.

Having said this, it will be easier to allow full value to the illuminating suggestion as to the tendency in labour-saving machinery which it is the purpose of the *Manifesto*, to which we have already referred, to define. Its description is not merely an Individualist manifesto: it calls itself an "Electro-Individualistic Manifesto," and powerfully suggestive of enormous changes in industrial enterprise it is. Electricity is displacing steam as a servant power: a commonly-observed fact but of which few have noticed any important implications. The import of electricity in relation to industrialism is according to the *Manifesto* this: its use will abolish the machine of enormous magnitude: its natural "bent" favours the miniature machine which is a "tool": whereas steam-power favours the machine of enormous magnitude which cannot be individually owned on any extended scale. The use of electricity means therefore the return—after an enormous sweep round the circle which includes the machine—to the tool: not indeed as it was harnessed to the human energy of hand and arm, but to a power which can be regulated to almost unlimited strength or shaded off to the most delicate

fineness. But the unique importance lies in the possibility
of such miniature tools being individually owned: the personal possession of the user: capable of being stored and used
in the home. The break-up of the factory-system therefore:
break-up of the towns: decentralisation and disintegration of
the industrial system! No wonder Mr. Charles is intoxicated
by his imaginative sweep into the possibilities of electricity.
He quotes T. A. Edison and his comment on this modern
Prometheus he shall make for himself. He says:

> Thomas Alva Edison has spoken *ex cathedra*:
> "Not individualism but social labour will domi-
> nate in the future. You can't have individual
> machines and every man working for himself."
> *Pace*, Mr. Edison: you may be a great inventor
> and a magnificent organiser of inventive talent,
> but don't prophesy until you know. What for in-
> stance is your endeavour to make a form which
> would cast in one mould a complete cement-
> house in a variation of styles, but an attempt to
> create an individual machine in house-building?
> Is not your electric vehicle an individual ma-
> chine in locomotion? Is not the tiny motor on
> the sewing machine a magnificent example of
> individual miniature machinery? Is not all the
> inventive talent busy now to invent a practi-
> cal tractor for the small farm? Is this not an
> individual machine? Almost all inventors of
> modern times are in the direction of the indi-
> vidual machine.[1]

---

[1] ≠ Heinrich.

Of how it will be possible to "burst the steel trust" without striking a single blow at its armour, the *Manifesto* illustrates by the following from the *Scientific American*. (It is now possible to produce steel by electricity at almost a commercial price in a miniature cylindrical furnace about 18 inches high and 14 inches in diameter.)

ELECTRICALLY-REFINED
STEEL FOR AUTOMOBILES

Apropos of the recent article in the *Scientific American* on the growth of electrical refining of steel, we note that the automobile manufacturers are availing themselves of the new process for the production of mild steel castings. One of the largest English automobile manufacturers has installed an electric furnace for supplying castings of this kind for machines made at his factory.[1]

The *Manifesto* would be made more valuable by an augmentation of its list of such instances: but those who are on the look-out for the first appearance of a type of labour-saving tool which can be used apart from a herd will be sufficiently heartened by the sight of a single instance. That others will follow there is no need to fear. The *Manifesto* prophesies that by the year 2000 a single unsupported individual will be able to produce almost without manual labour, and certainly without overwhelmingly harsh labour, the entire round of tasks necessary for the complete service of his needs. The regulation of light and heat which electricity gives promise of suggests the creation of artificially-created climatic conditions which will make the present vast transport trade of the

---

[1] ≠ "Electrically-Refined Steel for Automobiles." *Scientific American* (August 16th, 1913) p. 123.

world appear a costly and barbarously crude effort. Indeed if economy has any voice in the matter, the transport trade of the world will cease, seeing that the present cost of the transportation of goods averages out at 100% of the cost of production.

In view of the foregoing it is easy to arrive at an intellectual estimate of the value of those communistic-writers who have been endeavouring to scarify the much-though-miserably advised proletariat into an acceptance of their particular nostrums. We can take as typical of the rest a recent jeremiad of the Editor of the *New Age* in reply to a challenge from one of the capitalistic press to refute its defence of the South African Government's action during the recent disturbances. The "reply" contains the following:

> We come to that aspect of the problem which as we said at the outset will raise the question... of the very existence of society... Does it not exist in part... of the class we call the proletariat?... In all affairs concerning society... they have as much title as any of us, to ask where, and exactly where they come in. But their only means of existence... is to sell their labour. What is to happen... if nobody chances to think their labour worth the cost of reproduction and... if human labour power ceases to be of sufficient value to command the price of subsistence? Under these circumstances the proletariat is in the position of horses... threatened with the extinction of petrol... the fact that... the obsolescent material consists of human beings, each made

in the image of God does not disqualify it from
falling under the general rule of Economics...
Economists measure the advance of an industry,
not by the increase in the number of men it
employs, but by the increase of production at
a diminished cost... and the economists, as we
say are right in measuring progress by the ease
with which production is maintained... Such
schemes, of labour-saving appliances... are nu-
merous as the Armada, and as threatening to
the existence of the proletariat as that was to
England. Now will Mr. Strachey begin to see
where retrenchments for economy may carry
us? *Now* will he look like a Statesman, etc.,
etc. Would we... stop science... put a period to
progress, cease inventing proletariat saving machinery?... We would not! What then? There
only remain two means of dealing with them...
one is castration and the lethal-chamber for every proletarian,... and the other is the... social
device for at once saving part of society from
extinction which is known to our readers as the
National Guild System[1].

In the same calm hypnotised way one could imagine an insane
mathematician attempting to prove a proposition to an understanding listener, by a careful proof of its contrary. It is the
concept, dear reader, which has made this hapless writer mad.
By generalising from the verb "to produce"—a word which
to mean anything at all requires specific limitation by subject
and object—he has arrived at a "conception," a "thought,"
i.e. production, to which by the very act of generalising he

---

[1] $\neq$ source unknown.

gives absolute unconditioned existence. After that of course he has no control over it; it simply runs away with him, to the extent that he is driven to make proof to workers, who would not willingly produce a pin did they not think they were producing something to live on: he assures such that "the economists are right in measuring progress by the ease with which production is maintained!" Ease with which the production of lethal-chambers is maintained! Might not the worker be "right" in thinking them maintained somewhat too easily—even with progress at stake?

It is this kind of mind which accepts slavishly an accepted but erroneous mould of speech in the face of common sense—a mind unoriginal and conventional, which is ready to be hypnotised by an existent, what though hateful, mode of labour. It cannot think or imagine beyond it. It fails to appreciate that creator and creation are not on equal standing: that the intelligence that created a monster can create its destroyer; that only by the consent of its creator and user can the machine do anything either for or to the mind which creates it. The machine is powerless to vary itself or its powers: its use even lies at the mercy of men of whom the only constant thing which can truly be asserted is that they change, who can destroy it or supersede it: or simply neglect it. To base a way of living on the assumption that a type of machine is permanent and that men will submit their variable ways permanently to it, is to be dazzled and therefore deluded by a single chance discovery of a facile way of handling the vast inanimate power stored up in the world. It is sure that there must be billions of possible alternatives to this present way of handling, but that the sensitive observation of a Watt happened to concentrate, probably if the truth were known on account of a habit of mooching over the fire, upon this one, which suggested to him the possibility of steam-machinery. Had Watts had the type of mind which is hypnotised by its environment, deadened in its powers of observing new relations by a too strong "set" towards the accepted conventional way of regarding them, he could never have been impressed by a commonplace phenomenon in such a degree. But it is just this "set" type of intelligence which has seen finality in the system he established; who are persuaded that men must either adapt themselves to its ungainly services or present themselves at the door of the lethal-chamber, unwilling but persuaded that they must die.

Of all these "means of production" to which one philosopher says that the workers must either become adaptable or succumb, the *Manifesto* makes very short work: "Why not make every proletarian also a possessor? Why use legal and revolutionary methods to gain possession of something that will be of no value in the near future? Electricity will do all the necessary dispossessing and expropriation. It will rapidly put all the present means of production on the junk heap."

It seems a little ominous to be speaking already of "making" the proletarian into a possessor. Is he never going to throw off his non-possessing character on his own account and become a possessor without waiting to be made? Is he in fact going to dodge the uprising—the insurrection—after all? For it is not the question of dispossessing and expropriation that anyone is much concerned with: it is the appropriation and possession: and who or what is the benevolent despot which is going to make him proprietor save at the length of the only efficient demand—*i.e.* the power to take.

And, once given—or taken, though one might like to think that if work is to be reduced to the level of pressing a button, the button to be small and modest enough for a humble man to consider its possession not wholly above his station, and in the limits of his own home too, he will surely have the spirit to stick to the button and defend the home. But there is no knowing; to those of the serving habit there is no limit to the number of ways they will devise for slipping into the mud and sticking in it, just as there are a million ways to the intelligence of a Napoleon who wants a continent or an Alexander who wants the world, for getting what they want. What for instance instead of the happy dream that with electricity's advent each member of the proletariat will be presented with a neat little electric outfit, with land and climate, all complete, merely requiring that he shall "press the button"—what is to prevent some erratic genius being seized with the quite conceivable and quite overpowering dislike to their faces and devising a machine to wipe them out of existence? Indeed until now electrocution is the most familiar of the dramatic forms in which the ordinary public have been made aware of its possibilities. There is nothing moreover in the past service of machines sufficient to induce men to set them up as saviours of Society, and electricity fitted to no matter what kind of machine, unless it is kept in its place as a servant will become the master of the unintelligent. Everything turns on courage and temper in the long run, and if it is absent mechanical labour-saving power might as well have developed in the direction of a ring through the nose and a clamp through the foot for any virtue it might have to save men from slavery. There will always be men who will contrive to be masters as long as there are men willing to be slaves. The temper which will submit itself; adapt itself easily to systems either mechanical or spiritual, to anything other than its own personal preferences, is the dry-rot in the spirit which makes slavery. It may be objected that this temper is born and not made. Very well then, why kick against the pricks on its behalf? If men are born with that kind of temper they are born slaves and will sink to slavery in spite of every effort of born masters to hold them up. Whether they are or no remains to be seen. At any rate the passing away of the dead weight of an industrial system, fitted to the requirements of huge composite machines will give the egoist temper a chance to breathe if it exists though ever so feebly.

The same brand of counsel which expounds to the "poor" how the true and inevitable economy of production is that which must lead the majority of the populace to the electro-cuting chair, also expounds to them the doctrine of "ought." The Editor of the *New Age* must recently have frightened the capitalist press greatly by giving them a good talking to—administering rebukes all round, ranging from the "Boom-ing impertinence" for the *Times*, "omniscient twaddle" for the *Nation*, "yap" for something else, down to one which he distinguishes as being the "meanest jackal-pup of the lit-ter" because forsooth all these have not interpreted the true truth of the South African business for the proletariat as they "ought" and because, even its untrue truth when supplied was late—the old dodge of leading the poor to expect outrageous philanthropy from the enemy, but not the spunk of a chicken from themselves. The Capitalist press is the Capitalists' press, the lips and tongue of the Capitalist body. It is the mouth-piece contrived, bought and set working for the one purpose of telling forth their praise and aiding their own schemes. Why should it give utterance to anything that would make difficul-ties for capitalists or give away the secret where their strength

lies? If it can give the impression that their supremacy pivots
round a question of "Right" or "Wrong" and can keep their
journals such as the *New Age* busy debating it, why not? The
Editor of the *New Age* would do well by himself if he were
to re-read the story of Samson and Delilah, which applies
very pertinently to the situation[1]. No one we think from the
day that story was written through the thousands of years
down to this has seen anything but wisdom in the giant's
fictions concerning the withes, the plaited ropes and what
not. Where men have seen folly plainly visible was in finally
putting an enemy in possession of the truth. The capitalist
press is quite capable of learning a lesson like that even if
the "humanitarian" journals are not. If the poor want true
descriptions prompt and to time they must become articulate and supply themselves with a mouthpiece of their own.
At present they have neither the brains to conceive nor the
strength to produce nor the intelligence to devise the like. If
such a one were created and run in their interests they would
look on at its slow strangling as calmly as they would regard a
military garrison. Both phenomena would be to them equally
devoid of significance. It is not the poor who maintain such
scattered shreds as exist of a poor man's press. Then why
whine because they are not told what it would be very good
for them to know, but not so good for those upon whom they
rely to do the telling.

---

[1] ≠ Judges 13-16.

64

5. The Chastity of Women

"Our best work we do to satisfy ourselves."

[. . .] IT is clear why as long as the "pure" women persist there can be no abatement of "lust." It is not merely that by their very distinction they stand pointer in hand as it were stimulating it first by concentration and then by a refusal which is in itself a further stimulation, a retiring which is flight inviting chase; they make the error, as negative persons, of mistaking for lust love itself when it is offered to them. We have already elsewhere made the distinction between the two, and the phrases in which the "pure" refer to their conduct in marriage unmistakably show which of the two they are looking forward to in anticipation. They "give" themselves in marriage: that is, they permit: as negatives they submit themselves to a positive will: they feel in short that a deed is done to them which they, in virtue of the consideration that they are now married, allow. They are the true "womanly"; the attitude they adopt is not that of persons who satisfy their own desires, but of those who in kindness allow others to satisfy theirs.

Having held back during the requisite period which serves to keep up their value as saleable goods before marriage, the bargain being struck they allow themselves to be "touched" as Miss Pankhurst would put it, that is, they submit to what to them, is lust. That is why they feel that they in "giving" themselves have given so much: given so much in fact that they have a reasonable claim for a lifetime of devotion: and a sound grievance if they do not get it: quite naturally too, since they have for so long set such unparalleled importance on it. During their fleeing period they have kept themselves in good countenance by imagining a sentimental heaven as an inevitable return to be made for what is so persistently sought. That is why the "pure" women are always disappointed with marriage. They find themselves in the position of the remnants of a dinner after a hungry person has dined; a position which is the Nemesis of the womanly woman: the person who thinks it of more importance to charm than to be charmed: to be the repast rather than the diner. They make the mistake of commiserating too much, and putting too much weight upon the outcry and woes of the person with an appetite: of putting the value of the request and the refusal on the same footing: whereas they are of as wholly differing orders as are the appetite and the dinner, for the latter of which almost anything will serve, provided the appetite can be maintained. However—to get rid of this material metaphor—let us rather say that the temperament which seeks first and foremost to be charmed is of an altogether higher order than that which seeks first and foremost to charm. To have someone who charms us is a matter of infinite importance to us: as to whom we charm, provided we can keep our special magnet sufficiently within our vicinity as to keep hope alive, is of little importance at all—to us. It is the question of what we want, not of what others want—even though it happens to turn out that we are the wanted article—that is of material importance to the positive, dominating selfish master mind. Those who charm us we adore because they mean so much to our own life and growth. It is not their growth or their convenience that matters: the reason that gifts are lavished on them and their conveniences and wishes served as soon as they are spoken, is to keep them fixed where they will be serviceable to us and as token of how much they mean to us. When therefore Miss Pankhurst with a toss of the head speaks thus: "There can be no mating

between the spiritually-developed women of this new day and
the men who in thought or in conduct with regard to sex
affairs are their inferiors," she speaks—true, to the womanly
woman—in the terms of one who rebuts the efforts to win her
to that which she allows but does not desire[1]. She speaks as
one who is administering a rebuff to someone else, not as one
who is obstructing the satisfaction of her own needs. Nor is
she. Womanly women do not pretend to love: they are loved.
Their attitude of pride is strongly illuminating: in love we are
humble, in miserably-happy fear of our fate; but the "pure"
women having no desire in the matter fear nothing, having
nothing at stake. Their pride is the subtle expression of their
nothingness: the unconscious expression of self-contempt. If
they knew anything of the positive element of love, of being
charmed, they would understand that it is the most valuable
thing in the world: the one which stimulates growth from
within, increases capacity and stimulates effort. With the
verdict of the world in general in view, one does work just
sufficiently well to escape its active censure for scamping. Our
best work we do to satisfy ourselves: but the work which
we achieve by a sort of inspiration beyond our best, by the
establishing of a new record, we do it under the influence
and to please the one or two people in the world who have
the power to charm us—for the sake of an "It's rather good"
from them. It is not so much that the charm they exert
helps to surmount effort: it removes the sense of effort; it is a
lubricant: or a powerful magnet capable of drawing one up
a steep place. Why then this hoity-toity "Spiritual women
will not mate with... " any whatsoever? The personal value
of charm to oneself is such that were a tree or a lamp-post

---

[1] ≠ *The Great Scourge and How to End It.* Christable Pankhurst (London: E.
Pankhurst, 1913).

capable of exerting it, women would mate with these. The "health" or "record" of men and women does not enter into the matter: the only question is: whether they can do it; be charming, to wit. It is a question of power, not of an adjunct intellectually considered desirable, and the vision of "suitors" with aspect as wholesome as sound field-turnips each having a doctor's certificate in his pockets is powerfully unalluring: because, one must suppose, the efficiency of one to charm must be proved by the sole fact of charming.

It is the failure to appreciate the fact about life that it is only its positive aspect that matters, which causes such radically different attitudes towards life. All the negative things, fear, hopeless misery, all forms of the thing called "disease" are specific forms of weak vitality[1]. It is more important to heighten vitality than to combat disease: which as a matter of fact can only be overcome by increased vitality, and there is more danger to "health" to be awaited from the misery of renunciation and the dull heats of virginity than from the ills of syphilis and gonorrhoea. There can be no disease of "matter": it can be broken but it is incapable of contracting disease. There can only be such a breaking down of the spiritual unitary stream as to render it incapable of penetrating the material which it has assimilated and organised into a body. The sole thing which can be called a "cause" of disease is low vitality and of all the things which tend to lower it, the chief is dullness. (Miss Pankhurst should have referred to the "health" of the virgins as also to our vigorous "virgin" civilisation.) Both the "pure" and the "vicious" are in and to themselves dull and stupid: they are duller still

---

[1] ≠ see Bergson, p. 79.

to those associated with them: the obsession in their interests of necessity makes them so. The "pure" moreover add
to their lack of interest a pose of virtue which creates the
close atmosphere to which we have referred: they assume the
pose instinctively for a defence because fundamentally they
know they are not genuine. They cannot be truthful and by
contrast with their theatricality the frank bargaining of the
prostitute is a relief. So the "purity" atmosphere lays a pall
of dullness all about: no one escapes it: whatever the role
we adopt we are caught in its folds. Dullness is death in life:
disease has at least the relative advantage of being discomfort.
In disease life is afflicted, but it is petrified by dullness; any
form of torture is preferable to it; any small "vice" which
offers a trivial variation of sense perception. The seeking after
the "vicious" is a small ineffectual wriggle which life makes to
escape the boredom of the "pure," but "vice" cannot throw
off its "pure" character. The two are one—related to each
other as the obverse and reverse of a coin: the under and over
of the same psychological condition: as the prostitute is the
twin-trader of the legally-protected "pure" woman. Where
there are excise officials there are smugglers. Let therefore the
womanly women abandon the "privileges" which enable them
to make a corner in a commodity the demand for which they
sedulously stimulate, and the pirate brigs which ply on the
outskirts of the trade will become purposeless. The entreaty
of the cry "Virginity for men" coming from so favoured a
class as those of the "pure" women has a comical sound, and
Miss Pankhurst's disease-story is overdone. If seventy-five per
cent of men have one form of venereal disease and twenty per
cent have another and both kinds are contagious and possibly
ineradicable, it follows that the number of those who are free
from it neither means nor matters: that we are all tainted

and presumably all inoculated in fact. If Miss Pankhurst desires in the interests of a fad successfully to exploit human boredom and the ravages of dirt she will require to call in the aid of a more subtle intelligence than she herself appears to possess.

6. Mainly Anent the Decalogue

"When it is a crime to breathe?
When someone has you securely by the throat."

F OR a period of eight months or more we have been explaining that "ideas" of the static kind commonly called
"absolute," *i.e.*, those which do not with more or less speed
dissolve into ascertained fact, are delusions of intelligences too
feeble to be quite aware of what they speak. It appears that a
proportion of our readers, mindful of past benefits no doubt,
have tolerated the broaching of this subject with only a very
strained patience: and that now, at long length, with a pained
realisation that the theme shows no sign of flagging, they are
driven to ask whether we are not buffooning. "Are we in
earnest? Have we *none* of the standard (*i.e.* absolute) ideas?"
We therefore propose here to make a number of forthright
statements on the absolute virtues which are associated with
the injunctions promulgated in the decalogue. After that, we
shall make no further comment on questions as to whether we
are "earnest." Before dealing with the concepts bolstered up
by the commandments it will serve us to notice an assumption
relating to the "Search for Truth," for supported by "opinions"
and "beliefs" merely a critic will only feel justified to the
extent of advancing opposing arguments: but on the strength
of his assumptions he will base reproaches. A reproachful
one writes: "It is silly to be contemptuous of people who
are *trying to get at Truth*." The assumption is clear and it
is very widely adopted. It is considered that the making of
an earnest Search for Truth should of itself ensure immunity
from scoffs and jeers: that the "Search for Truth" represents
an activity the worth of which will be self-evident, and that

not to be in earnest about it is the mark which separates
the "frivolous-minded" from the "serious" man: "Are you
in earnest or are you buffooning?" means "Do you enter
into the debate on Truth seriously?" Our answer of course
is that we are as earnest in the inquiry into the nature of
Truth as—but no more than—any one of our readers would
be in debating the question "What is a Boojum: or a Snark:
or the Jubjub Bird?" We are quite prepared to agree that
in the hunt for the Bird of Truth (whereon see Miss Olive
Schreiner) as in the Hunt for the Snark, all methods of search
are equally worthy of respect, and equally admitted of, and
that the choice should be left to individual preference.

"Do all that you know, and try all that you don't" is
applicable in both cases.

> You may seek it with thimbles and seek it with
> care,
> You may seek it with forks and hope,
> Threaten its life with a railway-share
> Charm it with smiles and soap.

Or if you are a modern reformer—a rebel or a suffragist—you
will go as well in the search and as far by vigorous clapping
of hands, by a tract on venereal disease, or best of all by a
throb and a whirl inside your head.

> For "Truth" is a peculiar creature and won't
> Be caught in a commonplace way!

but like the Snark, if and when discovered may be put to all
manner of uses! One may

> Serve it with greens in shadowy scenes
> Or use it for striking a light[1].

---

[1] ≠ Quotes, with some variations by DM, from *The Hunting of the Snark (An Agony*

❧

It was our set intention to rule out from these notes on the Decalogue every ambiguity, all irony, every suggestion of the frivolous and pert which possibly might mislead. It is therefore in order to be unmistakeable or nothing that we protest the serious, profoundly important philosophic character of *The Hunting of the Snark*. With uplifted hand—not that it matters—we declare that we are most lugubriously solemn in making this stipulation that we be allowed—generously and without reservation—to laugh at all Searchers after Truth. It is precisely what they are there for: to be laughed at at the start when the searchers are fresh: jeered at when they keep the performance going to such length that we become tired. They are in precisely the same position as a comic singer, who sings his songs to provoke amusement at their initial essaying: perhaps he may rely on the quality of its jokes to risk repeating it before the same audience twice: but he would know what to expect were he to repeat it half-a-dozen times. Similarly with the methods of the Searchers for Truth, which though varied in detail have a common accompaniment of noisy reiteration, apparently resulting from a species of convulsion brought on by the chanting of words. These methods though amusing at the outset, if continued swiftly become matters meet only for jeers; jeers appearing to have the salutary effect of putting a brake on the wild whirling of the word-intoxicated heads. (All the searchers, by the way, claim not to be searching for Truth but to have found it.) Bacon's observation to Pilate's scoffing question "What is Truth?" "And did not wait for an answer[1]," is striking because it is prompt, not because it is discerning: it is really as inept as it is facetious. Probably the answer

---

in 8 Fits) by Lewis Caroll (London: Macmillan, 1876).

[1] ≠ "Of Truth" from *Essays or Counsels, Civil and Moral* by Francis Bacon (1625).

74

was beginning to be offered to Pilate when he cut in with the words of the Bellman, "Skip all that"; at any rate, Bacon might have reflected that the Roman governor would have had long to wait seeing that fifteen hundred years after, Bacon himself is only prepared to make a quibble concerning it. The fact of the matter is that Truth is one of a class of words which have been born under the two-fold impulse of (1) haste to make a finished statement, (2) doubt as to the grounds on which to make it. In the introduction to the "Hunting of the Snark" the process is beautifully analysed. Explaining how the "hard" words in the poem such as "snark" and "boojum" have come into existence, the author shows how they are the natural outcome of doubt and haste. "Supposing," he says "that, when Pistol uttered the words:— 'Under which king, Bezonian? Speak or die[1]?' Justice Shallow had felt certain it was either William or Richard, but had not been able to settle which, so that he could not possibly say either name before the other, can it be doubted that, rather than die, he would have gasped out 'Rilchiam?'" We can surmise that subsequently, if the memory of the circumstances under which the name "Rilchiam" had been coined were forgotten while the name still lingered there would undoubtedly have been established in history a puzzle which would have corresponded to the "ethical" puzzles of philosophy, "What is Truth?" "What is Justice?" "What is Chastity?" It would have run "Who was King Rilchiam?" All of which should explain why in refusing to take the conceptual ideas seriously we feel we understand the impatience of a Pilate or Bellman who dismissed these ancient wrangles with a "Let's skip all that."

---

[1] ≠ *History of Henry IV, Part II* by William Shakespeare (circa 1596).

❧

It should now be clear to the most verbalised intelligence why we should consider it a ridiculous waste of our space and our readers' time to engage in any debate concerning "Morality" in gross, or sub-divisions of "Morality," such as Honesty, Truthfulness, Piety and so on, in particular. We consider them one and all the "Rilchiams" of language, and far from being debated seriously, their forms should be expelled from Speech: except for purposes of gammon and make-believe. However, just as from the generalised form Rilchiam, a vague associated with an individual William or Richard can be made, so from the vague generalisations called "Morality" or "Honesty" special forms of action can be considered to be related. When therefore a correspondent asks in a bewildered way whether or no we believe in "Honesty" and then goes on to ask whether we run up accounts with tradesmen and shirk payment, we get a perfect example of the workings of what Weininger would have called the *henid* mind: the confused mind which works on a basis of loose association[1]. (Weininger's description of the *henid* mind is extremely able and well worth attention. It is diverting to note that he used the term to characterise the intelligence of women and yet at the same time one of the principal points which he endeavoured to make against them was that they were incapable of constructing a generalisation!) However, no matter how achieved it is a mental relief to see the interrogation change from "What is Honesty?" to "Do you steal the goods of your grocer?" Though we capitulate at once to the difficulties of the first, to the second we can answer at once that it is not our privilege. We are not sufficiently well-off to make the experiment workable. But richer people are quite successful in this line, and we hasten to add

---

[1] ≠ *Sex and Character* by Otto Weininger (London: W. Heinemann, 1906)

that we have no scruples against robbing the grocer. We
do not "respect" grocers' goods on any sort of principle: in
fact we have been pointing out for months that the goods of
the grocers of Dublin for instance could with great wisdom
have been regarded as the strikers' own. "Snatch in as suave
a manner as you can" would be our working basis; that is
if you want something, but if necessity drives then "Snatch
anyhow." The difference in method is such as that which
exists between the methods used by bankers, financiers and
the professional classes in general at the present time and
that used by an army which commandeers food in war-time.
It is a distinction in the amount of fuss, that is all. Do it
gently if you can—and like it gentle—but anyhow "Do it."
Those who can wait until their "share" is given them, will
have a very wry story to tell: the tale of the "industrial
problem." The poor who are too modest to "take," complain
because more is not "given" them. They make the enormous
mistake of thinking that "shares" are allocated on a principle:
whereas in reality, each fixes his own share. The injunction
in the decalogue is purposely (presumably) left unfinished,
in order to allow an individual choice in the matter. "Thou
shall not steal" means nothing. Not merely does it neglect to
say "Thou Shalt not steal"—rent, profit or interest; it does
not even specify "tradesmen's goods" nor even free rides on
the London Tube, on the manœuvring of which we think we
could give valuable information to penniless and foot-weary
pedestrians. It just leaves it conveniently blank for those to
fill in whose particular "order" happens to be uppermost at
the given moment. For it is obvious that the whole of "life" is
based on a system of "stealing": that is a forcible laying hold
of required commodities without permission. We "take" the
life of bird, beast or vegetable, and cut short their struggles to

survive without as much as a "by your leave." It is only where one power or confederation of powers has become supreme that the question of "theft" arises at all. The proper answer to the questions, "Under what circumstances is 'taking' tantamount to thieving?" And "Under what circumstances is 'stealing' 'immoral?'" can be found by asking the analogous questions "When is it a 'crime' to breathe?" or "When is breathing immoral?" The answer being of course, "When someone has you securely by the throat"—"When you can't manage it, that is."

It is manifest even to the least observant of human beings that the embargo on appropriation of goods is laid only by those who are powerful enough to retain possession of them. It has no relation whatever to the producing, *i.e.* the growing or making, of them: and we venture to say it never will have. If the time ever arrives when "each produces his own" and the "right" of each to retain what is produced is "respected" it will be because the power of defence of each, either singly or in the requisite combinations is such as to produce "balance." As long as there exist those whose power of attack and defence is obviously lower than that of others there will be an embargo placed on the appropriation of produce even by the producers. The power of self-appropriation and of self-defence will always dictate the terms in virtue of which property is held: will always decide what is "just." If men could only size up the confused phrases and bid their orators "justice them no justice" and then turn their attention to the term "just" they would find it very well directed. That state of affairs is "just" which is presented by the balance of all the forces implicated. If one person can trample another down, rob him and leave him to make shift for himself as his remnant of strength will allow him: for him to do so would be "just." A thing to be "just" is to be as it can be: other things are merciful, pitiful and so on: but they are not "just." The best instance of the accurate use of the word "just" is in the little phrase "Just so," which means "Exactly"—a concurring that things are as they are. When therefore the mob are persuaded that they must not steal in the manner prohibited by statutory law under the impression that to refrain is not merely "legal" but "just," they are acting under the hypnotism of habit and familiar association. The most efficacious way of dealing with this hypnotic spell which at present is so forceful that a policeman's job is on the whole one suited to the powers of superannuated invalids—soft, because the necessary work is performed by that mental inhibition which plays the police-man, *i.e.* the thing called Conscience—the most efficacious way of dealing with it is by reflecting on the reason why two terms should invariably be placed together. The command-ment "Thou shalt not steal—in certain ways"—is embodied in a legal embargo as to method issued in the joint names of Law-and-Order. When a particular embargo becomes too annoying attention is usually directed on the iniquities of *Law*, but the meaning of "law" and of the "state" which gives "law" weight only becomes intelligible when what is supported under the name of "Order" is clearly understood. "Order" has nothing to do with "tidiness" or "harmony," or any "concept." It is merely an *arrangement of things* to suit an individual whim. First let the individual know what he wants at any particular moment and the arrangement which fits in with that want to him is "order." A "model" housewife will consider things "in order" when the chairs and tables are in those places which please her fancy (and very probably that of no one else); a gang of assassins arranging to blow up a city by means of dynamite would consider everything "in order" when everything was *en train* for the successful accomplishing of the deed. One General Smut is now maintaining "order" in South Africa by well-known lamblike means: "order" is successfully maintained in England on a basis of squalor and want. "Order" then may be defined as the arrangement that fits in with the whim of a particular person or that of a rough compromise of a group of persons: that and no more. There are therefore as many forms of "order" as there are people: each individual and unique; and each one's plan of "order" may vary from day to day according to needs. There is then not *one* "order" as it is left to us to conjecture when we are told that "order" must be maintained, but literally innumerable orders. It is as though people were agreeable to dividing up numbers on a regular plan but with the lengths of the divisions different in each case: one taking alternate odds, another alternate evens, another every third number and so on. Bergson has worked out the theory of "order" of course in *Creative Evolution*[1]. As far as we are aware its application to "law" has still to be made. This application is pretty obvious. A statutory law is the expression of some one view of order, some arrangement agreeable to an individual whim, forced on the rest of the community under threat or execution of physical violence—which violence under the guise of armies and police–is maintained by the assistance of the very people whose own plans of order will be crushed by its agency. Mainly because they are stupid but also in some degree because they are timorous and mean-spirited, what though well-meaning and industrious, the "people" who support the "state" acquiesce in the self-abnegating ordinances

---

[1] ≠ *Creative Evolution* by Henri Bergson (London: Macmillan, 1911).

of the state which are precisely designed to frustrate their own schemes of "order." This is the gist of "democracy," *i.e.* "government by consent." It is quite clear then why there are "laws" against "stealing" of one kind and no laws against far bolder "stealing" of another. The laws against "petty thefts" are made and administered with a right good will: the major thefts of rent profit and interest—the wholesale "lifting" of property are the admired achievements of our "governing classes." The "governing classes" represent a group of individuals whose schemes of "order" have a "natural" affinity for each other: as for analogy one might suggest that all whose numerical divisions happened to be multiples of others must coincide at points: he whose "plan" was "One, four, eight, twelve, sixteen," would find it coinciding at points with his whose plan was "One, eight, sixteen, twenty-four," and so on. The rough compromises arrived at among the members of this group in nowise cancel out the individual differences; the members of the "classes" are prepared to wrangle among themselves, as in the party-system. But they understand their position and smother their dissensions and close their ranks immediately against those whose divisions represent "prime numbers" to theirs—the poor-poor. That is all there is in Law-and-Order. The "morality" red-herring which is dragged into the matter is the creation of the feeble-witted poor who have just so much spirit as would lead them to despise their cowardly acquiescing if it were exposed, naked in the light of day. Their retention of it is of course encouraged by the "governors" since it serves them in the capacity of a most efficient police.

In addition to the main injunction against unauthorised stealing, the decalogue works in the theme in two minor texts:

Number ten: "Thou shalt not covet," &c, and number seven: "Thou shalt not commit adultery[1]." The first of course is exhorting Conscience not to forget its vocation: to play up and be a policeman. Not merely "Do not allow the natural man whom you have in charge to steal what he shouldn't: don't allow him even to want to." It is on the principle of using preventive methods early, as one cannot be too careful.

In the seventh injunction one recognises in "Adultery" another of the class of "Rilchiam": and dismisses it. Concerning what this commandment means as distinct from what it says, it is clear that it is a warning against using other people's property. It would call for no remark additional to those made anent the eighth did it not illustrate how vain is the belief in the "rights" of possession: that possession is not merely nine but ten parts of the law: that an "owner" should be as ready to defend his property with as unremitting a zeal as that with which an early Christian guarded his soul to prevent the devil snatching it away. What is called the "free love" argument is an exposition of the vanishing of the claims of "right" in face of the power of "might": a fact which leaves a "conceptualist" as nonplussed as a merchant would be if bales of goods assigned to the ownership and warehouse of Mr. Smith were to find voice and legs and say "We are only labelled Smith: we prefer to belong to Mr. Jones." If thereupon they held to Mr. Jones and Mr. Jones held to them, it would be poor consolation to Smith to know that he had a "right" to them. He would find himself in the same situation as the "workers" who work and think they have a "right" to what they produce and can prove it to you by ten different lines of argument; but who are bereft of the goods none-the-less. One can only say that it is their business to

---

[1] ≠ Exodus 20:1–17.

find out why their ears are boxed: also why their pockets and stomachs are empty.

In the sixth commandment, "Thou shalt not kill," the ruse employed is identical with that employed in number eight. Obviously we live only because we are prepared to kill—bird, beast, fish, plant and anything which stands between us and the opportunity to kill these; to kill is the first necessity of living; therefore the injunction cannot be, as it appears, a general prohibition of killing; it refers apparently to "killing" under special circumstances and the specification is merely left blank to allow "governors" to fill in the bill to fit their convenience. When killing is done contrary to the specialised restrictions selected by governors it becomes "crime" and is called "murder." To understand why killing at times is, and at other times is not murder, one must turn not to law, but to the theory of "order." "Order" is that arrangement of things—including people—which fits in with the whim of an individual, or an individualised group. If the "order" of those who are maintained in their position of governors demands the killing of certain people, as it does in a war, in overworking to make profits, or any of the thousand ways in which the lives of the common people are jeopardised and "taken"—then "killing is no murder." It is instead, "patriotism" or "bold statesmanship." But if the common people begin to think that the ways of the governing parties are incompatible with their ideas of "order" and they take to killing: then killing is murder: double-dyed, heinous: a hideous, heart-shuddering blasphemous affront to God and man: to the universe, to "morality," to the heavenly host and all the troops of angels, and must be avenged. So, call out the entire army and navy and see that God and the Church are bustled up!!!!! Killing then is murder and no doubt about it.

To the fifth and fourth we need give little space. The fifth is one which most of us are fairly well able to reckon up. "To honour God"—or the "king" is one thing. We have not lived with God and the king: but with parents most of us have lived and very early in life the "command" to "honour" them becomes a dictate of supererogation. If we know people well enough, most of us are able to bestow credit where credit is due: and to withhold it on the same terms. Number four can be referred to any week-ender. We need not flog a dead horse. The meaning of the Sabbath day was that it was to be kept "holy": used for the indoctrinating of the "holy ideas." Six days are as long a period as a "natural" man can go without being reminded of the holy ideas: the seventh day is to be set aside for the renewing of allegiance to the "sacred" names. In an article in our last issue we explained why certain names were to be kept "sacred": because if questioned their "essence" would vanish: the name was the thing. We refer our readers again to that explanation, which will enable us to "explain" the import of the third commandment almost in a word[1]. "Thou shalt not take the name of thy God in vain: for the Lord will not hold him guiltless" and so on. That is: the name of God is not to be questioned: it is to be left—a name above all names–undesecrated by a "natural" man's inquiry. "God's" identity is not to be inquired into: a prohibition which puts the first and second commandment out of reach of a danger which very closely threatens them. "Thou shalt have no other gods but Me." (Of this the second is a continuation and

---

[1] ≠ see "Men, Machines, and Progress," p. 47.

enlargement.) It is only the fact that inquiry into the identity of the "Me" is forbidden which prevents the identifying of the two persons of the injunction. Suppose the "Thou" and "Me" are one and the same? If they are one and the same, the whole heavenly structure dissolves in mere sound in the ears of the natural triumphant man—the egoist. Valuable indeed to the conceptualists are the uses of the "Sacred!"

Of the ten, the ninth remains: the injunction against "bearing false witness," to which we would add "lying" in general, we have purposely postponed to the last, because it has to do with a different order of values from the remaining nine. To be forbidden to "bear false witness" and to be forbidden to "steal" implies that one is in possession of the power to effect their contraries: an assumption which can by no means go without question. It is within the power of any either to steal or not to steal (within the prescribed limits): but it is not in the power of all to "bear true witness." A dog—or a member of any other sub-human species—can steal: it can also be terrorised into not stealing. But to "bear witness" either truly or falsely is a business which involves a development of the power of being "aware" to its self-conscious degree. It is a power of life as yet in its incipient stage, and for the majority of human beings it is in too confused a period for them to be able to say with certainty what their perceptions are, except in the simplest and most often repeated operations of sense such as seeing and hearing. Even these often lie within a mist too hazy for many knowingly to bear "true" witness. Many witnesses for instance in police-court proceedings could not say whether they were speaking truly or not, if they became excited, and if finally it should be proved that they have been "lying," it is not proved that they have deliberately "borne false witness": it is quite as fair to believe that they were incapable of deciding what was true. It is not often that witnesses lie handsomely. There are comparatively few people who can lie boldly and deliberately. To do so requires too precise a perception as to what is "true." The reason why the "evidence" of so many witnesses who arc half-consciously "lying" breaks down under cross-examination is that the witnesses have not perceived the facts well enough to know just how these will be effected should some of them be described contrarily to the manner in which they occurred. Apart however from either the confused or deliberate lying about simple facts, we have the great stack of lies concerning emotions which has been piled up half-consciously and half-unconsciously by more highly developed people, under the name of Culture and which are supposed to comprise "Truth." "Culture" is the outcome of Gadding Minds—minds, that is, which are dull "at home," and which have fallen in gladly with the notion that there is a "Truth" which can be come at by assiduous and ingenious manipulation of phrases. They are very willing to attempt short cuts to understanding especially if they can in that way travel with a crowd of gadders like themselves. The culture-epoch of the last two thousand years will have to pass before the Searchers for Truth begin to inquire "at home": to understand that the only things which are "true" for them are the few things which their own individual power to perceive makes them aware of through the channels of their senses. Their present habit of Hunting for Truth with thimbles and forks, anchors and care, clappers, tracts and a wild whirling sound will help them as far towards awareness as—to use an analogy we have used before—the presentation of bound volumes of the works of Darwin will help the jelly-fish up the ascent of being. The clutter of cultural concepts—mere words—are choking the frail fine tentacles of perception: preconceived notions hang as a film over the eyeballs and until they can slip the entire burden their way in life will be mad and melancholy.

The great difference therefore between the eighth and ninth commandments could be gathered from some such summary as this: "Steal as efficiently as you can if you want to or need": it is the unquestionable method of regal and noble appropriation. But, "If you can avoid lying, or can bear true witness, do so—from your own advantage." The power to do so is a capacity, feeble but capable of growing, and is on the one line of human growth discernible. It makes that which is merely conscious self-conscious. It needs every encouragement: practice and training. It is not that "bearing false witness" is wrong (if swearing away the character of a threatening tiger falsely would save one from danger, it would be a strange person who would refrain from swearing falsely; and the same holds good in respect of many of the "tight corners" in relation to fellow human beings, which we occasionally find we have run into in this life.) Right and wrong save for conceptualists have no meaning: but that bearing false witness, and every form of lying and half-lying tends to weaken a power which is weak enough, but which is the highest reach to which vital power has, as yet, risen. To bear true witness comprises human genius. No wonder therefore with a culture made of lies, *i.e.* false observations, genius looks as though it were about to flicker out, or that, though we may do many apparently despicable things for money and property, we are aware of what we are doing when we regard the man who plays the charlatan and prostitutes his powers of observation as a fool in the deepest sense of the word.

7. Anent the Decalog

"The strong and alert are never moral: when they
appear upon occasion to be so, it is by mere coincidence."

PERHAPS the most striking illustration of the unquestioning habit of mind common to us all is the tone in which we use the word "immoral." Actions may be all things else and be tolerated, but if they are voted "immoral" their case is closed: the are damned, though most of us would need to be hard-pressed before we were able to say why. For obviously all that is said when one says "immoral" is "not-customary." It is informing to note moreover that while not-customary conduct is to be damned, it in nowise follows that its positive opposite is to be blessed. People are not prepared to admire enthusiastically "customary conduct": they have in fact no very high opinion of it: why then the working up of fierce indignation at the prospect of its contrary? That the "faithful" have been aware of the difficulty is shown by the extensive searches they have made to find the justification of "moral" conduct both as to foundations and superstructure: what inquiry into the Fundamentals of Ethics has shown to be missing the Metaphysics of Morals has attempted to make good. Indeed to enjoy the spectacle of human beings indulging in the full tide of talk in their least graceful moments one must turn to them when they are presenting the "philosophy" of morals. On no other occasions do they twist, shift and cant with so little effect of grace. And they are still hard at it and still stick at nothing. If moral conduct does not suit men, then change the men. The latest Defender of the Sacred, Eucken, unconsciously puts their case neatly. He says:

Before all else the natural world keeps man bound down to the mere ego; ... it becomes clearly visible that, as compared with the strength of the mere man, something impossible is being demanded. *Therefore man must become something more than mere man.* The original affirmation has become intolerable, but out of the negation has arisen a new affirmation. Here are great demands and great upheavals, gigantic tides of life sweeping men along and transforming them an inner infinitude becomes increasingly manifest. If anything can show us that our life is not a matter of Indifference, that in it something significant takes place, it is morality that can do it[1].

And there we may leave them.

"Moral" conduct is, as its name implies, "customary" conduct. Its advantages are the advantages of all repetitive action which is facile and foreseeable because habituated. Moral conduct is mechanised conduct and possesses all the advantages of mechanical reliability. It fits almost perfectly on to the routineer. Its disadvantages are the same: it plays havoc when it comes into contact with the new and unexpected: meets the unobserved factor which was not taken account of in blocking out the moral plan. To fit properly, moral conduct would need to be the activity of a "living automaton"—of a combination of forces which are denials of each other. It is the conjoining of these two contradictions which enables men

---

[1]≠ Eucken, Rudolf: *Main Currents of Modern Thought* (London: T. Fischer Unwin 1912) p. 392.

to construct "tragedy." The recipe for the production of a Tragedy, *i.e.* a play upon a simulated Terror, is as follows: a collection of living beings with an appetite for experience, adventurous therefore; a recognition of a species of conduct customary to the people to which the special collection belongs (*what* species of course being quite immaterial); lastly a "respect" for the second in the "intellect" of the first. These three ingredients mixed well together will account for any of the "great tragedies" known to men. Every "tragedy" has a "problem": playwrights spin their brains to shreds to concoct one: a new "problem" will win fame for any playwright: so anxious are men to enjoy the sensation of mock Terror: the so-called purgation through pity and horror. To understand the fascination of "Tragedy" it is necessary to realise that all Tragedy is melodrama, that is: actual living judged by a "concept" of living. It is worked by dint of an acceptance of the hoisting of a sky-scape, a canvas stretched across the mental heavens whereon is painted the moral scheme to which the herd below make effort to comport themselves. The "tragedy" is achieved by concentrating attention on the movements of those who being the least herdlike venture to ignore the sky-scape in order to follow their own bent for experience, thereby inviting the onslaughts of the terror-stricken herd. If the playwright can make it look feasible for the "hero" himself to participate in the herd's horror at his "sacrilege," the chances of success are heightened, the "heinous" effect of the situation upon which the "Terror" of the tragedy depends thereby having been increased.

The effect of tragedy on an appreciative audience appears to be a subconscious one. Of a certainty its effect is not what

Aristotle said was the function of these representations of woes of heroes—"to purge the mind by pity and terror of these and similar emotions[1]." The unconscious effect of tragedy is to reveal as the slang phrase has it "the greatness of man" as against the cobweb-like mesh of "thoughts" to which men lend the moulding of their actions as an affair of sport and make-believe. Melodrama purges terror of its basis of terror: as the turning up of a light in a dark room at once makes an object which in the half-light looked fearsome and strange, obvious and harmless. Those most swayed by concepts relish "tragedy" most. They enjoy it because subconsciously they are ceasing to respect the reality of the concepts which are the making of it. Melodrama because it displays in so garish a light the nature of "morals" is the subtlest sapping of the framework it is built on: which accounts for the unfriendliness of advocates of the sacred for this attractive but too destructively bright exhibition of their holy ghosts—the moral concepts. The churches for instance cannot be friendly towards drama: half-tones are among the foremost of the churches' exigences. So too, it is obvious that the arch-conceptualist, Plato, must demand the rigorous suppression of tragedy in his model republic.

It is clear that the one emotion which the moralists cannot afford to permit to weaken is: Fear. (They would call it reverence, but no matter.) Whatever strengthens human fear is to them the basis of "good": because "Fear" is disintegrating, and throws its owner in submission on to the breast of any and every concept which is thrust forward and called "salvation." The moralists exploit and play upon the feeling of smallness and loneliness which is the first outcome of that sense of isolation and separateness which is called

---

[1] ≠ Aristotle: *Poetics.*

self-consciousness. It is because men are in the first place lonely and afraid, that the feebler sort move in herds and act alike: hence the growth of "customary" action: moral action. The outcry against the "immoral," *i.e.* the unusual, is the expression of distress of the timid in the presence of the innovation. It is the instinct which feels there is safety with the crowd and danger as well as loneliness in adventuring individually which puts the poignant note into the epithet "immoral." To be "immoral" is to be on precisely the same level as the unconventional and the unfashionable: that and no more.

Although "morals," *i.e.* the collective term applied to automatised action, are based on the all-too-commonly observable phenomenon that the actions of herds at a given time run to one pattern, in the course of time it is a patent fact that certain influences acting on the herds tend to change the pattern. "Fashions" give the best illustration of how "morals" change. When crinolines for instance are "in," all women wear crinolines; when they are "out," to wear a crinoline would be a mild scandal, but something else is "in," and all women like sheep are approximating to that. So with "morals." They change but when they do the herd changes with them as by a common impulse. It is therefore only on account of the little extravagances of the rhetoricians—who will do many things to come by a good-sounding mouthful—that we hear talk of "the changeless law of morality." Morals are fashions in conduct that are constantly changing: but change as they will they will find their faithful attendant crowd of timorous and ineffectuals. The strong and alert are never moral: when they appear upon occasion to be so, it is by mere coincidence.

It is the realisation of this fact that they are catering only for the needs of the feeble which puts zest into the ambitions of great "founders," "leaders," "teachers." They can lay down precepts fit for followers with easy minds because it is only the born followers that will follow. So each new "leader" has his "precept" for the guidance of the faithful: the "pattern" according to which they must work. Each "New Dispensation" has its "law," and it would be a pity to leave the precepts of the decalogue without turning over the commandment of the newer dispensation which in a curiously odd way has worked itself haphazard in and among the pattern of the older which still verbally holds good.

The commandment "Love one another" is an advance in subtlety as compared with the injunctions it was intended to supersede. It is an attempt to establish an intra-conscious police in the shape of Conscience. It is what the Webbs for instance would call a move in the direction of "efficiency in administration," as the spy-system is more "efficient" than an ordinary police-system. More efficient because more intimate, and more effective because it is easy to control actions once feeling has been surrendered under control. The favour with which the command to "Love one another" was received is evidence of the strength of the desire for neighbourly espionage and democratic control of "each by all" of which all modern legislation is but the grotesque parody in action. (Now with democracy merely an infant, "loving one another" only mildly, we control each other in the realms of marrying, being born, housed, clothed, educated, fed and similar minor matters only. When all "Love one another" with zeal our inter-neighbourly control will begin to show something of what it can be.)

It is therefore quite clear what motives of economy would operate in the point of view of "Authority" in substituting "compulsory love" for "compulsory circumspect behaviour" such as the decalogue enjoins. If only universal "loving" could be made the fashionable habit, the supreme "moral," how easy the work of "leaders" would be. When individuals love one another how easily they work together: how they appear successful in overcoming the otherwise unmanageable ego. Then why not make love among the herd compulsory: and hey presto: the New-Dispensation: the Christian era.

How grotesque a failure and how offensive, the pose of "love according to conscience" has been no one need pause to state with the history of two thousand years written before them. Of all the attitudes which men have struck in emulation of painted canvases which have been stretched across the heavens for their guidance, none has given such good cause for individualist contempt as this. As long as conceptualists in the interest of their large concepts press only *thoughts* into service, the strain is little felt. But "love" is not a thought. It is worth while, in face of revivalist efforts in the cult of love such as, for instance, in the "gospel" of Tolstoy, to consider what people seek in those aspects of love which are not "sex": in the passionate friendships and tenderness of love: the wider emotional needs which have made their appearance with the intensification of "culture." The irony of the efforts of the advocates of the new dispensation to press "love" into the service of the "moral concepts" is not immediately apparent. It is customary to regard "love" as the outcome of "culture" and therefore in some special way amenable to the service of culture. It has become too much a habit of speech with the "civilised" world, *i.e.* the moralised, idea-ised world, to look on "love" as in some sort a means of "salvation," to expect it to analyse why it does so. If it did men would realise that the explanation is the reverse of the current one, *i.e.* that love is the consummation of moralisation. It is in fact an effort to escape from it. The heavy incrustation of habitualised actions, *i.e.* morals, increases in tenacity as life goes on, forming a sort of hutch which is half shelter and half tomb. The taking on of its earlier incrustations is called "growing-up": as they grow more obviously oppressive it is called "growing old." To be "morally-minded" is to have lost the instinct which revolts against this walling-up of the changing spirit: revolts that is against either growing up or growing old. As most people are morally-minded the world is left with a tiny remnant of individuals of whom if we spoke of them in terms of time-*measurement* we should say ranged in age from two years to five: the people of genius and charm. The age of maturity, if we may put it like that, when all that we mean is the age at which the soul has made itself familiar with its new dwelling-place and is at its best, brightest, most inquiring and "true," is from two years to five: not twenty-five or fifty-five as the moralist would like to pretend. From five onwards the browbeating process which is called moral education begins, and as we have said only spirits which are bigger and more resistant than their would-be instructors resist it and stand firm at their height of growth. The rest are slowly driven back by "culture" to the state of automatic living which was their pre-natal existence. The irony therefore of the moralists' efforts to capture "love" in the interest of their already too successful canvases lies in this: that in seeking after the "tendencies" of love and the "understanding" of friendship the morally-bound individuals are seeking a refuge free from the attitudes which make them grown-up. Because they cannot appear what but for fear and a brow-beating education they would be: *i.e.* unashamedly children, they have tried to build a refuge in "love." The tenderness of love or friendship (they are in fact the same thing) are the instinctive means which we seek for ourselves and offer to others, to enable us, in one relation at least to be unashamedly ourselves, very little removed from new-born children. This is the reason why the efforts of those of the "love-cult" to "ennoble" love appear— and appear so particularly to the quite ordinary conventional person—so irredeemably damned. To introduce an attitude into a relation whose very existence is a revolt against attitudes is to snatch from the conventional what is literally his one means of salvation, and that none too certain. It is a sufficiently rare thing for one individual to meet another with enough native sympathy with him to encourage him to show "himself," with all his weakness. It is inevitable that what we feel to be ourselves should in comparison with the harsh-set incrustations of our normal "moral" attitudes, appear "weak." The fact is overlooked that as long as the "weak" thing is there, we are still alive: and that only when the genius in us has flickered out: when we have become one with the herd, do we feel strong in our moral worth.

It is natural that "love" should have attracted the attention of the most thoroughgoing types of moralists, the churchmen or such moralists as the feminine theorisers who call themselves oddly the Woman Movement. The more powerful the agent, the more admirable if pressed into their service. It is unfortunate—for them—that in all cases where "love" has been utilised to further a "system" it has turned and gnawed a yawning gap in the system. But that is part of another story. The fact remains that the chief value of the law of the New Dispensation "Love one another" has been to make evident to men that they will have to, willy nilly, dispense with all dispensations: that there exists for them no "grace" to be "dispensed" which they have not first called up from within themselves. And with the passing of the set manner of "dealing in grace" which is "dispensation," there passes the ghostly basis of mechanised action: "duty" and "morality"; and men begin unashamedly to judge the quality of life by its flavour in actual living: by their own "taste" in regard to it, forming thereby their principle as to what they accept and what they reject in it, which is living by a "principle of taste"—a principle which is no principle. It is living according to personal desire: life according to whim: life without principle: the essentially immoral life.

8. Anarchism

"A tub for Diogenes: a continent for Napoleon:
control of a Trust for a Rockefeller: all
that I desire for me: if we can get them."

"ONLY let us make the draft of the people's pious resolutions, then let who will make their laws[1]." The time has come to rehabilitate the pious resolution which—people being what they now are—is at present held in wholly unmerited contempt. Resolutions are arrogantly despised because, forsooth, they are all "talk." As though "talk" could be despised by any save those who act in confident self-assurance: as the "people" *never* act in fact. People who cannot hit out straight off their own instincts, so to speak, fight their first rounds in talk, just as a person unable to use a sword might use a club. A club, though not a sword, has its uses and any whose only weapon it is might as well see to it that it is not worm-eaten. To return then to the combat by talk: the fight waged in a campaign of "resolutions." Let it be granted that "resolutions" might have a value. Provided they are opposite to facts as they actually exist, they can crystallise for consideration an actual existing relationship: and by so doing neutralise the verbiage of orators who rely for their rhythm and sonorousness as well as their innocuous effects upon enlargements concerning any or all of the things which aren't. Granted therefore, for instance, a campaign of talking: a preliminary skirmish with apposite "resolutions," one might safely risk giving a guarantee that in a measurable distance of time, the fight would be progressing on more drastic terms. [...]

---

[1] ≠ DM paraphrases "Let me write a people's songs, and let who will make their laws" (variously attributed).

It is a wise editor who knows the name of his paper's creed. It appears that we are to be counted among the not-so-wise. At all events, one who is perhaps the best-known living exponent of Anarchism and hitherto an unwearying friend of *The Egoist* has informed us that we are not Anarchist. We are rather "Egoist and Archist," that "combination which has already figured largely in the world's history[1]." The first thing to be said anent that is, that if it is so we must manage to put up with it. If to be an Archist is to be what we are, then we prefer Archism to Anarchism which presumably would necessitate our being something different. There is nothing in a name once one has grasped the nature of the thing it stands for. It is only when there is doubt as to the latter that it becomes possible for names to play conjuring tricks. It is therefore more because the mist of vagueness hangs over the connotation both of Archism and Anarchism than because we are greatly concerned as to which label we are known by that we find it worth while to discriminate, in the matter.

The issue of course turns upon the point as to whether in Anarchism, which is a negative term, one's attention fixes upon the absence of a State establishment, that is the absence of *one* particular *view of order* supported by armed force with acquiescence as to its continued supremacy held by allowing to it a favoured position as to defence, in the community among whom it is established; or the absence of every kind of order supported by armed force provided and maintained with the consent of the community; but the *presence* of that kind

---

[1] ≠ 'Why Not Put Up the Shutters?' by Benjamin R. Tucker. *The Egoist* Volume I Number 6 (March 16th, 1914).

of order which obtains when each member of a community
agrees to want only the kind of order which will not interfere
with the kind of order *likely to be wanted* by individuals who
compose the rest of the community. (We do our very utmost
to state the second position as accurately as possible, but that
it is difficult to do so, those who profess it know well from
their apparently interminable debates on this very subject of
definition among themselves.) The first is what we should call
Anarchism and represents one half of that Egoistic-Anarchism
which *The Egoist* maintains against all comers. The second,
which is that of our correspondent, as far as we can define it
has in our opinion no claims at all that are not embedded in
a hundred confusions to the label of Anarchism. We should
call it rather a sort of Clerico-libertarian-archism, and this
without any desire maliciously to "call names." It represents
a more subtle, more tyrannical power of repression than any
the world as yet has known: its only distinction being that
the Policeman, Judge, and Executioner are ever on the spot,
a Trinity of Repression that is a Spy to boot, *i.e.* Conscience,
the "Sense of Duty." Conscience, more powerful than armies,
"doth make cowards of us all[1]." Conscience takes the Ego
in charge and but rarely fails to throttle the life out of him.
Therefore as compared with the power of egoistic repression
the Ego comes up against in an ordinary "State," that which it
meets in the shape of Conscience is infinitely more oppressive
and searching. The Archism which is expressed in the Armies,
Courts, Gowns and Wigs, Jailors, Hangsmen and what not,
is but light and superficial as compared with that of our
Clerico-libertarian friends.

---

[1]≠ "Thus conscience does make cowards of us all, and thus the native hue of resolution
is sicklied o'er with the pale cast of thought." *Hamlet* by William Shakespeare (circa
1600).

❦

If therefore to be Anarchistic is to hope for and strive after the abolition of "The State" as by the force of governors and submissiveness of governed together compounded, a term with (one may hope) only a temporary significance, then we are it. If on the other hand it is to stand for "liberty," "respect for the liberty of others" and vague *ideas* of this nature, we incline to think the term would be most appropriately treated if it were abandoned to become the plaything of cranks and discussionists. For it will be found that such persons mean, as far as their elementary muddle-headedness permits them to mean anything, to substitute for the obvious repressive agency represented by Arms and the State, the subtler and far more perniciously repressive agency of Conscience with its windy words and ideas. The sum total of the matter amounts to this: We are all Archist: we believe in Rule. The question which divides us is: "*Whose* Rule shall *say* it is?" The reply is a matter of frankness or discretion. Whichever we select by name, in actual fact it remains our own rule: our own view of which "order" should prevail modified by a knowledge of our own fears and weaknesses. If we say "Let the State, *i.e.* the persons who are dominant at the present time, rule," it is because alongside the State's onslaughts by all its weapons of force, it provides some degree of safety under cover of which the timorous find shelter: and in their own little run, rule themselves. For which consideration they are prepared to "respect" the purely arbitrary conventions of statutory law, "crimes" and "criminals"—terms without meaning outside the circle of the respectful ones' timidities.

If in addition to fearing physical violence and consequently to accepting the State, men are submitted to the brow-beating of education, and are more than ordinarily timid, it is in response to a personal desire of their own souls that they put themselves mentally under the control of a system of words, the reaction of the weight of which system is felt in consciousness as Conscience. It is the pull of a set of "allowed" claims which are called duties, the disallowing of which claims are Sin. But the "Archism" is there all the same. The readiness to accept the weight of "Sin" and "Duty" is merely the outcome of an unreadiness—a dislike for self-responsibility. And the Clerico-libertarians, let them call themselves by what name they will, possess in reality this kind of temper. They will not openly confess an approval of the will to satisfy the wants of the "selfish" self. They will allow the self to "rule" but it must first *change itself.* It must nominally be a regenerate, dedicated-to-a-system sort of self. Like Eucken's man which is to be more than a man: the libertarian's self must be a self with the universe tacked on: and the "claims" of the universe must be attended to first. Now when we say that we believe the satisfaction of individual wants is the only "authority" we "respect" we mean the wants of the ordinary person: of any unregenerate Tom, Dick, or Sue. Not what after much argument someone persuades them they want: which finally they will agree they do but will still look as though they don't, but vulgar simple satisfaction according to taste—a tub for Diogenes: a continent for Napoleon: control of a Trust for a Rockefeller: all that I desire for me: *if we can get them.* Our wants are entirely matters of taste: and our tastes are bounded by our comprehension and awareness. We may be fools and gross beasts but nothing is gained by putting us to intellectual strain: making us attitudinising hypocrites. Our illness is that we are dull-witted and stupid without the power which feels things. Then give the penetrative power its chance to grow: wriggle and strain itself into comprehension:

when it can, it *will*: and when it *can* is soon enough. The exact tale of the wriggling and straining when it has found a voice is what one means by being "true" and "honest."

So "Egoist and Archist" let it be. There is—or we imagine it so—a sarcastic ring in our correspondent's comment, "a combination which has already figured largely in the world's history." The sarcasm is unfortunately wasted. If the combination *has* figured largely, it is apparent at least that it is one which will "work": and that is—according to the pragmatists—mainly what matters. The appeal which would have us turn a cold eye on the evidence as to what things succeed in this world wears thin at length. The time has arrived (it is we who say it) when worldly evidence as to what motives do actually work the springs of men's actions should be impartially examined. The evidence in a "cultured" community would no doubt be distasteful, but it is almost sure to be useful. The evidence might be treated, should we say, distantly but honestly as an analyst might treat sewage. In the process one might arrive at the reason why the libertarian, humanitarian idealist cure-alls won't go down: the reason why they won't and knowledge of what will. It will become clear that by their present hopes those that have nothing are deceiving themselves: and that those who know how things are got are quite willing they should remain deceived.

> The World is a bundle of hay,
> Mankind are the asses who pull[1].

Byron knew so much more of the nature of "temper" than the author of *Das Kapital*! It is not on account of the machine-system, nor the "surplus-value" it supposedly creates, that things are as they are, but because some men are reluctant or unable to pull. They have in fact a hundred reasons for not pulling: it is illegal, or immoral, forbidden by conscience, God and the Church: it is theft and Heaven knows what else: *therefore* because *they* can't or won't, "Stop the pulling." That is the socialist, communist and (in the main) the Anarchist solution of "Poverty." The bundle must be respected: not grabbed at without warrant, because, say the theorists, *by right* it is the "property of All." Whereupon the few "respectless" ones divide up the lot between themselves. The sooner the poor become "Archists" therefore the better.

---

[1] ≠ "Epigram: The World is a Bundle of Hay" by Lord Byron: "The world is a bundle of hay, / Mankind are the asses who pull; /Each tugs it a different way, / And the greatest of all is John Bull."

9. Rebels

"Not even the dislike of the sensation of squelching one's boots into another's vitals is likely to stop the struggle."

[...] So the task awaits us to define it afresh. A rebel, we take it, is a person who either for himself or others is dissatisfied with the condition of things—especially things connected with the possession of wealth—in which he finds himself situated; one who therefore concerns himself to alter those conditions. An agitator we might add is a rebel either "born" or "made," who from one motive or another takes it upon himself to make persons who are in the conditions to which he objects also dissatisfied with those conditions with a view ultimately to induce them to alter them.

Well, very estimable: what is there to cavil at in all that? Let us look at it. The characteristic of the "rebel" position is a feeling of angry temper against—something: *i.e.* conditions, presumably static. Now as a matter of fact "conditions" of a relative degree precisely in that relative degree under which the agitator conceives them, are an illusion. There are conditions which men would find absolute, as for instance an explorer without food in Arctic territory: but in a "land of plenty" such as these in which the "rebel movement" is trying to make headway: conditions—static—hard and fast—are illusory, and impermanent as the blocking out of light from a room by a night's frost is impermanent. Heat the room and the window-panes clear and the light streams in. Now seemingly-harsh conditions of wealth-acquiring in fertile lands with instruments of production such as we possess are as formidable as an army of snow warriors exposed in the glare of warm sunlight. Conditions dissolve under the thawing influence of human initiative, energy, and temper. What is amiss, in the worst (of these relative) conditions human eye has rested upon, is not the condition: but the conditioning human quantity which has enabled it to take shape. The condition was not there first: it followed in the trail of the human beings who allowed it to settle round them as an aura; and altering the condition is not the first concern: the seat of the agitator's offending lies in his trying to persuade the "poor" that it is: the folly of the rebels is that they believe it so to be.

Consider the "rebel" movement in England, which, one is not unhappy to note, evidently reached its high-water mark some considerable time ago, and is at present rapidly receding. The most spirited and distinguishing feature of its campaign was its onslaught on "Fat." Even its artist—one whose ability to English rebels must have appeared almost incredible, Mr. Dyson the cartoonist, spent his virtue in picturing the foibles and physical protuberances of the "Man of Wealth," thereby putting the "rebels" in great fettle. At the same time it must have been a source of the most genial diversion to the "Fat" themselves. The traditional gibe at the girth of an imaginary waistband can only be a piquant addition to the satisfaction of those who are well aware that it is a symbolic, what though envious, acknowledgment of the stoutness of their purse—an acknowledgment of their importance from a source which they could well understand being the most loth to furnish it.

The hypothesis upon which the rebel leaders—the agitators—press their propaganda is that "something" is amiss:

therefore that it is a "duty" for those of us who are not pleased with things, to be prepared to attack persons and institutions. An egoist would say that such an hypothesis is erroneous and that hopes built on working it out will end in failure and disappointment. He would regard the "poor" man (whom later we shall perhaps be able to distinguish further) *i.e.* the man who cannot engineer his abilities to the point where what he can get comes within measurable distance of what he wants, one analogous to the sick man in a community. Now for a sick man the first obvious necessity is to get well. If he were to spend what little vital power is left him in raging against those whom he sees around him who are well it would be concluded that his sickness had affected his brain as well as the less sensitive part of his person. If the sick man sees that a man in full health is getting ahead of him in the attaining of the things which the former wants, he may conclude that partially it is because the healthy man had a walk-over. Again, the only obvious thing for the sick one is—to get well.

Where the analogy between the sick man and the poor man is particularly important and altogether parallel and sound is in this point. The first necessities of both respectively, *i.e.* health and power, are not limited quantities: they are not monopolies in the gift of someone else: only in a very remote degree and under exceptional circumstances can they be conferred: they must in some mysterious manner–in the mysterious and miraculous manner which is the way of all life, be culled from within one's self. What the way is for each individual, he finds out not by rebelling but by acquiescing in the "make-up" of his own nature and in that of those with whom he will be in competition. Just as a student in a laboratory could get no way by being a rebel, by asserting that it would be better and safer all round if nitrogen became oxygen, if mercury and gold sank their differences and in the interests of the larger Unity became identical, so social rebels will get no way until they acquiesce willingly in men and women being what they are: accept their oddities and wayward differences and then make the best and most of them to serve their individual ends. It is comical that it should appear necessary to say things so elementary and obvious: one feels like the advocate of the lady anent whom Carlyle ejaculated "Egad, she'd better," when told that after due deliberation she had decided that "for herself, she accepted the Universe." Modern rebels are that lady's intellectual descendants.

The "poor" man is the one who lacks the power to get what he wants. This definition should meet the objections of a correspondent in this current issue, who points out that a non-aggressive man who does not desire wealth and power is quite as likely to be aware of what he wants and of getting it as is the aggressive person who desires "wealth and power[1]." The confusion is caused by putting wealth and power together as though they were terms of equal weight: whereas are they are quite other. "Wealth" takes its place alongside a thousand other things desired, which "power" can attain if its desires are set in its direction. Power is the first requisite no matter what the "want." Even to lead the quiet non-aggressive retired life, one must have power to insist on these conditions coming into being. Unless a man—even the most peaceful—has power to resist, one kind of spy or another with an armed force

---

[1] ≠ "Correspondence: Anent the Decalogue" by C. Harpur. *The Egoist* Volume I Number 6 (March 16th, 1914).

to support him will invade his privacy–the tax-collector, the sanitary inspector, the school attendance officer, and in the predictable future the recruiting-officer, the state-doctor and so on from little to more. The necessity for power can never be laid aside, if there be any wants left: aggressive wants or peaceful wants. With it, peace or aggression are available at will: without it, one must accept what is given. Which explains the speaking difference in the positions of Sir Edward Carson and his Ulster handful, and the nine South African "leaders" with the working population of South Africa behind them.[1] The situation is plain as a pikestaff: explaining it is like "explaining" the fact that most persons have noses somewhere near the centres of their faces: the basis of all concessions, whether from men, governments, or nature itself rests on the power to compel them. The "concession" is the mere act of grace which prefers to assume the pose of giving something, which withheld, would be taken. "Sing a song of liberty," forsooth[2]! Every one is at "liberty" to do what he can. A man's "liberty" is always at his elbow: always as much of it as he has of "power." Then what is the value of rebelling? It is an irrelevance, a waste of attention, time and energy. [...]

How the misconception regarding what this "problem (for-sooth) of the poor" is concerned with, is likely to end—the misconception that its remedy has to be sought in the "sys-tem" rather than with the individual "poor"—is becoming clear. It fosters in the weak an hitherto unknown arrogance concerning what they may regard as their just dues which

---

[1] ≠ "Views and Comments." *The Egoist* Volume I Number 5 (March 2nd, 1914).
[2] ≠ "Song of Liberty" by A. P. Herbert.

ultimately will lead them into a position they at present are incapable of imagining. Because they are "told" that the powerful have wrongly taken advantage of an "unfair system," the feeble-tempered conceive themselves as holding claims of Right and Justice against them. These claims are the actual instruments of their undoing: they the stumbling-block in their line of comprehension. They imagine that with these as defenders, ultimately to appear as another Castor and Pollux in the heat of the battle, any mouldering stick is sufficient to fill out their armoury for the struggle.

Indeed, with the assistance of "Conscience–working-on-the-other-side"— whom they postulate as necessary to Right and Justice, they have come to a conclusion which suits them: that in a "well-regulated" world there is no struggle: the libertarian trinity, Conscience, Right and Justice, can just conceive how it might be possible to muzzle the powerful in their varying degrees until the "pull" of every member of the community should just equal that of the sickest invalid on the list. "If only the powerful would be persuaded and give the system a run it was for their pleasure as well as for their good!" Meantime, while they are theorising, with their eyes in the ends of the earth, the already powerful are using their very theories against them. Under the delusion that in a community of brotherly democrats, each is going to govern all, the "poor" are submitting to a degree of governing which would never have been attempted had it not been glozed over by the fact that it was done *with their consent*. The deluge of powerful men's laws—arrangements to suit the schemes of order which will best suit them, has fallen on the meek little democrats, *by request*. They imagined they were contracting with men of their own weight: that in fact they were all to become equal, before the law. They imagined that having

proved themselves inferior in the open lists, they would be
allowed to draw up the rules for contests.

The "poor" cannot have it every way: they cannot fail
in the fight and then dictate the manner of fighting. How
are they going to persuade those who have beaten them all
round that the latters' needs are not what they think they
are, but what it is right they should be? How are they going
to persuade them that the "Morals" which serve them so
badly are better ways than the "Immorals" which serve their
conquerors so well? By talking, gush, pious sentiment and
rhetoric? They delude themselves. They have either to be
prepared to tug at the bundle of power and possessions or
take what is given them—if anything is given them—and
be thankful. Their dislike for tugging is not going to stop
it: simply because better men than they like it and intend
going on with it. To lay too much count on the sensitiveness
which is fretted by their discomfiture is to make an enormous
miscalculation, for no man is his brother's keeper except in
the sense that he is his gaoler: a fact which the working
out of all these philanthropic tendencies most unmistakeably
reveals. That enjoyment of struggle can be diminished by
the awareness that one is trampling on someone is due to
a repugnance, at the "feel" that one's foot is on something
which writhes and not on solid earth; but not even the dislike
of the sensation of squelching one's boots into another's vitals
is likely to stop the struggle: for the simple reason that healthy
people can't exist happily without it. What then will happen
to those who prove themselves incapable, in spite of much
friendly aid and substantial ends thrown, of maintaining their
foothold will be that they will be carried out of the way,
"employed" in a protected irresponsible position, legislated
for and controlled. For such as are useful, a legal status

will be guaranteed: they will be well-fed, well-clothed, well-housed, by means of a "legal" minimum wage: of the highest rank among the domesticated beasts of burden. This as long as they remain useful and well-regulated, hard-working and moral, that is. If they become too useless or too troublesome, they will, according to the degree in which they offend, be confined or killed off.

The staggeringly rapid increase in the number of indictable offences shows what direction governments and social reformers consider the line of efficiency in the confinement department will take. The eugenics movement on the other hand illustrates the line of efficiency in the extinction department. Segregation, castration, lethal chambers, elimination of "criminal" types along with the "feeble-minded"—these things although their advocates are mostly only sub-consciously aware of it, are the steady bearing out of the "principle" whereby the "tuggers" despatch the non-strugglers.

The responsible party of course are these latter: and in their arrogant setting towards disaster they are supported by the counsels of rebels, reformers, moralists and masters alike.

10. Democratic Times

*"There is a law for each man individually, be he rich or poor,
which is the resultant of all his powers: his strength,
charm, skill, intelligence, daring."*

IT will be quite clear to many persons if we point the sequence
out to them, why in these democratic times an indiscretion
is more discreditable to a man and more embarrassing to his
party than the most staggering of "crimes." In a household
where correct conduct is "not to scandalise these my little
ones," the little ones being children, pious women and men
with idealised minds, it would be the *rôle* of the devil himself
to speak as the plain blunt person, without regard to the
"doctrine." With his entrance in that household life would
thereafter and for ever be different. Sin would have entered:
the frank innocence would be gone: and the shifty eyes which
know evil from good left behind. And this is exactly what
happens in the democratic community when a governor is
indiscreet. His indiscretion undermines his creed, because it
undermines his creed's Assumptions—the pillars upon which
the fabric of democratic society rests.

It is not the custom to discuss politicians in *The Egoist*,
or in the accepted way, their works. Our present unusual
course in discussing Colonel Seely's recent political exploits
must be explained by the fact that Colonel Seely's conduct
was just now politically irregular: and concerning a politician
it is not possible to make a more serious allegation than
that. To be regular is the first and last word of a politician's
creed; he may traverse no least convention without custom's

warrant: nor raise the least whisper of inquiry into current and popular dicta. To act otherwise is, politically, to reach the giddiest pinnacle of the immoral at a bound. Therefore Colonel Seely, politically speaking, at this moment commands the fascinating regard an ordinary person would turn upon a Dr. Crippen or a Jack-the-Ripper.

He has questioned a democratic Assumption, and this being a democratic age a democratic Assumption is Sacred. That his conduct has serious consequences from the point of view of democrats, all—his friends and foes alike—will readily allow. They agree that democratic stability is threatened, that the democratic basis of society is being undermined. Naturally enough and obviously to be expected. If there be removed only one prop of a four-legged bench there can be no surprise if the board lists in the direction of the missing leg. How much more then if two legs; and so forth. No wonder that when a democratic government attacks two democratic assumptions in the course of ten days or so, the democrats—the eloquent women, idealistic men, the labour party and the poor, all these little ones should be scandalised. They are in fact in imminent danger of falling off their democratic basis, platform, what-not, and of being shot on to their own feet. Even if their platform admits of being propped up by some adventitious stump and they are able to maintain the lofty and erect attitude, it will never be quite the same after so undignified a scramble. Never the same sense of security, unquestioned stability, after so nasty a shock. "Doubt, hesitation and pain, forced praise on our part—the glimmer of twilight, Never glad, confident morning again[1]." [...]

---

[1]≠ "The Lost Leader" by Robert Browning.

It is this oppressed, powerless, yet credulous host "The People" which in the name of democracy flatters itself it is going to govern. Colonel Seely, inadvertently no doubt, has just been the means of producing some exquisite fun out of the indignation of the democrats which rage in the name of People and Parliament. Mr. Ward and other stalwarts of the People sound for all the world like the frog in the fable whom misleading flatterers had led to believe she was the Queen of Song. "Shall not 'The People' remain paramount?" How "shall" they "remain" what they have never been? If in order to trade upon the fact that the people are gullible it has served many persons' purposes, to tell them so, their misinformation does not alter the actual relation one iota: comfortable, shiftless, timid, the "People," the "Masses" remain what they have always been—the servants of those who are, or who are connected with those, sufficiently acute to understand their points. That there is one law for the rich and another law for the poor is a very inadequate way of putting the matter: there is a law for each man individually, be he rich or poor, which is the resultant of all his powers: his strength, charm, skill, intelligence, daring: the sum of his total worth and what it secures is a man's just dues. [...]

It is the making Claim by Right to that which they are incapable of securing by Might: the attempt to carry through the exchange by shouting and pious incantation which makes the democratic advocacy offensive. The democrats are *sweedlers*: from no point of view to be recognised as on a level of estimable equality with highway robbers who are gentlemen by comparison.

❦

Supposing then for the moment that through a misunderstanding the Ward-Thomases of the community should slide into the position of the intelligent, and advise the "arming" of their invertebrate unions. What then? Anarchy and the subversion of Society? *Pas du tout, messieurs.* The structure which threatens to come rattling down about their ears is not "Society" but a particular Conception of Society. We are in sight of the break-up of a Verbal System—not of the loosening of the ties of affection and common-sense as between men and men. Society itself is not based on any Conception whatsoever, it is based on the inborn predilections and instincts of individuals. When these instincts break through the overlying Verbiage and reveal themselves for what they are the "Stability of Society" is unaffected. For whatever these instincts are Society is and will be. That their character confounds the authenticity of some wordy interpretation of these instincts affects the stability of Society as little as an accidental error in the set of the angle of the axis in a pedagogue's globe would affect the sequence of the seasons. Summer will follow Spring although his little model make the poles lie on the equator. And human nature will get on as well when the blight of obedience has been chased from the miners' and railway men's unions and the rank-and-file of the Army, as well as from the sensitive ranks of the officers: even let us hope—a jolly sight better. When the assumption that we all obey is shattered, the sense of responsibility for self-defence returns, and a nerveless "People" will be galvanised into an Army, a consummation greatly to be desired by all save doctrinaire non-combatants, and even these suspicious-looking gentry would be forced into a position which would enable them to clear themselves of the charge of cant. To be non-combatants in a community which claims to have its combats waged by an arm worked by an involuntary nerve can be called a stoicism only by supererogation: its virtue is after the event: though doubtless in a military community they would be tolerated in a protected area as a luxury. Their desire not to fight would be defended by others fighting to make its fulfilment possible: even as at present: only their smug aspect might be removed.

The democratic armoury is of course not exhausted when "Society in Danger" fails to set things in a blaze. There is still "The horror of Civil War." Yet there is much to be said in favour of a gala performance of Civil War. A depressing Civil War is always with us, with its depressing effect due to its drab, furtive, hugger-mugger manner. No guns, no bands, no uniforms, swords, excitements, adventures, or thrilling bravery. Just a sordid, mean pressure: hunger, monotony, dreariness, squalor, filth, bailiffs, policemen, judges, jailors and hangsmen. Just for the tinsel on it there is much to be said for Civil War. Moreover Civil War would tend to put all questions to a trial of strength, and when such a test rises uppermost, even the feeblest must look to his resources. Moreover if existent moral conduct has done its hypnotic work: men of the poorer sort are dazed by the constant keeping in tune with the existent moral incantations. "Thou shalt not steal," good enough on the lips of rich men, makes tragedy on those of the poor. Civil War, with its different and far healthier proprietary "morality," would trouble the orderly waters, and to fish in them would come easier for a mechanised people than "fishing" is in face of an order malignant but nevertheless mesmeric. Civil War would furnish a springing board for the "poor" to open up new "lines" of "order." There are indeed more things to be made out in favour of Civil War than for the bastard variety which is being waged now. It would break lightly into the established order of things, which has too thoroughly in the minds of those who submit to it, assumed the immutable character of the progression of the sun and the stars.

This Carson campaign capped by the Seely incident and the dissolution of assumptions which this last puts into the melting-pot is going to prove the high-water mark of modern democracy. In England since Disraeli's time, the dominant classes have allowed the anti-democratic argument to go by default: no doubt because they lacked the brains to establish it. Since, with one name or another—Tory-democrats, Conservative Working-men—innocuous flirtations with popular democracy have been going on; it has been necessary for the "classes" to wait until opportunity made it possible for their instinct to instruct their intellect. Truculent temper is now explaining to a dilatory intellect why democracy won't wash. It will not now take long for them to get the hang of the argument: to see through the windy wordy business: this latter-day Cult of Humanity, the Rights of Man and all that is made to go with them. By challenging the conception of the Unity of the People—or rather by egging the government on to make the challenge—the supporters of Ulster resistance have snipped the one. verbal thread which, broken, lets the entire democratic creed run down like a broken chain-stitch. In this common Unity, the people arc One and Equal: rendering an equal obedience and receiving equal rights. Split the Unity, question the obedience and you disperse the Equality. With "Unity" questioned the criterion vanishes: the supreme dispenser of favours is confronted with a rival: the seat of

Authority is confused and Rights are the vainest of things
when Authority is called in question. Rights, Equality, Obedience, Unity, these four are the pillars of democracy. They
are bound up in this last—Unity; and who now seriously
discusses Unity? Who seriously discusses Democracy? None.
It is a dead issue. A little picturesque "strong man" play will
doubtless be enough to divert the vagrant attention of the
mob and so save the government and the politicians' salaries:
but for democracy itself a quiet conversational scrutiny—far
removed from oratory—will already have been begun: and
before it has gone far modern democracy will have found its
place in the list of Forgotten Causes.

11. Democracy

"'Free' marks the limit of one's individual power."

THE offending aspect of the pretensions of "democracy" is not that in the name of what the "majority" supposedly thinks we are supposed to be pleased and happy to be "ruled" by a clique for "our good." Far from it, since, in truth, but few of us are "ruled" at all. It is merely our little foible to pretend we are. We give our "rulers" to understand they "rule" us because it pleases them so greatly to think they do: and then there is the consideration that a docile demeanour serves to divert their too too kind attention; probably the most servile-seeming member of a "state," the most bent upon fulfilling the role of step-grandmother fundamentally is untouched by "rule." The obedient attitude is a very convenient garb for the perverse to wear: and if the mere doing of it does not jar the temper too much, appearing to submit will define the line of least resistance to doing what under the circumstances is what we please. Thus under the shelter of the servile demeanour there forms a residue of mulish waywardness, especially in those who appear to present their parts to receive the kicks which keep them going between gutter and cesspool: a waywardness which even more than temper succeeds in making them into a kind of clay unmeet to the hand which would govern. The great unwashed will accept the infliction of the bath which cuts a slice off the space of their limited premises with resignation and reflect that it will indeed have a use as a wardrobe and coal-place. Though they are cast down by such things they are not defeated. "Rule" slides from them, as water slides from a duck. "Rule" has effect only on those who are indoctrinated

124

with the Dogma: those who are under the spell of the "Word."
Even these—these intellectuals—are not placed in bondage
by the rulers: theirs is a voluntary bondage—true freedom,
according to the Word—and if they act as automata it is that
they subscribe to the dogma that it is their duty to be as
automata. They submit themselves to the law: because they
approve not always indeed of the law, but of the attitude
which submits to law.

It is not therefore for its supposed prowess in the line of
government that democracy's claims are obnoxious. It earns
its odium through the commodity which the "rulers" offer
in exchange for their investiture with authority to govern.
"Rulers" appear contemptible not for what they take but what
they give. That they lay hold of authority and all the ready
cash which their positions render available is, if regrettable,
yet tolerable: the machine will go until it breaks; the vexatious
thing is that in order to become installed in their position
of advantage they must needs undermine and bemuse by
flattery the intelligence of those whose lack of it is sufficiently
evidenced by their willingness to have truck with them.

Once upon a time, we heard—or read—about a soldier
belonging to the ranks who by the workings of some chance
which we forget, found himself dining at the officers' mess.
Finding himself unable to guess the use to which he might be
expected to put ice which was placed before him, he hazarded
putting it in the soup; whereupon the officers laughed: all,
that is, save one—the highest in rank. This noble one, in order
to administer the rebuke to the manners of his brother-officers,

and further to cover the confusion of the guest, straightway placed ice in his soup also. This edifying story as we remember it did not stop at this point but went on to explain how true gentility and true democracy reveal themselves in so fine an essence of Christian good-breeding, but it will serve our purpose better to regard the story as here finished and use it as an analogy in a totally different use, it is: those who use the flattery of the democratic "equality" argument in order to win the support of the mob do their uttermost to confuse the import of "gentility": how far they have succeeded the influence of the concept of "natural rights" bears witness. They encourage "claims" to be laid to things which from their nature can only be freely given. A delicacy which merely seeks not to press the confusion which error brings is misconstrued into a concession that no error exists: rather, indeed, that those who fail to perpetuate it are themselves in error.

Every new creed is ninety-nine parts *réchauffé* of all the creeds which by virtue of its hundredth part it is supposed to supersede: the fact that the ingredients are incongruous proving no bar to such rehashing. To mince the whole to a uniform state of non-recognition where possible, and to accept whole what resists the process according to its external merits, is the method of treatment. Naturally therefore in the cult of equality-cum-democracy it is not surprising to be met with the spirit of *Noblesse oblige*. notwithstanding the fact that democracy knows no *Noblesse*. How this curious combination of exclusives is worked in together is illustrated by the incident narrated above. The "noble" officer acted in the spirit which lies behind the attitude *Noblesse oblige*—the attitude that a superior can always afford to concede a point:

it is the spirit of chivalry: the meaning of the handicap: it is to be found almost everywhere where the relatively strong and weak, superior and inferior meet together. It is the swagger of the superior at their subtlest and suavest, since it wins a conscious recognition of superiority by the very act which would seem to minimise it. Now the confusion which is effected by the demagogues: those would-be rulers who in order to win their way to authority must flatter the mob, lies in the implication that while still *Noblesse oblige*, the tacit acknowledgment of relative merit on which it is built is there no longer. It has been submerged in democratic equality. Therefore a superior not merely *may* ice his soup: he *ought* and *must*; in fact, we supposedly, all prefer iced soup now: the new creed having created a new procedure. If incompetence is the equal of competence and the incompetent outnumber the competent, then by the "right" of democracy and the "will of the greatest number" the incompetent must set the procedure. There is nothing of course in the ways of procedure already existing which is not the result of "class" prejudice and autocratic naughtiness: nothing in the relative quality of men's intelligence and the nature of things otherwise to explain why the relative positions have arranged themselves as they have. All this wicked disparity is purely superficial and will be combated by a judicious mixture of scolding and pleading. Hark unto Mr. Lansbury's paper on the subject: "Every private must be as free as any dandy officer." "Must" no less! Suppose he had said "can be!" Why did he not? Presumably because "he" can't be. Then what is the route, between point and point of which, "Can't be" becomes "Must be" in a mind like Mr. Lansbury's? What magic human alchemy is worked on the way and who works it? Mr. Asquith or Mr. MacDonald or even Mr. Lansbury himself? Or does Mr. Lansbury find hope in the temper of "privates" themselves? To us they seem to be conspicuously silent. We may be sure the privates are as free as they can be, and when they can be more free, they will be. "Free" is such an odd sort of a word. It has the power of suggesting itself to be something which can be conferred, like rations and uniforms, and yet when it has been followed through a long series of disillusionings it lets one down to the truth that it is in itself representative only; it merely marks the limit of one's individual power, like the index-needle on those machines where one hits on a sort of anvil with a hammer to test one's strength. The index will move up and down the scale in the most obliging manner within the limits of one's power to strike. And similarly with the privates' freedom: it is anything their power can make it. If their power of "freedom" were equal to that of officers: why did they not become officers and so become "free" and dandy too? They would then have avoided the grounds of suspicion that it was less. It is to be assumed they did not become privates because in comparison with being officers they preferred to. Parents' poverty? But we must accept parents. Our parents are our one not-uncertain inheritance. What they are and what they do is part of what one inevitably comes by, inevitably as we come by our features and our gifts. Unequal opportunity? But there can be no *equal* opportunities. Moreover Fortune keeps in stock at least ten thousand opportunities per man. It is not the opportunities that are lacking but the power to accept them. And if all, out of a man's ten thousand opportunities fail to suit, it always lies open to him to create a wholly new one unique for himself. All of which may well appear if not indeed, but doubtfully true, at least quite unhelpful as to the telling. To which the reply is that it is quite true and would be helpful to a real democrat, if only one could find such. As a matter of fact, this "democrat" is a very rare bird and not a nice one. The illusion that he exists in his hundreds of thousands is a simple fiction put into currency by journalists: "democracy" a label unmeritedly attached to a community of self-respecting egoistic common-sense people, who only very occasionally and shamefacedly talk about their abstract rights, equality, the will of the people and the rest. There is not, for instance, one person in one hundred thousand who could recite this tirade of Mr. Lansbury's with an unembarrassed countenance.

> There seem to be two recognised and main ways of serving humanity. The exponent of one method deduces from his love of people in general a love of himself in particular. Charity, he argues, enlightenment, idealism—these must begin at home; and with a loyal and logical conscience he proceeds to bleed out of that same suffering world either fortune or social position, influence, power. And for the damnable wholeness of his flesh (if men had but the eyes to see it) the leprosy of humanity festers and reeks the more.
>
> —*Daily Herald*, Saturday, April 11[1]

In fact, the conclusion to which one is pressed is that we—that is the people who talk and write—take all theories, politics and propagandas too seriously: far more so than ever was intended by those who amuse themselves by such species of Sport. The permanent role of propagandists and politicians

---

[1] ≠ "The Greatest Tragedy" (1914). p. 12.

is that of public entertainer; and they stand or fall by the answer to the question, "Do they entertain?" And it must be admitted that they still exert a draw. Star turns like Sir Edward Carson or Mr. Asquith can compete without shame with a football match before the season gets exciting: with a "cinema" entertainment. It is true that they have the entire strength of the advertising power of the Press of both parties to boost them and create a fictitious interest. The minor characters of course have a harder time of it, though for these the services of the Press are always available. The "principles," the "creeds" of politicians have nothing to do with their pull on the public attention: everything depends upon their ability to organise a good display (whether they run a one-man show or a team matters nothing) which will provide a reasonable excuse for the backers of the favourite, or the home team, shouting themselves delirious with delight. When politicians, through some defect of horse-sense, mistake their vocation, and imagine themselves to be teachers and preachers with a message and think that the message will make good their failure to entertain with the public, they are quickly put to rights. The present unpopularity of the suffragettes following so rapidly on their former popularity will illustrate the case. When their "propaganda" was worked as a smart, prompt, unfailingly successful *show*, it was an enthusiastic success: a sort of Vesta Tilley on the political stage. Now that it has betaken itself to seriousness, to stretchers, "tragedies" and ugly scenes, it is vaguely disliked by its former enthusiastic backers. Their "principle" is exactly what it was, but because the entertainment they put on the boards is voted a poor show, what were "heralds of the dawn" are now labelled misguided fanatics. Sir Edward Carson offers another instance. It is because he has made it clear he can put up a smart exhilarating show that the "people" are prepared to offer to the Conservative Grand Opera Company a prospect of future patronage; and Mr. Balfour showed a sure "statesmanship" in picking up the cue and appearing as stump orator in Hyde Park. Again—Mr. Asquith. He was intelligent enough to see that it was not an argument the recent "political" situation required: it was a counter-hero: and did his best. Very nicely too: his success can be gauged by what his audience was prepared to swallow whole. A more laughable speech was never uttered than the one this gentleman offered at Ladybank a week ago. Had he not been a "hero" it would have been riddled through with laughter. Consider the remark: the top-note on which he was bold enough even to pause—for applause: "The Army will hear nothing of politics from me, and in return I expect to hear nothing of politics from the Army[1]." You bet he doesn't. The "Army will hear nothing of politics from me." Of course not, but to make a "ruler" gaily ruling hear something of politics from them is the Army's very proper business. One must confess that so finely-nerved a stroke commands one's admiration. After this master-stroke "your army" is merely the purring approval a pleased operator will show to a patient who has stood a trying operation well.

Still, Mr. Asquith must have felt he was making a desperate, neck-or-nothing experiment. It must be a wearing method of providing for a wife and family of an elderly gentleman to accept all odds offered, on the strength of one's ability to move to slow music and talk vague theory in a *recitative* calculated to hypnotise any intelligence which may be lurking–hidden in one's audience. Melodrama is danger-

---

[1] ≠ "Two Souls With But a Single Thought." *Daily Herald* (April 7th 1914). p. 3.

ous as an occupation for people past their first youth: one snigger from a devotee suddenly illumined with an intelligent gleam might destroy the career into which have been built the hopes of a lifetime. It seems inevitable politicians will be driven seriously to consider the advisability of getting a little ahead of the more lagging intelligences, by changing their role from melodrama to comedy. The change will melt away their dignity; the sense of the actual thrown on heroics is a sure solvent, but on the precipitate of comic relief which the process ultimately throws down will be laid a far surer foundation for those "careers" from which they hope so much. There is in short a far greater scope for display of talent in a character of W. S. Gilbert, than in the most heroic of Grand Opera heroes, and a Dan Leno will go far deeper into the affections of the public than can a Sir Henry Irving; accordingly a politician who worked indiscretion into a conscious habit, who allowed *fact* to make its commentary on the *interpretation* of facts, baiting the interpretation with the fact as the comic spirit baits the "noble" one, such a one would really enrich the community with a new kind of art. If a clever man entered political circles with the realisation that by the side of, say, the collected political utterances of a "correct" politician like Sir Edward Grey, the simple narration of a servant girl's carryings-on with the butcher's man is an artistic document of relatively high worth, dulness which is the only evil would take wings and depart. The actual doings of politicians must have some human interest: whereas those by which they choose to be known in public have none. Instantly the veil slips aside, things become luminous. Turned indiscreet side out, they lose their smug smoothness. An indiscreet politician assisted in well-doing by an indiscreet press would realise that their proper business is just with those things which at present are enabled remotely to tickle our sense in the shape of the scandalous memoirs of circles now fifty years dead. Scandal, in short, is the only news worth retailing. It represents public life in earnest whereas at present we get public life by pretence. There is scope for a "creative" genius in such a rôle.

12. Property

*"Our view is that all men and women should
equip themselves with weapons of offence and defence
as deadly as the deadliest of which they can hear tell."*

ON property. The mischief in all the debates which turn on
property is that unconsciously the debaters are infected
by the clerical habit of labelling as to quality. They are so put
about to decide whether property is good for one or bad for one
that they forget that their first concern is with what property
is. The subject is by this means landed in the thorny region
of attitudes, oughts, and duties where the controversy born
of ungranted assumptions takes the place of the unrestrained
tale readily told. Out of the great clamour which in modern
times has raged about property two themes only can be picked
out: one, that property is "bad" for a man, therefore must
men be influenced to acquiesce in the placing of their property
in Mortmain: in the Dead Hand which cannot be harmed by,
or do harm to, it—the corporation, the commune, the state,
the guild; and two, a fainter-sounding but more tenacious
one that it is "good" and that therefore the "influence" must
be exercised to find out ways and means whereby once got,
property may remain attached to its possessors.

Now both these lines of theory become obviously futile if
one starts from the point of what property is. Property, as
its name sufficiently indicates, is what is one's own. What
makes a thing into property is the fact that a person owns
it. Apart from this power of the owner to work his will upon
objects, "property" is not property: it is mere substance—part
of the objective world, whatever we will to name it. The light
little problem with which a modern tendency of thinking is

faced is, how at one and the same time to retain and abolish property, how to make commodities one's own and yet not one's own. When this has been solved, "collective" ownership will begin to show livelier signs of being acceptable to blunt sense, but until then, "collective" ownership will remain what it at present is, and always has been, the cover under which after winning a more or less grudging "consent," the few who are sufficiently powerful to mount to "control" will own the various properties which nominally are the possessions of the collective group. That is, the few will as long as they remain in power, work their will on the "organisation"–the Dead Hand, and aforetime property, after having been transmuted into "substance," will again become property: the property of the controllers.

Property is "one's own," and driven from one owner it finds another as inevitably as water seeks its level. And an owner is a master—one who does with what he possesses according to his own nature. Accordingly when a group vests its "property" in a Dead Hand, the Dead Hand of necessity must elect living agents: the property finds its owners in the agents. It is inevitable. Should the official be one who cannot "own" on an extended scale he at once appears the "nithing," the "weak man" in the system. The "group" detest him in a sense and a degree very far different from that in which they fear a tyrant, for he reflects their folly back upon them. The "group" appreciate even if they could not explain the difference between being governed by a Napoleon and a Praise-God Bare-bones: even between a Sir Edward Carson and a Labour M.P.

The reason is that what one can own, *i.e.* control, gives a measure of what one is: and the instinctive knowledge which the masses have, all phrases to the contrary notwithstanding, that the official in control is the owner is revealed by the fact that they reckon such a one, being elected to the position and not acting as owner merely proves himself to be incapable. They realise that they have not merely divested themselves of their own powers to own, but have perpetrated the foolishness in the interest of one too feeble to profit by it.

The misunderstandings which are rife in relation to the holding of property are due to the fact that we endeavour to limit the area over which it extends. We own not only land and money (supposing we do): our "property" extends to the limits exactly of what we are: the nucleus of our property is what we are born with: instincts, family, grace, beauty, manner, brains, and the original dower of power which we have which puts them into evidence. These are, in a more absolute sense than material possessions—our property. In relation to what these are, the toll we can levy of such material possessions as we desire will be. Human calculations are likeliest to work out aright if we regard our "property," that is, our "own," rather as a native endowment, than as something which can be post-natally conferred, as for instance, our kind of education; if we regard it as fundamental, a hazard of which the die is cast at birth: like our breathing apparatus rather than a muffler or artificial respirator. In fact, the analogy between the power to acquire property and the power to breathe might be usefully extended. Both are native endowments; both are necessary to continued existence; both are powers which can be adequately exercised only on one's own initiative; both require for their exercise access to a medium external to the body through which they exercise;

136

both require their needs to be measured by their wants; both invalidate the entire person by any failure to work effectually, both have a minimum of specific requirements which they draw from the environment in which they are placed; and these failing in either case, only an advanced stage of inanition explains the failure of fight to the last degree of savagery in order to enable them to augment their powers to the necessary degree. That one acquires food and clothing for its first satisfaction while the other acquires fresh air makes no real sort of difference to the parallel. The ones are as essential as the other and their acquisition to be considered as much a matter of course.

It will of course be maintained that the power to acquire property and the actual coming by it are two very different things; it is because they are regarded as so different that those debaters who uphold the "theme" that property is "good" are so concerned with the ways and means of keeping property "stable"; ready to go to any length towards the creation of an authority which will guarantee that men shall remain secure in their property. Yet after all their efforts the nature of property defeats them: it remains fluid. It gathers as a refulgence about the individual powers, grows dense and dissipates exactly according to the force of the individual will about which it settles. The authority which was to keep it fluid, itself becomes the property of those who choose to exploit it. All properties are as fluid to the acquiring as air is: they know only one authority: the will which can command them; and the means which can command them can be as readily sought and found in the individual will, as can the force which primarily conceives them as desirable. There are no firm and fixed methods: there are merely convenient ones. Whatever method serves best to the getting and holding is best. The line of least resistance to actual possession is the line for successful competition. Phrases—"morality," "legality"—from the point of vision of the person on the make are negligible quantities: they come into the reckoning only as possible factors with resisters one might encounter on the way. They belong to the kind of forces which, while not respected, are recognised: they enter into the calculation in the account of resistance to be met, but not in the account of the force which is to meet it. Moral and legal forces are part of the machinery whereby those who think property "good" try to make us "respect" our neighbour's property: whereas the fit and feasible thing is for each of us to respect our own. The respect due to our neighbour's property is the affair of our neighbour. Minding each other's business—and property—is a dull laborious and irritating affair. Minding our own is our native interest; the proper affair of a swagger person. For the possession of property is nothing more than the expression of our personality and will, the material with which we are able to do as we please. The seeking to acquire it is the endeavour to get a free scope for the exercising of our own power: it is the avenue to self-expression and self-satisfaction. Those who do not force open such an avenue to some extent, are those who have nothing to express. A deterring "respect" that the avenue is other people's property is a smug excuse provided for those who cannot attend to their own proper concerns. It does not hold with stronger powers, nor does human admiration go out to it. It goes to the "strong" men: whether it is the exploiter who sets out to buy human stuff—body and soul—to express his will upon—like Mr. Ford; or any "tyrant" who will sacrifice his fellows' life and limb—to please himself. They like it. When men gather up all their scattered conceptions of what is admirable and create God, they create him in their image and give him the world to play with. The world is his: we and all that therein is. He makes his will through the world and us: anything less would be a derogation of his dignity and power. It is not an accident that men have conceived "god" under such an image: he is the embodiment of the strong will which they fundamentally admire. That the image entails their being hustled somewhat is matter for grim satisfaction. There is a real pride in being treated *sans cérémonie*.

If it is felt occasionally that God goes too far, he does not lack apologists. "May not God do what He likes with His own?" Of course God has the advantage over earthly strong men of being very remote and is thus saved from administering those aggravating personal pushes for which well-beloved earthly tyrants usually pay with their necks: though even a Job ultimately cursed him, in spite of his good opinion of him. In short he ceased to respect him though he continued to like him: and that is precisely what happens with the strong-willed here: the great of the earth—those who work their own will in the world—are admired and liked but, of necessity, tripped up, kept as much as possible on a leash; as for the small, the feeble-willed who respect their neighbour's possessions—they are neither liked nor respected; they are trodden upon: then actively disliked because they appear so messy and disfigured.

If then the person who respects only his own property, placing on his neighbour the onus of respecting his, is the one who instinctively is appreciated as the worthier person, it remains to consider why the apparent practical forcing into effect of such instinctive impulses is spoken of with disfavour: why, in short, the seizing of property is regarded with abhorrence. It is mainly accountable to the uncalculated effects of the efforts of those who seek to make property stable, by guaranteeing a man's "security" in his possessions. What actually happens is that property follows its natural trend in the wake of the strong will. The net which the invoked "authority" lays manages only to ensnare those too feeble to break through it. It is like a spider's net which will catch flies but through which a man's boot rips without recognising its presence. In effect the pains and penalties which the state attaches to attacks on property turn out to be handicaps attached to the slowest runners. Prison is the potential home of the poor: the crust and ha'penny stealers. The big thieves regard prison as outworks of their various enterprises: the houses of correction which a kindly state for some unaccountable reason supplies them with gratuitously. It is not strange that the strong and rich believe in the state and the penalties it imposes: because these things suit them; there is no need for them to be hypocritical: they believe with all their heart and soul that the poor should not steal: it would be quite awkward if they began to: like two people both trying to get through a stile at the same time. So to encourage them they will, unless it happens to be seriously inconvenient at the moment, observe the demeanour of one who does not commit petty thefts: in fact they would honestly be ashamed to. Let Justice be done and preserve the Law-Courts!

The really queer and odd factor concerned in the morals clustered about "theft" is that the propertyless take so readily to them. The praiseworthy efforts of the rich in maintaining the "tale as it is told," are based on common sense and are comprehensible, but the acquiescence of the "poor" is only explained by failure in intelligence. Not only do their instincts fail to prompt them to the adequate assertion of their will to acquire: they are not strong enough to resist the laying-on of such an interpretation of their situation as makes a bad case hopeless. They permit themselves to be bamboozled into the belief that the piping voice of the magistrate saying to the poor, "He that takes what isn't his'n, When he's cotched'll go to pris'n," is the thundering voice of the Lord saying from everlasting to everlasting "Thou shalt not steal." What really means nothing more than "Mind your manners," gets mixed up with odd queer things like Universal Law, Religion, Space and Everlasting Time, into which mixture the figure of the policeman and hangman appear as the agents of an Eternal Justice which deflects them—mere specks—into time.

Not all the "poor" however are thus pathetically and be-musedly silly. They are not all putty made for the moulder's hand, ready to be shaped by the "statesmanship" of the perfect statesman. Quite a goodly proportion would be able to appreciate Mr. Winston Churchill's remarks anent Sir Ed. Carson: appreciate them perhaps a shade more caustically than they doubtless appeared to their author.

> The great democracy is watching. So often we urge these millions to be patient with their bare necessities of life—the audience in India—in Egypt—all are watching, noting—native soldiers, native officers—the devastating doctrines of Mr. Bonar Law... I thank God that I have

not to play for the stakes to which you are committed. "We are Tories," you say, "no laws apply to us. Laws are made for working people—to keep them in their proper places. We are the dominant class and it will be time enough for us to talk about law and order when we get back to office." Yes, indeed!

— *Daily News*, Wed., April 29th.[1]

What the intelligent "poor" in their present perilous position are set to solve is the "calculation as to consequences." The boomerang effect of any aggressive expression of the will returns on them in the shape of consequences—a bill to pay. The antagonisms, the rage of frustrated schemes are roused in just those persons who are empowered to get their own back with interest.

An accepted "value" which more than any other to-day stands in need of overhauling is that of a guaranteed security: more particularly that of security from physical violence. In the civilised world this supposed good has long outweighed every consideration which might have seemed to vie with it. It has become the sacredest of the sacred. It has had a long run—a fact which has the merit of leaving its effects too defined for doubt, and its present sublimation in modern democracies and modern industrial civilisations calls out for judgment to be passed on its worth. Three main charges can be brought against it. It destroys the stamina of the people, whose young men fritter away their strength in talk. They are as garrulous as old women, far more sentimental and far less shrewd. Their battles are fought—in talk. It encourages the peoples' most dangerous vices: they become self-deceptive: at once cocksure and timorous, swaggering yet having to seek

---

[1] ≠ 1914.

a vicarious vindication; vain of their "freedom" which is yet merely "freedom" to obey and submit. It provides a system which offering a common protection for all alike defeats the ends of contests in which men might become apprised of their true level. They are all "equal" because "security" at once makes unnecessary and forbids the putting of their full powers to the proof. But more than these: the promised benefits which were the considerations which led to this apotheosis of Guaranteed Security turn out to be a complete hoax. Against whom do the "people" seek to "secure" themselves? Not against each other, but against the top dogs: which they do by doffing off responsibility for their own defence, and leaving themselves bare and weaponless with their defence left in the charge of—whom? Just these top dogs. The workings of the machinery inside the heads of these democratic peoples is extraordinary and funny. They are like men working in a pit filled with poisonous gases supplied with the necessary fresh air by men at the surface whose only concern is to keep them toiling down there for their benefit. At any moment they can switch off the supply, and the workings of the cage which would bring the toilers to the surface they are placing in their employers' hands also. And they imagine that making great to-do banding together in the depths of the pit will have an effect, not realising that they must approach more nearly to equal terms before their organising together can do much for them. To abandon a straining simile: the re-assumption of responsibility for self-defence, the self-provisioning of weapons of offence and defence which will compare with those of their present masters is the first concern of the propertyless who now depend upon "employment" by others as a means of livelihood.

❦

A correspondent, Mr. Henry Meulen, asks how far the advice given to starving strikers to seize food would go with persons in less desperate straits[1]. No distance at all we should say, since for unarmed men to take to courses of violence is to court the possibility of desperate reprisals, and common sense justifies such action only on the understanding that it is an alternative to an otherwise still more desperate situation. Moreover, it stands some chance of success because of its suddenness, its obvious need, and from a wholesome fear which sees in it a lesser evil than a more ferocious which might come later. But it remains an affair of wild impulse, and impulse cannot be adopted as a policy in a dangerous situation. Our view is that all men and women should equip themselves with weapons of offence and defence as deadly as the deadliest of which they can hear tell: that only by this means can the people be in a position to make terms with those who can call in such to support them: that under such conditions the "property" question would cease to be the festering class problem which it now is, but would unravel itself on the lines of natural ability, human self-respect and kindliness. The present paralysed condition of an unarmed "protected" mob in the power of a handful of armed "protectors" supplied by the state, and called a condition of law and order, peace and security, is the real problem: not a "property" problem but a "power" problem.

---

[1] ≠ "Property and Theft" by Henry Meulen. *The Egoist* Volume I Number 9 (May 1st, 1914).

13. Salvation, Service and Saviours

"People can only serve themselves."

SALVATION, service, saviours: the alliterative trinity whose kingdom does so alarmingly spread. The reason that this phenomenon of modern times—the raising up of "Saviours" by the squad so to speak—gets less attention than its significance deserves, is to be sought in the existence of a certain clashing between the "deliverers'" modesty and their vocabulary: their business, without a doubt, they conceive to be the "saving of society," but remain a trifle deprecating labelling of themselves boldly and assertively Saviours. It is a pity, for the special kink which is the mark of the saviours is quite considerably interesting. The thought that the existence of even their least little one should be overlooked for want of its proper designation seems to make it worth while lifting the name of the species into the currency of recognised labels. So as Saviours let them be known for our better appreciation of their unique quality. [...]

The argument has made a wide loop round but is now ready to return to the gospel of "service": to the saviours who are believing to save the world by serving; an argument competent, we hope, to make clear to these persons who are misguided more than willingly by erring; that their avocation is futile and distressful; that they in concrete fact actually spoil the landscape for those whom they believe they serve. Their mistake comes from a belief that people can be served, whereas people can only serve themselves. They can and do serve themselves to what they are competent for, but what balks is not merely what may be a limited power to serve themselves but a real meagreness in the repast to which their powers must be related.

Those of our readers who remember the days when they were settlement workers will remember how the fact was borne in upon them that it was not the faithful ever-ready but rather plain tract-deliverer and district-visitor who was really appreciated by the "settled" ones. It was the graceless and charming person, who came down once a session garbed in her best clothes for the occasion whom they voted it had proved worth while accepting the invitation ticket for. One could in the light of such experiences ask the Saving-Classes to calculate precisely, without flattery and without excessive modesty, what they think they can be worth in a saving capacity to the "world," and the "poor." To begin with these leisured ladies: women of position such as Lady Constance Lytton and wealth such as Mrs. Pethick-Lawrence and other moneyed persons who have, for instance "run" the W.S. and P.U.[1] Were the acuteness theirs they would recognise that they themselves and the family and moneyed interests which make them "respected" are a direct charge on the "poor": before the "poor" feed themselves with crusts they must first feed these on whatever expensive things they can conceive they want. In the second place, for the execution of these tasks which make the production of this unequally distributed wealth possible, the "poor" are competent: equipped with strength and skill: their saviours but rarely supplied with either: in this sense therefore the "poor" serve their would-be servers and there must be some humour for them in the suggestion that it is otherwise. It is true of course that they would not serve could they avoid it, but until they can

---

[1] ≠ "W.S. and P.U.": Women's Social and Political Union.

themselves increase their competence, this forced service is a necessity and in accepting it for the time being they look about for compensations. They serve themselves as far as they can to what there is, and among the choicer dishes of the feast at which they may fare, there is chief the graces and aspect of those who have served themselves better. If those of the leisured female aristocracy who are thinking of plunging into Salvationism will hesitate a moment while they turn over a few points, reflection will give them pause. Apart from their own incompetence to do anything beyond remaining leisured, *i.e.* do-nothings, they might remember that they form picturesque points in a landscape. If they require to learn in detail what we mean, they may purchase the kind of literature which the "poor" devour in quantities: the novelette which costs a copper, and they will see how important a part they play in the world of the poor. Or the novels of Ouida will guide them aright. They will realise that for anything short of saving their own souls it would be sheer brutality to shatter these visions of the poor. They will realise that the difference between the view-points of the poor and rich is as that between persons who occupy a hut in a park and of those who inhabit a mansion in a slum, and we believe it will dawn upon them why the wardresses in a prison for instance do not wax enthusiastic over the distresses of an earl's daughter among them. They are rather cast down, as perhaps some self-mortifying saint might be who accidentally got a peep into heaven and saw the real thing. The root of the misunderstanding which leads saviours astray is that people do so tend to narrow the number of things of which we can make use: serve ourselves from. The rose-tree is as useful as the cabbage patch: a delicate vase as a slop-pail: a friend more useful than a servant; an expensive wife than an economical housekeeper: the mistaken notion that these things are otherwise comes from a too misleading divorce of what we need from what we want. A closer linking of the two together may guide these disturbed leisured ladies to a more satisfying decision as to whether they are to save or not to save. If they feel it is for their own benefit, in their own self-interest, if to intrude on the "poor," to drag tired feet along evil streets, to go to prison, or to starve or anything else is *to please themselves*, that should settle the matter: by all means let them do it. It is what they want and doubtless the "poor" will survive it, for they lead a tenacious life and when one interest fails they put a firm tentacle round another.

In the foregoing remarks, we have dealt rather with Lady Constance Lytton's assumptions as to "Women's" mission: to the tenets which her atmosphere and the remarks and assertions she makes in passing imply she takes as established; but inextricably interknitted into the structure and phraseology of her book there is something far more curious and arresting. It is too insistent to be counted as an impression, or as something implied: it refuses either to be ignored or fenced with, it must be faced: the book is either it or nothing. It was a first intention merely to count the number of references made to the subject and dismiss it in that way: but as one read on it became clear that to do so would be to bone a skeleton. One must either refer to this preoccupation with the exigencies of the alimentary system in *Prisons and Prisoners* or merely fence with the book. One might if one wished, make a comment on the apparent mental effect of persistently wearing the white flower of a blameless life, and of doing the other thing, and draw a parallel for instance between two productions—*Prisons and Prisoners* and "The Ballad of Reading Gaol," one a trivial account of sanitary arrangements and one the vision of souls in pain. *Why* this one feature of prison life should have loomed so importantly in the author's account we do not dare definitely to say, but after conceiving and rejecting various explanations we alighted on one conclusion and give it for what it is worth. It is Lady Constance Lytton's contribution to the "sex question." On the "touching pitch undefiled," "to the pure, all things are pure" principles she sings on this one note without a tremor and considers it a daring deed done for purity[1]. Oh Saviours! Oh brains!

We suppose that it would mean little to the "movemental" mind if one were to say that when one has invoked a label one has advanced no further towards explaining the thing to which it is attached. We remember just before one of the suffragist processions, one of the leaders of subsidiary hosts, in telling over the prospects of her own muster, who said "And I've got four prostitutes coming too," in a tone which revealed how overcome she was with her own daring. Afterwards we looked to her contingent for four in scarlet: but no: these members of an alien species if they were there were labelless and not to be distinguished from the lady's daughters. Happily for the "movement" however prisoners are much easier quarry because they wear the garment: hence they may rise to the interest level of "hobbies."

Prisons as you know have been my hobby. What maternity there lurks in me has for years past

---

[1] ≠ Titus 1:15

been gradually awakening over the fate of prisoners, the deliberate, cruel harm that is done
to them, their souls and bodies, the ignorant,
exasperating waste of good opportunities in
connection with them, till now the thought of
them, the yearning after them, turns in me and
tugs at me as vitally and irrepressibly as ever
a physical child can call upon its mother. The
moment I got near the Suffragettes the way to
this child of mine seemed easy and straight, but
I knew the temptation to think this must make
me doubly sure of my ground. I have felt from
the first that I could not take this woman's
movement merely as an excuse for Holloway...
It is my yearning after the hobby that sucks up
my soul like a tide, my Nile sources, my Thibet,
my Ruvenzori. If you... will only help me in
spirit that the little spark in Sven Hedin shall
not fail in me. I am no hero, but the thought of
other travellers' much worse privations on that
road will, I believe, fizzle up my flimsy body
enough for what is necessary[1].

It is difficult to get into the mind which chooses prisons as
a hobby. One supposes prisons are selected on account of their
human content—the prisoners and in order to "help" them:
yet one would doubt whether there are many "prisoners" so
hard put to it that they would choose prisons as a hobby:
nor indeed so little capable of satisfying the human loneliness

---

[1] ≠ *Prisons and Prisoners* by Lady Constance Lytton (London: William Heinemann,
1914).

which the prison-hobby seeks to fill. They are not of the kind which tolerates things easily: not so humble and submissive as their saviours seem: nor so lost for ways and means of personal salvation. A servant-girl would not waste words over the "yearnings for motherhood," nor take to hobbies as alternatives. Out of the many "fallen" in prisons whom Lady Constance would "raise up" and "save," if the two cases were plainly put to them—hers and their own—they would account their own the more preferable. But it is very possible to take all these "yearning" women too seriously: there is an air of unreality about their phrases; if it is children they want when they can so easily get them, is there sense or reason in being fobbed off with a "prison?" If only they would insist on having a few minutes' serious discussion with themselves we should probably henceforward hear less twaddling cant about motherhood. When we are unblushingly presented with the following as a soul-to-soul talk which the author has with Annie Kenney ("through (whose) whole being throbbed the passion of her soul for other women": "marching arm-in-arm around the garden, under dripping trees"):—"She told how amongst these offices of women was the glorious act of motherhood and the tending of little children. Was there anything in a man's career that could be so honourable as thiss[1]?" what can one say except that Miss Kenney is really quite too sudden! Lady Constance makes the comment, "All that she said was obvious, but in it there was *a call from far off, something inevitable as the voice of fate*[2]." It is as likely as not that it will be a call from the attendant of a lunatic asylum unless they pull themselves together.

---

[1] ≠ Lytton.
[2] ≠ Lytton.

Perhaps they would claim that mania has its advantages: undoubtedly these two women mooning about in a wet garden, persuading each other that the "act of motherhood" which they share with the cats and dogs, birds and trees placed a special halo round their heads were having the time of their lives: as men driven mad by money worries may grow happy under the mania that they have inherited great wealth. One can question the kindness of restoring them to sanity. But however this may be for the patient, to onlookers their condition conveys a serious malaise. To them the complaint of which the sufferers are oblivious is the most salient feature about them, and these women, the victims of tepid emotions too frail to rise to the consummation-point where they strike their definite image and define their nature, are genuine sources of distress. The obvious course to take in relation to them would be to forget them: but in these times their numbers are legion: they rule the roost, and it is difficult. They emerge everywhere, in literature and affairs—everywhere. Only when the Art of Living grows better known will they be catalogued in their proper place: forces too feeble for knowledge. Till then we must all perforce swim in their treacle-ish stream of emotions too feeble to clarify themselves. [...]

14. Next Saviour

"Give the 'salvation of the world' the slip."

NEXT saviour. Mr. H. G. Wells. We by no means exhausted the topic of salvation in our last comments. The "salvation of the world" is not a theme to be regarded as a swan-song poured forth alone by spinsters and eunuchs in straits, its actual and fitting setting is oratorio with star-turns, minor lights, orchestra and chorus all complete. The Salvationist company includes all those who now orate—all except ourselves. We are, in fact, their only audience. The only reason therefore, let it be said, that Mr. Wells is chosen in preference to other "god-gifted, organ-voiced Salvationists" such as Mr. Shaw, Mr. Chesterton, Mrs. Besant, or Mrs. Pethick-Lawrence is that we have just now read his newest book: the latest of his songs of salvage—songs which he produces with such prodigality that should we postpone him until a succeeding issue he will have another through the press and we shall be behind the times. Therefore let Mr. Wells' be the next saving word. In the title of his newest sketch, *The World Set Free*[1], there is a brevity which might suggest that he had fallen into the practice common to all other Salvationists: that of losing sight of one of the parties involved in the warfare: a sort of glorifying of St. George before they have found the dragon. But Mr. Wells is not guilty. The brevity turns out to be the outcome of purely æsthetic considerations connected with the graces of its outer cover. Mr. Wells is quite explicit and not merely tilts his "world" boldly over against the "lives" which are in it: he even tackles the conundrum of the metaphysicians, "What is in the

---

[1] *The World Set Free.* By H. G. Wells. (Macmillan, 6/-)

'world' when the life which is conscious of what is, is removed?" Without pause sufficient even to take breath he has his answer ready: there is an "over-mind," a "purpose," a "life-force" (minus lives of course), a "race-consciousness" (minus the stuff of the roots), an "impersonal body of knowledge." [...]

It is curious that Mr. Wells with his ardent enthusiasm for the "Spirit which desires to know" should never have taken the trouble to find out what knowledge is. What is knowledge if not feeling sufficiently strong to become clear and definite? How can we know more than we feel? Why then suggest that the "spirits which desire to know" should leave the low plains where feeling is passionate and strong for Himalayan heights where there is snow and one scratches back one's hair and wears white drill overalls? We offer these fruitful questions for Mr. Wells to consider before he writes the first sentence of his next volume, which event we suggest should be postponed for a period of at least three years' duration. In the meantime we can explain to him why his prose is such as would lead a schoolboy to expect getting his head smacked should he try to make it pass criticism. We forbear from reiterating a tag and explain why literary style bespeaks the man. The growth of literature is the increasingly precise outlining in words of images felt clearly enough to make their features definite for the one who feels them. A poor writer is one who writes before his images are clear—before he knows in fact. For some reason, either because he wants money badly, or because popular acceptance and publishers' indiscriminate generosity as to pay, fosters a belief that the world is thirsty for the works of his pen, good or bad, the poor writer writes, and neither his taste nor his character forbids. He assumes the certain tone in regard to that of which he is uncertain. He is untrue, and in his taste there is nothing exacting. It does not demand a complete image and therefore the expense of time while waiting for it to round to its completion. Respect for his own sincerity is not available to veto the publication of anything which would undermine it. The "style" is such because the character of the writer will permit it to be such. That is the gist of what we imply when we call a writer a poor writer. Now Mr. Wells is occasionally a good writer; but more and more he produces execrable writing. Although his writings have made him rich financially he is too poor to wait until he knows what he feels. He has a vague buzz and whirr in his head and straightway his pen is out and he will write down phrases such as "banked darknesses of cumulus," "civilisation the simplification of complications," "The ruling sanities of the world," "The spectacle of feverish enterprise was productivity[1]." He will unblushingly produce a volume out of less emotional evidence and material for thinking than a truer person—even with an empty stomach—would feel honest in making to fill out a paragraph. And he trusts to a vague diffused energy to carry the performance off. And if we are asked what concern this has for us, we reply first that we have met so much of it and are bored; second, since we have a paper to sell and minds soaked and soddened in a hash-up of blurred images are incapable of bracing themselves to the effort of understanding it, draining off some of the slop is part of our struggle for existence; and third, Mr. Wells is not a fixed quantity and a little grandmotherly admonishing may be enough to induce him to mend his ways: give the "salvation of the world" the slip and save himself in fact.

---

[1] ≠ *The World Set Free* by H. G. Wells (London: Macmillan & Co. 1914).

15. Long Years

"If a person is determined to do as he likes in a certain anti-lawful way, the government is powerless to stop him. It can only kill him, a fact which the government well knows."

L ONG years ago—five perhaps—there existed in Manchester a colony of suffragettes, real ones, faithful of the faithful, who sped to do Mrs. Pankhurst's will before she had well breathed it forth. And at the very kernel of the community was a tiny group which in its intimate moments and as an unholy joke called itself the S.O.S. They were Sick of Suffrage, and meant nothing more than a scarce-whispered weariness at the interminable reiteration of threadbare arguments and probably a definite wearying of the unending donkey-work of the gutter and pavement. As a joke it was considered quite enormous: but the element which gave it all the humour it possessed was that it was true, and by as much as it was true of the "true soldiers in the cause" in that springtime of the "movement" it can be safely gauged how much it was and has been true of those suffragists who reluctantly made themselves suffragists afresh because of all that "these brave women are suffering for the Cause." If ever a generation were fed on seeming good food which refused to go down it is this female one which has had the "principle of the suffrage" thrust upon it as an urgent issue.

The fact of the matter is that the modern suffrage "move-ment" has been only nominally concerned with suffrage: a fact doubly unfortunate for suffrage. Not only does the genuine impulse in the direction of a certain "something" fail to derive its force from the suffrage, but by filling a false position in the "Cause" the suffrage becomes embarrassed by an attention which is really fired by something else. By a bad misnomer the suffrage finds itself in the unenviable position of a makeshift thrust forward to fill the gap made by the non-appearance of a celebrity. Which explains how Mrs. Pankhurst has, unwittingly, led tens of thousands of women out on a wild-goose chase. She organised so exhilarating a hunt that the value of the quarry was taken for granted. That the hunt was everything and the spoil next to nothing—the "good fight which justifies any cause"—unfortunately did not dawn upon her or them. The "suffragists on principle" whose interests in their principles was quickened with life only by Mrs. Pankhurst's "good fight," the "constitutionals," were left with the shell from which Mrs. Pankhurst's host had withdrawn the nut. These last were wisely "rejoicing by the way," leaving to the suffragists on principle the straining towards "an end" to be enjoyed when won.

That Mrs. Pankhurst had struck her rich vein by accident and was only vaguely aware of what constituted her good fortune is of course amply shown by almost everything she has said, and likewise by most of what she has done in her personal relations with her own devoted host. She was as much deceived by her rallying-cry of Suffrage as any constitutionalist who hastened reluctantly to the "Cause" to claim her vested interest in it and challenge Mrs. Pankhurst's large utterances in speaking in its name. Moreover, it was the "vote" she wanted—not the "good fight." The vote was necessary to her if she was to make herself count among the crowd of Labour-politicians, all scrambling to make themselves a position of importance out of the rich mud of politics. Her lack of a vote placed so heavy a handicap on her that she was unable to make distances with men who were hopelessly her inferiors as politicians. Mrs. Pankhurst was and is a politician. All her interests are political as are Miss Pankhurst's. But alongside only very ordinary intelligence she possesses a biting, enduring aggressive temper—a rare feature among public women. Miss Christabel Pankhurst's dramatic first arrest and subsequent stupid imprisonment (Miss Pankhurst is an enigma: no one knows what she is: she has lived in the public eye for eight years, she is setting well towards forty and has been known to express only two candid opinions: one on Mr. Asquith and one on the White Slave Traffic. One watches with interest for the third.) drew to them crowds of women too intelligent to be politicians: but too little politicians to be a match for the Pankhursts. They combined like natural affinities. All women who thought at all considered their proposals seriously: the majority were prepared to give them support. Thereupon, the Pankhursts selected from the best available, what was necessary and then pre- [sic] themselves[1] to be exclusive, since Mrs. Pankhurst had her political axe to grind. She required at the outset, for the sake of backing, women with money and with some capacity: when she had obtained these she drew the limiting line which would keep out women with accepted followings and too much ability: that is unless they came with ashes in their hair, repentance in one hand and passivity in the other. Then on the principle of the Eastern potentate who illustrated the practice of good government by lopping off the heads of all the stalks of grain which grew higher than the rest, she by one means or another rid her group of all

---

[1] ≠ text missing in source.

its members unlikely by virtue of personality, conspicuous ability, or undocile temper, to prove flexible material in the great cause. The gaps thus made she filled up with units of stock size. These readjustments of course took time but there resulted no harm from that, for before the talented or the conspicuous had shown sufficient signs of restiveness to make it wiser to clear them off, they were tractable enough to allow their talents to be exploited. Thus all was grist to the mill and the "great cause" went marching on.

As one learns from that mournful and monotonous institution, the suffrage-speech, Mrs. Pankhurst's nominal movement is not the first woman-suffrage movement. There existed one before which fortunately fizzled out, and it is mainly those associated with this former genuinely-suffrage venture and their connections who remain the non-Pankhurst suffragists. Their holding aloof is due partly to the fact that having questioned Mrs. Pankhurst's authority to speak in the name of the Suffrage movement, they roused that lady's implacable ire, and as we have said they could make their entry into her ranks only in abject terms. On the other hand their policy of separation is partly explained by the feeling that they might very well regard the suffrage propaganda as a sort of vested interest of their own, and that if show and interest were to be made out of it, they might as well endeavour to share in the credit. Hence they become as little willing to sink the goodwill of their tradition in Mrs. Pankhurst's organisation as Mrs. Pankhurst is willing to allow them to share in the authority over hers. Two camps therefore—old and new, "constitutionals" and "militants," the former saddled with a white-elephant in the shape of worn-out untrutsworthy, specious tricked-out arguments in favour of the "principle of woman-suffrage," who can rouse no feeling, but are given a respectful hearing from the people among whom conviction bites no sharper. And they can do nothing to help themselves. They are afraid to try anything beyond the most superficial of arguments for fear of being entangled in the entire theory of Representative Government. It is a sheer accident which the suffragists can merely deplore without being able to alter, that all the high hopes set a century ago upon the working of the Representative System should be finally petering out just as a few ardent women are waking up to the fact that the system exists and that they are not in it. On the level of intelligence at which the suffragists tell their sad story they can get no effective opposition: their audience are not capable of thinking out just the right refutation of the plausibilities: on the other hand they cannot attract any mental force, and as for the crude emotional force, that goes straight past them to the militants. Their least little sparkle is secured only when they manage to manœuvre themselves within the shine of their rivals' halos: a dubious manœuvre since they can never be quite sure in which regions these halos will shine as halos, and where as false lights. Moreover, they stand in danger of being warned off rudely, as Mrs. Pankhurst's band feels always that they are reaping unearned advantage: that their waste-land of dead suffrage propaganda has become valuable only through the fact that it lies adjacent to the centre of an interest with the creation of which their suffrage-principle has had nothing to do.

This is the reason why for all suffragists who do not begin and end with, simply "the vote and Mrs. Pankhurst" there is a never-ending fluctuation. The suffrage argument, taken neat, is hopeless: broken-down beyond hope of putting together. All that it can hope for is to be towed along the track behind some interest which gets its supplies from another source. The commonest way is to get behind the militant organisation: the societies which are non-militant but which are friendly to the militants are all of this order. They are innumerable: their motives are identical: pledged to support a boring subject, they gravitate naturally towards the only visible halo, the only point at which interest seethes. They flirt with the militants–if they are only on good terms enough: the Actresses' Society, the New Constitutional, the "Fellowship," the Freedom League, the Church League, the Conservative Women's League, and the rest. The traditional society, Mrs. Fawcett's, is not sufficiently friendly: it therefore is left to make a different shift for itself. It pledges itself to give the pious sniff and denounce the ways and works of its rival: that doesn't carry it far: then, it makes alliance with a very curious party: the very people to grapple with whom Mrs. Pankhurst was inspired to make her bold bid for the vote: the party which by its ways and works has unconsciously added the last touch to the farce of representative government: the Parliamentary Labour Party. This makes a doleful combination and it is small wonder that they are constantly on the look-out for "ideas" to stiffen things up a little. The constitutionals would like to be, if they dared be, the "intellectual" party: unfortunately strict suffrage and intellect will not lie down together. Their experience with the "White Slave" business will do something to teach them how wise was Mrs. Pankhurst in the early days when she directed all argumentation to be strictly on the vote, and nothing but the vote. "Give us the vote, never mind why, or we'll

burn your house down if you don't"—that is the only safe
argument intellectually speaking. Deviate into this notion
or into that, no matter what, and a watchful opponent will
catch you out. It was what happened when certain official
English "constitutionals" were sufficiently ill-advised as to
have truck with such a journal as the former *Freewoman*. Mrs.
Humphry Ward promptly caught them out. But for our own
compunction at their woeful case, we might have enabled her
to lay their twists and subterfuges barer than she managed
to do by her unassisted observation. Apparently, judging by
our correspondence columns, a precisely similar episode is
now being enacted in America. If suffragists will accept our
well-meant advice, they will postpone their thinking until
they feel less deeply pledged to their suffrage opinions. The
two together can only end in difficulties—for them. They
must be prepared to leave the one and cleave to the other: it
is the price they pay for loyalty to be content to say as in the
jingle "we want, we want, we want the vote," with as little as
possible about "why" and "what for."

We might here reply to the American correspondent who
asks for a statement as to where the *Freewoman* (now the
Egoist) stands in relation to woman-suffrage. Replying on
impulse, we would say "Nowhere," since the suffrage is wholly
a matter of indifference. We should, for instance, hear of the
existence of a Party Compact to withhold votes from women
for an indefinite period with the same absence of feeling with
which we should hear that the measure was to be put through
next week. That as regards the "principle."

As for the genesis and development of the *Freewoman-
Egoist*: the *Freewoman* marked the term of an emotion: the

militant suffrage enthusiasm. It was a seeking for the seat
of the illusion which is all-powerful while heat is in it: but
which becomes quite ludicrously patent with a lowering of
temperature. The zest there is in a good fight when one
is in the mind for it explains something, but not, one felt,
everything. There must be something besides the joy of a
good fight to explain why men and women set out hot-headed
after first one hunt and then another: the long list of good
"Causes." The first clue led in the direction of the hypnotic
words, the words saturated with the associations of the zeal of
centuries for other—causes: Morality, Freedom, Right, Justice.
The source of illusion lay perhaps in a misinterpretation of
these: therefore re-interpret and illusion will vanish in "True
Reality." So!

However, the closer scrutiny which re-interpretation of
these words demanded promptly revealed that it was not re-
interpretation they required: they had received interpretations
enough and to spare: what was required was a comprehension
of their nature and function and the confusing of intelligence
to which their use led. The exposition of "The New Morality"
turned into a study of the words Morality and Moral; the New
Freedom, into an inquiry as to what one meant by being "Free."
Far from being erratic the development of the *Freewoman-
Egoist*: the *Freewoman* has been in one unbroken line: a line of
inquiry which has gnawed its way straight through difficulties
where the "faithful," the "loyal" would have broken down or
turned back. It is not a "new" morality which is required,
but an understanding of the "moral" in order to put it in its
proper place. (It is to be remarked that when the journal was
gibbeting existent "morals" and proposing a new set, it was
called "immoral"—and was dearly beloved of the suffragists.
When it limited itself to explaining what everyone means by

"moral," and left both existent and new morality to find what status they were able, the cry of "immorality" ceased: and the love of the suffragists ceased with it. For the change was going to rob them of their thunder and at the same time burst their halos of self-conscious virtue.) Moral conduct, it became clear, was nothing more than the habitual conduct of the great majority: sometimes, hurtful habitual conduct, sometimes beneficial: requiring to be varied with time, person and place: above all it is varied by the intelligence of the person. The habit intensifies only for the unintelligent: and it is the dead weight of the latter's support which secures it respect. An intelligent man resists the habit and holds himself ready and alert for readjustment. To call him "moral," is to class him with the herd: to call him immoral, is to prejudge him: it may just suit him to fall in with the custom. Both descriptions for him are idle terms, indicating a silly and useless division, like water-drinkers and not. It is no use, since we all drink water at times, because it suits us, or it just happens. An intelligent man is moral and immoral in the same way.

The "New Freedom" goes the way of the "New Morality." The term Freedom (foolishly objectivised, like Morality, Rights, and the rest), the term apart, an unswerving inquiry dissolved the glamour which hung about being "free." When we say "One is free to do..." whatever one may have in mind, we mean "One has *the power* to do... " such and such. We cannot be "freer" than we have power to be. So-called freedom is entirely a matter of power and popular speech about being free is merely confusion. To be aware of the confusion is a first step towards acquiring that which is essential—power. It prevents one wasting energy and breath claiming to be "free":

that one needs to claim and cannot act as such, proves the absurdity of the claim. Such claimants are, in fact, asking for protection, *i.e.* that others should forego the exercise of their power in order to give them an *appearance* of power. Claims are the reproaches of the powerless: whines for protection. All the suffragists' "claims" are of this order, and it was to disentangle the journal from association with these, and with the long list of whines, Free Speech, Free Love, Free Assembly and what-not, that "Freewoman" became *Egoist*, which title is a sign hung out above the seat of authority: the centre of power: the self. One has the "freedom" if one has the "power," and the measure of one's power is one's own concern.

We must not leave the subject of suffrage without reference to militant affairs, since the periodic agitation which the press works up in the public mind is just now at its height. The newspapers skilfully agitate the question as to which side appeal shall be made: and should both sides fail to respond, what shall be done. We think it should be clear by this that it is waste of breath appealing to the militants themselves: as—by the way—it is idle to talk of the work of destruction being perpetrated by paid persons. There would be just as much pertinence in saying that Mr. McKenna or the judges who convict the women are *paid* to do their jobs. Nor is much likely to be done by attacking the society's funds. The newspapers could do far more by ignoring the whole subject: a procedure which would necessitate the spending of funds on forms of publicity now freely provided them by their censors. To think that it will is to commit the childish error of under-rating an opponent. To be sure, the Pankhursts are not sincerely trying to get a vote: but then they are quite sincere in trying at all costs to make something else secure: they are backing their prestige—their own policy because it is their own, quite apart from suffrage considerations, exactly as a man would shout on the horse on which he had put his money without regard to the racing merits of its rivals. In this they are so deeply sincere that they are able to give an air of sincerity to all they say and do: and it gives the explanation why strictly they cannot be accounted charlatans, although in the name of one thing they acquire and use up support which was given them on considerations quite other. And as it is hopeless to appeal to the Pankhursts it is hopeless to appeal to any of their followers while the glamour of following is on them. It has to be realised that after full deduction has been made for sensational appeals upon minds confused by swollen rhetoric the suffragettes are enjoying themselves tremendously, and this in spite of the physical strain and horror and weariness. Militancy has, in fact, in the emotional life of those upon whom it takes firm hold answered a want in the lives of woman which is all the more insistent because it is but rarely put into words. Unless exceptional ability has opened up unusual avenues of interest, or unless they chance to be under the influence of some other satisfying emotion, women are haunted with the vague realisation that they do not count much otherwise than passively: they feel non-responsible and unnecessary save as accessories. Moreover, usually they are burdened with more undirected emotion than they can well carry—vague emotion continuously suppressed until it acquires the energy of a tightly-wound spring: and there is no prospect of securing its release save upon the initiative of some hypothetical person whose appearance even in imagination is still to make. To young women, educated perhaps not much, but still more than the scope of their activities seems to have any call for, to young women of this sort, and there are thousands, pleasant, emotional, untrained and untried, the Pankhurst call comes, having in it almost the sound of the inevitable "Thou art the young woman[1]" Here is a sphere where she can count: action as simple as a child's with the ready flattery of the great leaders to put her easily among the line of the great. From Sappho to Jeanne d'Arc or Jesus Christ—anywhere she chooses she becomes one with them. From being nobody among very ordinary somebodies she feels she has become a person among those who count: name in papers, a celebrity: government solemnly discussing how by stretching its powers to the utmost it can deal with her: a problem. Secrecy, glamous [sic], action, a cause, big phrases, leaders, she has carved out a niche for herself in the scheme of things[2]. And no more suppressed emotion. Emotion stretches itself out to the utmost: there is the abandonment: the breaking of conventions: the stretching out to one's full height: the touch of the "O Altitudo."[3] A very jolly time surely. Far from being paid to live it, it is worth being paid for. The physical distress is an undercurrent: not wholly felt. It will be felt later, when the emotion has died down, but neither the determination nor the endurance will fail, as long as the emotion lasts. It is plain, therefore, that the suffragettes cannot, neither leaders and followers, be appealed to. We can take it for granted they are going to continue to the bitter end. As an object of appeal there remains the government. It is true that as far as the general public is concerned the pressure upon the government has never been so weak. The government's stubbornness in this matter in former times has often seemed inexplicable: it is

---

[1] ≠ DM paraphrases 2 Samuel 12:7.
[2] ≠ "glamous" as in source.
[3] ≠ "O altitudo divitiarum" by Giaches de Wert (1581)

for the present, at least, quite explicable. The women it is felt have tried bounce unsuccessfully, and it is a human commonplace that the reaction when bounce miscarries is always stubborn and unyielding. Still, the government has to keep in view the fact that the public temper is very fickle. That it is favourable to them to-day is no guarantee that it will be so to-morrow even should they follow the very course for which to-day it clamours. And it is not easy for the government suddenly to become harsh when it has from its own point of view shown itself hitherto very sensitive. It should have remained inflexible from the beginning if the cry "the law must be maintained" was to have any force. The present Home Secretary inherits the results of Mr. Herbert Gladstone's "flexible" policy in 1909. Otherwise it would have been easy considering the present state of public opinion to take the "heroic" course advised, i.e. to let the sentences run their usual course: throwing the responsibility for what may happen on those who cause it to happen. Moreover, in clamouring for a change of treatment of suffragists the public makes the mistake of imagining that there is only one question under consideration, whereas there are two. First there is the question of punishment used as a deterrent and second there is the question as to what course can be expected to minimise the probability of further damage. Now as a means of inflicting hardship the "Cat-and-Mouse" Act is certainly far better than the ordinary action of the law: for instance, being subjected to resisted forcible feeding means greater suffering than being allowed to die if one really wants to. By first setting the prisoners free and then again imprisoning them after a brief interval is very deadly simply because it is a wearing-down process and proportionately hard to bear. It also tends to depress onlookers, whereas a death or two would make all the supporters of the "victims" feel that they were bound in honour and consistency "to do something" in order to make the tragic events appear less futile. The "Cat-and-Mouse" Act is, as we have pointed out before, very good government indeed, well calculated with its waiting policy, depressing action and punitive features to break the strongest spirits. As regards the prevention of further misdemeanours—the notion which is actually agitating the public mind—no government, and no act of any government, can prevent them. Government rests upon an assumption that it possesses the assent of the governed, and the suffragettes have realised so much of political reality as to be aware of that. Against the recalcitrant individual, government can only defend itself. The power of government is built up from the acquiescence of the governed: which is why a people whining against its government presents so absurd a spectacle. If a person is determined to do as he likes in a certain anti-lawful way, the government is powerless to stop him. It can only kill him, a fact which the government well knows. The disturbing element in this present situation is that it doesn't want to be connected with the killing of these women—for entirely sentimental reasons. It is no good saying that it would treat men quite differently. Of course it would. It would treat them as men, but how can it treat women as men when they are women? Men would, in fact, never put themselves in a like position unless they know that strong public feeling would be with them: they would never rely upon a kindly regard for their beautiful eyes to save them from the legal consequences of their acts. Sir Edward Carson does not rely upon being soulful and of tender build when he defies the government. But the women do. It is, shall we say, humorous, that the crucial point about which the women have made their defiance of man-made laws turn should be just this ancient womanly one. The hunger-strike is a gamble—heavy stakes laid on the certitude of men's chivalry towards woman. That is why it is so strong a card. Even if, in a fit of exasperated temper, it should happen to fail them just now, it will have to be brought into play in the long run when things have been allowed to get a few degrees worse. Well then, what? It requires some spokesmen of the Order of Masculine Chivalry who realises the lie of the case to give the cue for action. The person at whom the Fates obviously are pointing is Mrs. Humphry Ward. The rôle of the great Duke of Wellington is obviously destined for her: to advise a course which she distrusts and dislikes to put an end to a state of affairs which she dislikes and fears still more. Her creed rests on the maintenance of men's Chivalry towards women with, in addition, the acknowledgment in deed and word of a reciprocal attitude in women towards men to make it possible. There now exists therefore a unique opportunity of offering to the world a perfect working model. The anti-suffragist leader's most virulent opponents have in "Deeds not Words" actually hung the thread of their lives upon men's chivalry. They have, as Mrs. Ward declared they would, by their failure to adopt the reciprocal womanly attitude, made the working of chivalry almost impossible. The loss of their lives would merely demonstrate what can already be foreseen: the point at which exasperation brings chivalry to the breaking-point. They have put themselves into the delicate and painful position of drawing too largely upon the fund of interested kindness, and someone would do well to extricate them: the someone by preference: a woman. Mrs. Ward has her opportunity: that in consideration of the larger ideal of which her opposition to woman Suffrage is but a part, she waives the claims which the present strength of those considerations has given the predominance and beseeches the government anti-suffragists to combine with the government suffragists to put through without delay a non-contentious measure which will confer on these women the parliamentary vote. If the womanly woman is returning, it would be fitting that her triumphal re-entry should be made in her best rôle: the subtle, courteous, persuasive, kind. Why not?

16. Just and Moral

"The decisive powers are indicated, as in a scale, by the outcome of a struggle which is always after the nature of a fight."

[. . .] IT is worthwhile lingering over this tendency of the "down" to ask for the "generous" when they are offered the "just," since from such an attitude follow many implications: which is the reason why persons with spirit care little for the ousting of the "just" by the "generous." For one thing, the action of the latter is uncertain, unreliable, and, worse than all, expected to cut both ways. He who has been generously treated must, in his turn, act generously or be considered—something which he does not care to be—mean. They would prefer to be "just" because it is expedient—and be "generous" by whim—only when they please. Plans of their own, by being generous, might be interfered with: moreover, they care little for the feeling of having been generously dealt with: they feel it to be either an investment or thinly veiled patronage, and would prefer to carve a career irrespective of it. To accept favours with indeterminate obligations attached is an irksome proceeding for able men. Only favours which are done outright, for the doer's own satisfaction, are suitable for acceptance. In short—to be "generous" is purely an affair of individual taste, while to be "just"—in this secondary sense of fulfilling fairly whatever one undertakes—is the basis of tolerable social existence.

There is, however, a sense in which "to be just" cuts more deeply than it has been seen to in relation to bargains: it touches individual quality so closely that it becomes a question of linguistic suitability as to whether the word "just" should be used in respect of it, especially as it has to do with a something in human character which is called—quite erroneously—"moral." The decisive powers which give configuration to the grades of a community, and which fix its members' status, are not fundamentally based on bargains: the spirit which allows of bargains follows after. The decisive powers are indicated, as in a scale, by the outcome of a struggle which is always after the nature of a fight. The struggles are waged almost to exhaustion before such a scale is arrived at, and it is roughly on calculations based on their outcome, that the spirit in which subsequent bargains are struck takes its tone and temper. Before one arrives at the point where one can be "just" in the secondary sense there has been this preliminary assessment of values which have decided what is "just" in the first degree.

Assessment of one's worth precedes all one's bargaining: what is a "just" bargain for one is absurd and fantastic for another to contemplate. What is "just" for one, is based on what one "is" and "has."

This account—the basis of agreement—comprises the sum total of one's entire competence. To swell it fraud, deception, misrepresentation, bounce, swagger, "honest" miscalculation—all these things may enter in an attempt to confuse the exact value. They are all means endeavouring to conceal what is just: to make assessment inexact, not-nicely balanced on the precise worth of the parties with intent to confuse others as to one's just dues. Now one's just due is what one can obtain if one chooses to put the particular issue to a test of trial by strength. It is a corrollary following from one's competence.

Now it is one of the most obvious facts of life that the "competence" of individuals varies: varies to an enormous extent: and it follows, therefore, that what each individual can, in subsequent bargains, "justly" demand (justly, *i.e.*, with due regard to the individual's powers effectively to back up his demand), varies equally. That is why the equality argument never cuts any deeper than sound. That men are "equal" is the cover instinctively sought by precisely those sentimentalists who "claim" the generous because they dislike the "just." For just as it is an obvious fact that individual competence varies enormously it is a fact equally obvious that nothing hurts the humanitarian (*i.e.* the rhetorical Salvationist, equality-cum-rights) temperament more than an open recognition of it. The patent fact that men are not equal in the only sense that matters, *i.e.*, in power of life, is the humanitarian's skeleton in the cupboard. It is the universal secret known everywhere, mentioned nowhere.

We can perhaps make this primary aspect of what is "just" more clear by turning to a consideration of the "moral" for a while, and returning to show the connection between the rhetorical meanings of the two. Accurately "the moral," as we have pointed out before, is the "traditional," "the customary." The fact that it belongs to the crowd, and describes the way of the crowd, explains why it exists in such good odour with them: it explains why it is the ready catch of all those who seek to win the favour of the crowd. To advocate a thing because it is moral is obvious flattery: it means "your"—therefore "good." Quite possibly it is "good" since it appears as such to them; and since they cling to it, it shows itself a reliable habit for them at least. The moralists, however, are not content with this account of the amount of merit in their appeal to the populace for favour under the aegis of the moral. They endeavour rather to imply that the "moral" is one and the same with that force of spirit which is the kernel of all personal competence. It is worthwhile being quite definite as to what this "spirit force" is, and since there is a popular word which is used in almost the exact connotation, this should not be difficult. The word "character" (which only inasmuch as it has been erroneously identified with the "moral" is synonymous with stodge) the word "character" will serve. Character is the living energy—varying in strength and differing in quality which, strong, weak or indifferent, is the ultimate individual competence which must be there before it can be directed towards any activity whatsoever.

More often than not strong character turns to new kinds of activity, leaving the moral, and courage being justified of her children, manages to inaugurate a new practice: which weaker characters later will doubtless make moral, *i.e.*, imitate, and probably vitiate by imitation. Character is the worth—the power—in an individual apart from the thing he does though what he does is determined by what it is. The differences in character are not differences in "morals," "ways," "habits"; they are such differences as exist between a strong magnetic current and a feeble one: or between a scraggy bramble and an oak: both "good" to themselves, no doubt: but not needing and certainly not receiving identical treatment. To speak of morals when one means character is to speak of attitudes when one actually means "values."

In order more strongly to assert that "men are equal," weak but kindly persons choose to slur lightly over this question of individual force: they are afraid to seek out the one reason why some men are cuffed while others do the cuffing, and because they dare not face this fact, upon which what is "just" primarily is based, they change their cry from the just to the generous: and practise a little innocent but highly misleading bounce by calling the desired generosity—Justice. The bounce will go just a little way—but not far: certainly not far enough to make much material change in their condition.

Let us take as illustration the present outcry against the wage "system" (so-called). The "system" is to be abolished because, forsooth, it is "immoral" and "unjust." Just note: the very same breath which states it to be immoral, and against the deepest instincts of men—also declares that it is almost ineradicable, that it has worked itself into the very tissue of civilisation, so much so that men's minds are hypnotised by it—their very speech is at one with it, and that they cannot shed the phraseology which embodies it, but having shaken off one phrase will use another in which it is as deeply implicated. To settle down to work for subsistence wages, whether under the old slave order or this new wage system is shown to be an instinctive level to which the mass of men have set themselves throughout history. Well then: whatever the receiving of wages may not be—it certainly is the custom: it is habitual: Moral. More than any other feature common to mankind throughout the ages the custom of being paid for labour done in terms of wages—kind or coin—is the most unmistakable. Working for wages is certainly moral—so exceedingly so that we shall feel compelled, one of these days, to go into the reason why. It is hurtful, too, we are told. If so, let those who are hurt by it tell us how. If it is hurtful it is a very interesting example of the undoubtedly "moral" being only questionably "good." Doubtless what such writers mean when they say it is immoral is that wage earning is not compatible with the temper of persons of strong and original character. Which seems fairly true, since wage earning for the masses has involved the labouring on other men's schemes in which the labourers have little or no personal interest; in the main, their toil is menial, servile, obedient, submissive, and they themselves are open to suffer insult and contumely.

Then why do they persist in it? One tells them that it is hurtful: but they should know best. As to whether the shoe pinches it is the wearer who is the best judge. All that an onlooker can say is this "wage shoe" is of such a shape as would make the wearing of it torture to feet of certain mould. But the wages-shoe seems to suit wage-earners very well: they require a very great deal of persuasion before they can be induced to say a word against it, and even then the very words which would seem to rebuke its strictures look always to its continued wear. Names matter little: they take it off as "shoe" and promptly put it on again freshly labelled "slipper." The fact is, it appears to be made to measure: it adjusts itself to the total of their actual competence. Certainly masters and men are not bargaining in the dark: from time to time they have tried their strength, and their present relations are the adjustments which have followed as the outcome of these trials. The competence of the wage-earners cannot be put at a high figure when one bears in mind that they have barely arrived at the point where bargaining is at all possible. They come to the masters as beggars: begging to be allowed to accomplish their purposes for them, and at their own request their energies are bought up for that purpose. On the strength of their own powers they are not in a position to make an advantageous bargain. Nor do they. When by combination with others as incompetent, *i.e.*, powerless, as themselves they are able with some show of success to ask that rates be at least thus much, it is often accorded by the employer because it is more convenient not to haggle: or because he can afford it: or because it pleases him to be generous and he pities the poor men's plight.

That the trade unions by a device called the monopoly of labour have managed to secure a certain semblance of bargaining has given the union wage-earners a sense of heightened status which is likely to prove highly misleading: they are likely to confuse a reluctance to incur inconvenience into a recognition of existing competence which belongs only to positive exercise of power. The results of the exercising of a monopoly over labour, of strikes and other obstructive tactics are purely negative, and in the long run will prove nugatory. Men are not irreplaceable: an ominous feature for those who would establish monopolies. Machines will go a very long way with such work as the mass of wage-earners perform. The crucial test of competence is not what men can force others to disburse, but what each has the power to set about producing for himself. That employers set no great store by the "claims" of the trade unions is proved by their determination not to yield over the question of non-union labour. These "negative" shows of power, in effect, exhibitions of absence of power, are not likely to bring people with the long purses down on their knees. If then, we were to sum up the wage-earners' dues in terms of what is primarily and secondarily just, it becomes clear that their case has to do with character rather than with morals and will find its way out of the slough of wage-earning when they can rely on what is just and dispense with the generous.

First, as to the sorts and sizes of wages. No honest-minded man can contend in the main that these are unjust: that they

offend as violating the terms of a bargain. On the contrary,
wage-earners are seldom in a position sufficiently strong to
make a bargain. They beg and receive—work with wages
attached. They do the work which is given them, tolerably.
They take their wages whether the concern pays or loses: on
the whole they hope it "pays," since of a certainty they would
not be employed for long unless there was a prospect of profit
from their employ to the one who employs them. Just as
they know that they would not work but for the certainty of
wages, they should know that an employer would not employ
them but for the hope of profits in one form or another. If
the wage-earner does not like the arrangement, he can always
leave and start a concern of his own. If he will face "justly"
the actual reason why he has not already done so, he will
allow that it is because he feels he has not the competence
behind him either in ability or possessions, or both, to start
a concern for profit to himself: otherwise he would set about
it. If in the future he ever feels he can—he will. His present
talk about the "surplus value" which he "creates" is so much
self-deception. He "creates" nothing in the initiatory sense.
He does the work he applied for, is paid for, and would get
the sack for not doing. He had no thought for the "created"
profits when he undertook the work. His thought was to get
and keep the job. His "right" to make someone else give him
work; his "right" to make someone else refuse to give others
work; his "right" to a certain amount of pay; his "right" to
"surplus value" are afterthoughts, and poor ones. For if he
had had the "might," the "competence" to cover the wide
expanse of these "rights," he would not be in the position
of a beggar asking for the favour of a job from a master: he
would have set about being his own master: the one thing
which to this day the ordinary wage earner steadily refuses

to be. That he has begun to call his shoe a slipper in no way mitigates the obstinacy of this refusal.

Of course, his self-appointed apologists have a host of "reasons": it would, in fact, be strange if the wage-earners in common with everyone else, could not find an inexhaustible supply for not doing what they have no inclination to do.

But their intellectual friends have made out a pretty case for them: based on the quite questionable assumption that their present downtrodden condition is not a fair index of their actual competence, and that the primary assessment of their weight is "unjust." Their contention is that how they can be treated is no index that they cannot prevent themselves from being so treated: that their competential assessment is out of date, and that they are good for more now than when affairs became adjusted to them in their present subordinate position. And, of course, in the course of time, character values constantly change, but when they are changed in a marked degree there will be a fight—we call it a revolution—to assess anew powers to the extent to which they have changed. During such a struggle there exists a state of war in which scruples respecting the terms of contracts, the usages common to times of peace, the respect of property, and the like, will be abrogated: while the combatants will press into the waging of their contentions their entire strength, compounded of armed force, intelligence, cunning, present possessions, friends, past obligations, charm and grace, which may serve them to win allies or break the fierceness of attack. When the campaign has been fought out to exhaustion, in the lull which follows there will emerge the new estimate which each must take of other's competence: an estimate which will serve for many years to come. Whereupon the harsher terms of what is primarily "just" having been for another space decided, the period will arrive when that which is "just" in the secondary degree, and which applies to terms fixed by contract, can re-establish itself. Thus war—open war—is not in its nature opposed to peace: it is a necessary preliminary of peace. The years of peace are based on conclusions of relative strength which can only be arrived at in war: conclusions which assert what is basically "just" whether in relation to international or intranational powers. A class or a nation will from time to time precipitate a struggle on primary terms, and for the time will regard all contractual documents between themselves and their opponents as torn up. After the issue, what was before reckoned "primarily just" will be re-adjusted. That is precisely what the term "to re-adjust" means, *viz.* to make a hitherto accepted assessment fit more exactly to the powers that are. So we can state the conclusion: In times of peace if we make bargains it is expedient to he content to satisfy and be satisfied with their simple fulfilment: and it is in no wise feasible to attempt to bludgeon the contractors, employers or others, into doing favours. But war declared, all bargaining is finished for the time being, and what one may demand is about to be decided on the strength of arguments not verbal but competential. What is "just" is for the moment in doubt, but will be made clear by the lie of the combatants at the close of the campaign. A revolting class, which has not an instinctive feel that this is the gist of the situation is so little advanced on the path of revolt as scarcely to be entitled to bear that description. And nothing good for them or others—will come of hurrying them. One rises—when one is able.

17. I Will Be Good

"Each is responsible for himself and his but not for all."

IT was the late lamented Queen Victoria who immortalised
in a phrase a little gust of emotion which is familiar to us
all, but to which most of us are too shy, or too cautious to
give utterance. The incident which was able to knock this
august maiden off her perch, and betray her into a very human
indiscretion was the sudden announcement of her accession
to the throne, whereupon she ejaculated, "I will be good, I
will be good." Who is there who has not felt such a spasm,
and luckily bitten his tongue just as he was on the point of
giving expression to it? Luckily because people do so seem
to expect one to live up to one's utterances, when after all,
spasms are spasms—and horrible if they are mistaken for
permanencies, dragging a code of conduct after them. If only
some discerning person had been on the spot to explain the
correct theory of spasms to the new Queen, how might she not
have suppressed, instead of encouraging, all those dreadful
bores of her era, who emulated her in the role of being good!
Because, be it noted, she did not say she was good, which
would have been at least impudent, if not exciting: she said
she *would* be, obviously with her mind's eye on a manner of
conduct not altogether native to herself. So was she—good
and dull—and when ultimately she died, she unfortunately
omitted to take her spiritual progeny with her. We have them
yet, and they multiply and prosper, expecting us all to step
out to the rhythm of "we will be good—we will be good."

❦

Of course, one hears the endorsing chorus–"And a very good thing, too"— rising from the hosts of salvation. And we understand why. "Being good," in addition to being very plaguey for oneself, and being (could we say?) most interestingly "nosey" in relation to others, involves the practice of a precept too well rubbed into human consciousness to be wholly without effect. To "turn the other cheek" and receive a second smack from an offending individual instead of administering a smart one in return—is ideally "good" conduct of the modern version[1]. It is, in fact, to be "generous" rather than "just": which makes it clearer from whence a new species of revolters have imbibed their peculiar doctrines, and acquired the effrontery to express them. They believe that the "haves" *"ought"* to be "good" because this is the burden of all modern teaching. The gist of salvationism is to build up a communal tradition of conduct which shall be regulated by what is "generous" rather than by what is "just." To erect a scheme designed on a basis of goodwill is their heart's desire. And goodwill means to be fired with the intention to be "generous" rather than "just," a sequence Salvationists hope will have the same stability as its opposite. They take no count of the spasmodic nature of the impulse towards the "good," but hopefully persevere in their task of attaching wheels to an eagle. The latest example of this misguided attempt to put excellent forces to unserviceable uses comes to us in a volume of essays on *National Guilds* (Bell and Sons. 5s. net), which is offered to the public by Mr. Orage, the editor of our contemporary, *The New Age*[2].

A collection of essays intended to propound, in a reversion

---

[1] ≠ Matthew 5:39.
[2] ≠ *National Guilds* by A. R. Orage (London: G. Bell and Sons, 1914).

to guilds, a new version of salvation. The essays are, we gather, reprints of articles which have already appeared in *The New Age*, and are accordingly written in good "journalese": good, that is, none of the writers' sentences are left wanting in any of their parts. Now good journalese is a very telling form of prose-writing: excellent within its own limits. Its virtues are that it gets on with the narrative and tells a tale as effectively as it can be told with expedition. It reaches its readers because it does not mince with terms: but accepting them with all their confused associations of meaning, uses them without a qualm, leaving the selection of meaning to the reader. Journalese is especially appropriate as the language of "news"; it is in its right place in the relating of incident and fact. Latterly it has deservedly fallen into disrepute because it has overstepped its limits and attempted tasks for which, by its nature, it is disqualified, and where indeed its very particular merit of forthrightness is an added offence. Its efforts to disport itself in such an inquiry as that presented by the subtle complex woven by the interplay of human motives have effects as disastrous as those which would ensue were a racing car to try to show its powers in narrow streets and crowded thoroughfares. A racing-car requires a fairly clear track, and so does journalese; the words over which it makes such speed must be straightforward: stripped of all doubtful meaning. With such words as those whose vague and ambiguous connotations are the root-cause of philosophic controversies it can or should have nothing to do. And when, for instance, in addition a good journalist, *i.e.*, one who can write good journalese, will slip and write bad journalese, a quite definite word like "crime" in a sentence like this: "To reduce the untiring efforts of mankind to the level of cotton and coal is a crime and a sin against the Holy Ghost[1]" one can imagine how he will use such words as democracy, morals, ethics, justice, sin, and "surplus value." As the writers of *National Guilds* have had the misfortune to attempt to provide a basis founded on a valuation of human motive for their system, and as they have not attempted to look at the springs of human motives any deeper than a slip-shod acceptation of the popular use of such words as above mentioned, it follows, that they do not offer the preliminary part of their exposition to serious readers. Even putting the subtler evaluations of human motives aside it makes hard reading to see a word like democracy advanced as though there existed a common understanding as to what democracy implies or as though in this country its implication were understood sufficiently to allow of its merits being seriously canvassed. Accordingly, the insinuation that democratic institutions are without question advantageous, and an easy appeal built up on that makes it impossible to accord the preliminary part of this exposition anything beyond the recognition of ready speciousness which one allows to the usual stump orator. It must be dismissed as not having taken the first step towards serious inquiry; it has not started with an examination of the terms about whose meaning there lies the doubt. The writers have been content to profit by ambiguity speciously to "tell a tale": just where exposition is most needed they fix their base and take the position for granted. The result is propaganda: that usual misleading thing called a "constructive social proposal."

Apart from the introduction of unfortunate and ill-comprehended terms, perhaps dragged into the argument for elegance'

---

[1] $\neq$ *National Guilds.*

sake and a sort of curate's impressiveness, the book bases its
case upon two assumptions, both, we think, quite untenable.
The assumptions are: (1) That the present state of affairs
is intolerable, and (2) That it is leading to a condition of
even greater hatefulness, which is described as the "Servile
State." Now, when one endeavours to be honest about facts,
one has to confess that the present state of affairs is not at all
intolerable: we all seem to be bearing up very well, especially
the wage-earners, who are supposed to be resenting it with a
special intensity: it is indeed those who are not wage-earners
who appear to be conscious of a certain inadequacy. Of the
horrors of the "Servile State" itself we can fairly judge, for *this
is it*. To think that it is necessary to place the "Servile State"
in the future is to fail to understand what is implied by it. It
is doubtful whether we could average out at anything more
"servile," even in degree, than we are at present. Certainly
not in kind. Most of us serve, and appear to find it not
only tolerably comfortable, but to glory in it. Indeed, "I
serve" looks very well on crests and badges: while as for those
amiable and obvious persons, the politicians, who are made
out to play so sinister a part in the threatened conspiracy, *they*
are not making us "servile"—they couldn't–our own private
efforts in that line are not to be bettered. They appear to be
simply tidying up the mess a little, presumably to make them
feel happier in accepting the money they get for their jobs.

Let us brace up our nerves and look squarely at this word
"servile." There is no obscure connotation attached to it. A
person who has not the wherewithal to be independent to be
his own master, must needs be as "servile" as anyone need
be under any conceivable circumstances whatsoever; and it

makes very little difference who the master is or whether there is one, or two, or a multitude. Now, the very fact that it is possible for the theory of *Guilds* to be elaborated at this time of day, and with some show of enthusiasm, offers the best proof of how well the "servile condition" suits us all: for guilds present just another variation of the attempt to dodge the first condition of independence. To seek to establish industrial guilds is not an effort to work oneself free of a master, but to secure an additional and more powerful master. It is not an effort towards the acquisition of property, *i.e.*, possessions of *one's own*, which is the entrenchment behind which one can rule one's life after the manner of one's personal inclination: it is an unblushing announcement of a willingness to stand and deliver the little bit one has—one's energy—to the custodianship of a police possessed of far greater powers of preventing resumption of property than any individual or corporate body known to history. The very thin plea that each little "guildsman" is to own the whole guild should not, after the practical experience of a century of representative government, deceive an infant. It is, indeed, very odd that anyone, after being witness to, and acknowledging the disappointing failure of the representative system in politics, should have started out, bald-headed to apply the self-same system to industry. Matters of politics do not concern us more than a trifle but industrial concerns are matters of great and immediate importance. The line of mental development of persons who argue that a system tried and found wanting when applied to one set of affairs must therefore be all that can be desired when applied to more important affairs, is difficult to follow. The truth of the situation is that quite intelligent men have been misled by the concept of "bigness." They have, for instance, imagined one big world, whereas, in the actual, "the" world has no existence save as the various outlooks of each of those who make up the myriad of unique existences. "Reformers" have tried to get a comprehensive view of the "world's work"—which does not exist save in their own imagination—and they have come to neglect and hold lightly work viewed from its only real aspect—the personal satisfying of needs and wants as they rise up spontaneously from each varying individual: and from thence there has sprung an erroneous notion of "economy," itself in turn closely tracked by an erroneous notion of "waste." All this amalgamation of industries: this "elimination of waste" by joining up big businesses is a wild attempt to catch up with the initial error of imagining that "all" are responsible for each, which is a corollary following from that blatantly grotesque parody of a generalisation known pseudo-scientifically as "Society an Organism," of which "Members of one Body" is the theological variety.

Perhaps never since the days of the Chartists have the activities of those belonging to the lower-paid classes of workers been in the popular estimation regarded as possessing forces so vital and fateful as the forces known as syndicalist are to-day: and while they are hard put to it to give an account of the arresting quality, and are indeed inclined to give credence to accounts in proportion to the degree in which they are fantastic, they nevertheless feel the potentiality lying in it. Now the genius of syndicalism amounts to this: it gives expression in concrete shape to a revolt against the "Society an Organism" acceptation of social life. It expresses a revolt of those who, following the lines of this theory, must presumably be against filling the role of the trimmings of the beard

190

or the parings of nails—those parts of the organism which are sacrificed in order to enhance the beauty of the whole; it voices the objections of those who are reckoned as nail-parings and clippings where others presumably are head, heart and eyes, or other indispensable, honoured and well-cared-for features. Holding up the coal-supply or the means of transit or committing any of the sundry acts of offence and destruction comprised under the label *sabotage* is the protest of the less honourable members of the body against the direction of the higher powers—the brain-what-not of the body as a whole. It is as though the rebelling hair should swiftly convert itself into whip-cord or lightning to smite the barber or his client: or as if the sacrificial fingernail from which its owner seeks to sever himself should turn into a sword with will and intention in it, and smite the hand which manipulates the scissors. The directing power of such an "organism" would be considerably shocked, no doubt: so much so as to question the advisability of separating from such "members." The same notion is behind the "principle" of being good (the *principle*, as distinct from the whim). One returns good for evil *on principle*, on the same basis of reasoning as that on which one carefully tends a limb which ails constantly and gives its owner pain. It is because they are members of one body.

Syndicalism is a protest (vainly inarticulate) against a concept which has increased in strength steadily during the Christian era: it is an instinctive preference for the admonition "Call no man master" as against the democratic principle: "Ye are all members one of another[1]." That this revolting spirit now keenly alive in a limited number of wage-earners should have used trade unions rather than some other as an instrument of offence and defence affects the nature of its

---

[1] ≠ Matthew 23:9; Romans 12:5.

motive no more than the choice of a chopper rather than a garden-hose would affect our motive if one were suddenly approached by a mad dog: one would have chosen which ever was handiest for the occasion.

The fact, however, that they have used the trade unions as a means has been productive of certain very interesting but very erroneous conceptions. Of the misconceptions thus created, perhaps those indicated by the writings of the authors of *National Guilds* are amongst the most noteworthy. The advocates of the guilds have endeavoured to be in the swim of two fashions at one and the same time. Besides syndicalism, which is a practice rather than a theory, the most notable tendency of the last few years has been the swing from collectivism towards egoism. It is true that the crowd is just now surging in full tide towards collectivism—in social as well as religious and philosophical affairs: that makes no matter: the strongest forces are set against it: and the popular collectivist triumph is already tawdry and of the vulgar. Now, *National Guilds* is the effort of certain collectivism—honest enough—to cover the badges of their collectivism. They are wholly unsuccessful: everything which has of late years been said to discredit State-collectivism could be said with four-fold emphasis to discredit this double-handled engine of State-recognised, State-recognising, National Industrial Guilds. This effort to escape the reproach of State-collectivism has resulted in the conception of a State-fortified guild-collectivism. If the Servile State means anything more than a condition where in addition to the mass of the people being so propertyless that they must of necessity work for wages on the property of governors—the owners—it means the establishment of a police with powers to invade one's most intimate concerns and interfere with one's means of securing vital necessities; and the enormous industrial guild system possessing the "instruments of production," with the politicians holding the estate, is in a hundredfold stronger position to bring this latter about. Under the guilds the propertyless will still be propertyless—owning nothing fundamentally wealth-producing of *their own*. A political bureaucracy is to be backed up by an industrial one: which two, as organisations, will negotiate with each other. The mass are to serve: that is, do as they are told on the governors' jobs—for wages which are then to be decorated with the title "pay": the abolition of the wage-system, according to the *National Guilds* is to be effected by calling the "shoe" the "slipper." The volume contains a chapter enlarging on "pay" in the Army, which is so striking in its lack of penetration into the implications of wages and pay in general and pay in the Army in particular, that we hope to go into the causes which can give rise to a mal-comprehension so complete in a later issue.

Not comprehending that the importance which syndicalism gives to trade unionism is merely adventitious the prounders of the National Guilds propose to install them as the lungs of their new social system. Now in proposals of changes as comprehensive and vast as one must expect the effects of the guilds to be it should be necessary to take views a little beyond to-morrow Now the present unions have sprung up as local institutions to protect the labour which clustered into localities primarily decided upon by the location of machines. The trade unions are the outcome of the nature and (in addition) the *size* of the machines, and the stability and permanence of the unions primarily depend upon the continuance of like attributes in the machines. It therefore requires to be pointed out that if there are two modern and patently existent tendencies—egoism and syndicalism—which the "Guildsmen" have taken into account only to miscomprehend there is an incipient tendency of vast importance of which they have taken no account at all: the tendency following the advent of electricity to reconvert the enormous machine back into the individualised maniable tool. What the effects of this may be—geographically as well as industrially—the change from agricultural to industrial England effected by the advent of the steam engine will sufficiently indicate. It therefore becomes evident that the enormous organisation of which the trade union is typical is threatened not merely by the spiritedness of human temper, but even more by the inward sweep of its intelligence: and robbed of the integrating force supplied by the amalgamation of employed persons (servants) engaged in numbers upon a "master's" trade, the bottom falls out of the unions, and there remains nothing wherewith to create the national industrial guild.

To sum up: Syndicalism is in its infancy and is confused in its expression. What it means to say, and what it will say when it is more accustomed to itself is that the workers' great quarrel with employers has been a vast irrelevance: that the workers themselves are responsible each for himself and that if they are "down" it is their business to find the ways and means of getting up: that their task is a much nearer, simpler, yet more difficult one than that of "undertaking the world's work." It is attending to *their own* business—not a master's nor any other—themselves finding out the means how, and applying them. When they do that on an extended scale the spectre of the "servile state" not merely in its dressed out bogey-form of state or guild socialism, but in the existence of an actually "serving" population such as at present exists in this nation will have vanished. With the renewed realisation that "each is responsible for himself and his" but not for all, the questions of "the decline of crafts," "the economy of production and distribution," and "the elimination of waste" will be found to have eliminated themselves.

18. The Notion of Equality

*"To be satisfied to let the best man win in ungrudging
recognition of 'inequality': these are the
best traditions of virile peoples."*

THE notion which enables the Saviours of Society to develop
their steamiest heads is that of "equality," and to take
this notion to pieces is a process after the nature of a cold
douche which should do much to reduce the humanitarian
temperature to the level of common sense.

On the face of it the task is difficult because of the elusive
element in the enthusiasts' advocacy, for the first comment
which they will make after affirming that all men are equal
is that they are quite ready to grant you that they are not.
But one must have patience with a humanitarian: being a
verbalist he must be given ground-room to set up his catch-
words, and labels: else what is he? And if with patience you
let him run on with his discourse, somewhere approaching
the finish he will begin to show what he means as opposed
to what he originally has said. Out of the twisted phrases
one gathers that what the egalitarians mean is not that "all
men are equal," but that they are "equal in the eyes of God,"
or that they are "equal before the law," or that they ought
(blessed word!) to have "equal opportunities," or that they
have "a right to equal treatment"; Mr. Bernard Shaw would
say that they ought to have equal incomes. There are other
turnings of the phrases, "levellings up" and "levellings down,"
but these already cited will serve.

Between them there is little in common to serve as a con-
necting link. Each requires to be taken singly on its individual
merit. The most illuminating, if the most vulnerable, is the

one that men are "equal before God": and we need not worry to ascertain the meaning of God before seeking to learn why. It is enough to know where we may find him. It is commonly agreed that whatever God's nature, his abode is in the human heart, and that whatever response comes from that intimate quarter will be inflected with the voice of God. Now it is the heart which is the most emphatic in its denial that men are equal: the tricks of verbalism may go as far as they can but when feeling is more than skin-deep it remains unaffected by mere expression of opinion. Individual feeling is not merely aware that one is not equal to another but differs from all the rest: it acquiesces with a sense of satisfaction which is the secret of the hold which every form of genuine sport has upon the best elements of human nature. A desire to test and call into full evidence the amount of disparity between one and another is the motive behind every competition. To maintain a fair field and no favour in order to clinch the matter: to be satisfied to let the best man win in ungrudging recognition of "inequality": these are the best traditions of virile peoples, and furnish the evidence that worth is shown not merely in the possession [of] a high degree of power, but also in intelligence which is capable of recognising it even at its own expense. If the "eyes of God" have looked with favour on anything it has been upon the sporting instinct of good losers as well as good winners, and these same eyes have been always ready to frown on those who claimed to be equal with all men.

If in claiming to be equal in the eyes of God, inferiors have presumed on their merits overmuch, in maintaining that we are all "equal before the law," the superiors have presumed overmuch upon our lack of understanding, for it is a catch which could deceive only the excessively stupid. Before the law was, we were—unequal: that is why the law was necessary to perpetuate the inequalities of power and possessions. Consider, for instance, the law prohibiting theft, which is made to prevent those who have little or nothing from attacking those who have much. The poor man has scarcely anything that the rich man would care to own. He has the energy of his limbs, and the law is so framed that even this comes easily within the rich man's reach. The law is irrelevant as regards the rich who could have no sane motive in coming by possessions in the prohibited ways. Should they indulge in them it is, as a matter of fact, regarded as insanity, and "kleptomania" is a recognised feature of "pathological crime." That there are no laws against rent, interest, and profits, or against speculating for profit proves that by instinct the law has kept clear of any attempt to put a term to the obtaining of the lavish rewards which fall to the superiorly "unequal." There is to be no counting of heads and sharing up if the trend of the law is to count for anything. It assumes that initiative is, and is likely to remain, at a premium.

When the equality argument shifts to claims of "right to equal opportunity," "rights to receive equal treatment," "equal income," it becomes obvious that the assertion about all men being "equal" has in reality been abandoned, and the theory of what we should call the "Other Persons" has been resorted to. It is the shadow of the "Other Persons" which hangs over all these rights to deserts which one's own powers fall short of obtaining. It has its roots in the dependence on the feeding-bottle and apron-strings; it is the refusal of responsibility which seeks for the protection of the fostering parent in the outer world at the age when the fostering of the parent would naturally come to an end. It looks to the world to press opportunity upon it as it aforetime found the parent pressing the bottle. It is a misapprehension due to a

false analogy. Opportunity is not like cake which exists apart
from one's ability to eat it. An opportunity only becomes
one when it is seized. It is the power which can use it which
strikes the hour for the advent of opportunity. Opportunity
is the form in which power asserts itself. It is there or not
according as power is there. To ask for equal opportunity is
to ask to be endowed with the powers of someone else. What
can be another's opportunity might not be ours. What shape
our opportunity will take depends upon what kind of power
we have. Whether we have any opportunities or not depends
upon whether we have any power or not. If one has power
in one's self everything will turn to opportunity; if one has
not, the most obviously open avenues will appear blocked
as with impassable walls. Power exploits everything which
is amenable to it; lack of it means just inability to exploit
anything. To have an opportunity means to be able to exploit;
i.e., to use what is at hand. To ask to have opportunities
provided is to show inability to use an opportunity, as a
fretting infant turning from one nourishing food to another
will be unable to get benefit from any. A parent may care
to protect and arduously keep alight the unhealthy flicker of
life, but it is a mistake to imagine that others will do this
without demanding a price. What the price is reveals itself
in the sequel.

As for equal treatment. "Treatment" is the retort according to kind. Gunpowder is treated as becomes gunpowder,
gossamer as becomes gossamer. People are treated according
as they are, *i.e.*, for what they respond to. The egalitarian
would have men treated as they imagine some ideal person
called "Man," whom they have in mind, should be treated;
but as men are unlike this "Man" as cheese is unlike chalk,
the treatment is not forthcoming. A person who is a shuffling

hanger-on will not be treated as though he were a strong independent self-reliant individual. He will be treated, *i.e.*, used;
i.e., exploited for what he is, just as the strong man will be
exploited for what *he* is. He will get as his total income what
he appears to be worth to anyone to whom he cares to put the
delicate question: to his employer, for instance. Income is the
reverse side of "outgo"; divorced from the latter the former
is without meaning, and when Mr. Shaw proposes making
the first independent of the second he indulges a grotesque
fancy for his own diversion which he could not reasonably
expect to have any force with his fellows. For him it has
force as a whim, and that—his own: just as arctic exploration
has had force with certain explorers. Or rather it would be
possible to argue that it had such force with him, did he make
a *bona fide* attempt to practise it: which unfortunately for
the strengthening of one's belief in his genuine convictions regarding this matter, but unfortunately as regards one's belief
in his general commonsense he shows no sign of doing. And
with the enthusiasm of its arch-prophet at this low heat we
feel justified in leaving "equality of incomes."

However difficult it may be to coax from the egalitarians
a coherent statement as to their main position, it is not at
all difficult to track the notion of equality in its modern pre-
posterous democratic sense back to its source. The grotesque
misconceptions on which modern democratic theory is based
are the outcome of a misunderstanding of the forces behind
a tiny social experiment upon which sheer accident concentrated the attention of the civilised world. The nature of
American political institutions following upon the successful
issue of the War of Independence was not fixed under the
influence of an underlying intellectual theory. It was the
natural adjustment to the fact that the American rebels were

what they were—capable farmers—owning and working their own land, bearing and knowing the effective use of arms. There was no large servant class amongst them. They came of a picked stock; self-assertive and powerful; too powerful to brook control—as the history of the early American settlements offers sufficient evidence. If they were not the equals one of another, at least there were none so inferior in native power amongst them as to encourage interference with impunity. It was because they were just what they were that the American constitution fitted their needs. The constitution was an adjustment fitted to free men, *i.e.*, powerful men. The rights which it guaranteed them represented the terms of a bargain which each one could justly contract for. Their rights were a consequence of their individual might.

The European theorists, however, who were fired by this spectacle of American "free and equal" institutions, failed to grasp the fact that those social arrangements were secondary: wholly relative to the particular conditions in which they took rise. They deluded themselves into imagining that the conditions of free and equal Americans could be introduced *holus bolus* into ancient civilisations of which the foundations were fixed on a basis of slavery, mitigated here and there by local differences; a truly fantastic misconception. From a highly particularised situation they risked an impossible generalisation; from the mights of picked Americans they generalised upon the Rights of Man. How this generalisation has broken down it is now open for all to see—notwithstanding the fact that the "liberty" and "equality" elements of the American experiment have been so exceedingly well lubricated with the "fraternity" element, a foreign element which, at the outset, it became clear would be necessary to make the scheme work at all in the slave states of Europe.

There is something pathetic—as well as ludicrous—in this wordy attempt of modern democracy, boldly to assert "rights" which they are bankrupt of power to validate, *i.e.*, to justify, *i.e.*, to make good in power as well as in words. Its century and a half of a hearing is a standing monument of the extraordinary hypnotism which words wholly divorced from sense can exercise. Perhaps the delusion owes part of its success to the fact that the soil in which it settled was so well prepared. The religious notion that there existed an external authority from which all bounties flowed had much to do with the ready belief that rights and powers could be conferred[1]. The paternal version of faith was in keeping with an extension which saw in the State the temporal parent of the people: a parental authority as potent to bestow "freedom" as it was to clap its members in gaol. In fact, so superbly has the delusion flourished that far from giving way it has compelled the term "free" to develop a new meaning. In addition to its only efficient meaning of "empowered," it has developed the meaning of "unrestricted"; making the term—in consonance with all democratic thought—relevant to a duty laid upon the "Other Persons" rather than to any change in the personal force in one-self.

To be "free," in its meaning of "unrestricted" implies dependence upon the exercise of an embargo put upon the forces of the "Other Persons" in the interests of those persons who are to be kept "freed." It sets itself to the removal of obstacles by others to make clear the path of the particularised ones. By virtue of those refraining from exercising power when they might, *these* are permitted to be "free." They are "unrestricted," "left free," which being free is a fixed

---

[1]≠ "Praise God, from Whom all blessings flow; / Praise Him, all creatures here below; / Praise Him above, ye heavenly host; / Praise Father, Son, and Holy Ghost." Thomas Ken, 1674.

condition, and a permission granted them beyond their powers, by courtesy termed a "right." Thus a status accorded to the down-and-outs by others of a different order is called "being free." This freedom extends exactly the length of the chain of permission. They become "Freed men": a permitted status very redolent of associations with another. And the higher order is very paternal, very protective, very anxious for the good of its protégés as long as this does not interfere too much with its own. Let there be no misunderstanding about the fraternal spirit, the sand upon which the edifice of democracy is built. To recognise it for what it is is not to under-value it. Most of us are very good-natured and fraternal when it comes to the pinch, and when we are in the mood for it can be protective and what not. Only, people cannot have their cake and eat it. They cannot press for the granting of bogus courtesy "rights" and then complain that the respect which goes with genuine ones is not accorded them. They cannot cry out for the protective offices of a state and then cry out that the Government is grandmotherly. People who argue to the effect that the Government of a community made up nine-tenths of servants can be called "free" should be the last people in the world to mention the fact that such a state develops very servile aspects.

It is, indeed, only at the present time that the democratic theorists, though always mistaken, have become genuinely farcical. A protective Government, under which all look after each, which delivers "rights" out of hand so to speak, accords opportunities, finds you work, shelter, food, education, cannot let you run amok: it must look after you. A parent does not let a bottle-fed infant please itself: neither does the democratic state. The cries of the "Servile State" alarmists latterly gathering volume amongst good democrats are the vexed and disgusted comments which the creators have to pass on their creation. They look on their handiwork and see that it is bad: which would be all to the good no doubt were they aware that they are the responsible progenitors. Unfortunately they understand so little what it is in the Servile State which disturbs them that it would be too much to expect them to trace its parentage. When these alarmed democrats understand better the motive of their own outcry, we shall hear less not only of the Servile State but of democracy.

That the Servile State bogey promises to have a little vogue is due to the fact that skilful use can be made of an ambiguity in the term "servile." The term, when used as implying a detestable quality, means that certain persons elect to make a display of feebleness beyond what is necessary on account of their incompetence in order to flatter a stronger person with a view to getting more out of him. It is a sort of commerce in lowering of status in order to be accorded a measure of charity, over and above the terms of a bargain. In this connotation, to be servile is to crawl where necessity merely demands a walking circumspectly, to lick the superior's boots when the contract would be filled by merely brushing them: an overfeigning of feebleness to induce the throwing of a bigger bone of charity out of the thankfulness in the superior one's heart, when seeing the crawling object he can exclaim "Thank God I am not as this one." That servility of this sort is despised is just a matter of taste, for it usually turns in the long run to an increase in the servile one's competence. Though he sinks very low he has the reasonable expectation that his plunge will enable him to climb a little higher: that is, if he does not mistake his man and actually receive a sound kicking from the superior one's boot in a burst of repulsion against the figure he cuts. Nine out of ten even of the poorest prefer as a matter of taste not to descend in this particular kind of way, or to take such offensive risks.

But this meaning of servile is not the actual meaning as used in the phrase Servile State, though it is upon association with it that those who use it rely to make the notion odious. With utter futility, nevertheless, since the Servile State as intended by the alarmists who use it, is merely the description of any community where the great disparity between the power and audacity of certain of its members and those of others is so great as to deter the latter from the exercise of initiative. Wherever this disparity exists there must exist as the outcome of it two classes: one class which feels that it dare take certain risks; break away from the herd and strike out on its own; and another that dare not and therefore cannot. The latter will divide themselves up on terms of wages to serve on the former's schemes. So there obtains on the one hand, initiative, imagination, knowledge of human conditions and wants, and readiness for responsibility; on the other hand, toil, more or less heavy with skill more or less elementary; the two classes being joined together by the bond of wages for services rendered. One requires nothing more than this to postulate of necessity a Servile State, which less flamboyantly labelled would be a Servant-State, since services are paid for in wages; just as when services are paid for in kind it was a Slave-state. For the wage-system is not a cause, it is an effect; indeed, it is misleading to call the working for wages a system at all. A system is a design planned beforehand and laid on a situation, as an irrigation system, or a canal system, or a railroad system is a design laid upon the natural lie of the land or flow of the water. Working for wages is natural in the sense that the rivers of a primitive country are natural, or as the circulatory system of the body. It is bound up with the heights and depths of human ability; the natural differences in endowment of power back to which all changes (*i.e.*, all systems by which it is overlaid), must revert in the long run. It is not to demand its destruction or to assert that its destruction is possible, likely or desirable—it is only to describe it—to say that the present wage-system is merely an adjustment of the old slave-system, where, on the one hand, the granting of a certain amount of leisure and freedom from surveillance is balanced on the other by a corresponding disregard of the servant's welfare outside the hours of service demanded in the wage contract. Add to this lack of responsibility for the servants' general welfare, the utter divorce made necessary by modern "progress" between men and proximity to any base capable of furnishing an adequate yield of the elementary means of life, and one realises that the amount of initiative which would have been considerable for the needs of the old slave days, is relatively far less adequate faced with the needs of to-day. It proves that the wage-earners have not only failed to exercise initiative on their own account, they have allowed the initiative of their superiors so to plunge ahead as to make it increasingly difficult for them to become anything more than hired men. That they realise this and seek to decorate the terms of hire, by calling them salary, or pay, is evidence that the present generation at all events sees no prospect of wage-earners showing any such increase in natural power as will urge them to cease to be hirelings and become their own masters.

Consider the experiment of the letting direct to the workmen the contract for the new Theosophical Buildings. What does it prove? That the men can do the work off their own bat, and assert their power to absorb profits? Not at all. It merely proves that if a wealthy woman has a fad that can be run by money she will be able to give it a run, with exactly the same incentive which moves Sir Thomas Lipton, for instance, to keep on building new yachts. As long as the money holds out one can do as one pleases: pay as good prices as there are in the market, and so on. I do not see how such a scheme can be a failure. There is everything which ordinarily goes to make a job a success. Mrs. Besant supplies the initiative, places the order, dictates the the prices (good ones because it amuses her) she is willing and able to pay and the "workers" as usual work on the scheme of someone else. Not only are they working on the lines of other people's purposefulness and initiative: they are backed by the most skilful organiser of sentimental goodwill alive in this sentimental age. One hopes they like it: and like raising their caps and giving My Lady Beneficent three cheers when she graciously goes down to the works to say good-bye to the "dear poor fellows" before her departure to India. It would perhaps be too much to hope that they proceeded to add a pious if silent prayer that she would go to blazes, and felt a rebelling itch against this all too, too gentle touch: perhaps the democratic, paternal influence has gone too far to expect "workers" to be anything other than crosses between lap-dogs and draught-horses in their relationships with employers.

The experiment itself might very well be compared in one aspect at least with the system of "pay" in the Army. The very good-natured but excessively unobservant work on the wage-system to which we referred at length in our last issue[1] has this remark:

> Do officers ever dream of wages? Do they say
> they are going on half-salary? No. They go on
> half-pay... It is obvious, is it not, that these

---

[1] ≠ see p. 183.

verbal distinctions disclose substantial material differences[1].

Now Mrs. Besant's protégés might very well consider that they were receiving not wages but pay, as they do in the Army. For the difference between the two appears to be that wages are wages when the person who pays them—the initiator from the workman's point of view—in doing so is comparing them with a total computation which he has in his mind which he calls working at a profit, and by which he means that after computing his outlay upon wages and other necessary expenses his income shall present a satisfactory balance. When on the other hand wages are "pay," as, for instance, in the Army and Navy, the Government can go into the business almost regardless of expense: for the simple reason that they have sufficient money to do so. So has Mrs. Besant. Both she and the politicians can afford to be philanthropists—if they choose, and as long as the money lasts: that is as long as Mrs. Besant's popularity lasts, and the State's finances show no immediate sign of tottering. There can, of course, be only a limited number of such philanthropists since the wherewithal must come from somewhere. Mrs. Besant's supporters and the taxpayers to the Government must get their surplus from somewhere before the former can be in a position to do the graceful thing. And "surplus" and philanthropists are inextricably bound together. Not all employers could indulge in Mrs. Besant's hobby: as a matter of fact the Government at present does not propose to. It is not their whim: their good-will at present elects to run into other channels. If only people understood the arbitrary character of good-will they would save themselves from calculations which can only lead them in pursuit of a social mirage. It is the failure to apprehend its

---

[1] ≠ *National Guilds* by A. R. Orage (London: G. Bell and Sons, 1914).

208

spasmodic nature, and the fleeting and accidental conditions upon which it is based that keeps so many of us spending the best energies of our youth planning mistaken good things for a mythical class called the poor. And making part and parcel with all this miscomprehended goodwill is a sinister meaning which has come to be attached to the term "to exploit," which after all means nothing more diabolical than "to use" or to "bring out possible developments." It is not for those who know how to exploit anything whatsoever to attend to their ways: it is for those who hitherto have known but meagrely how to turn anything to use, to augment their power. It is their move: their turn to exploit. Attempted embargos upon other's exploitations will always fail in the long run: for those who know how to exploit know that there are many more ways than one to a desired end. Embargos are negative, empty of positive power. The positive power shows itself in use: in creative activity. To set about exploitation off one's own bat, is that initiative and enterprise on their own that the "workers" need. It is the lack of it which keeps them still in the serving class. It is its possession which makes masters.

We might here perhaps revert to the question of "moral wrappings" concerning which Mr. Stafford Hatfield raised some interesting considerations in our last issue[1]. Before doing so let us give a report of the progress egoist doctrine is making in the direction of the multitude. If any reader of *The Egoist* by chance saw a copy of the *New Statesman* Literary Supplement of June 27th, he must have been led to wonder how long Mr. Bernard Shaw had been a silent convert before breaking silence thus:—

---

[1] The Unconscious Self. H. Stafford Hatfield, The Egoist Vol. 1 No. 18 (July 1th, 1914).

> The highest forms (*i.e.*, of art), like the lowest,
> are necessarily immoral because the morals of
> the community are simply its habits, good and
> bad; and the highest habits, like the lowest,
> are not attained to by enough people to make
> them general and therefore moral. Morality, in
> fact, is only popularity; and popular notions
> of virtuous conduct will no more keep a nation
> in the front rank of humanity than popular
> notions of science and art will keep it in the
> front rank of culture. Ragtimes are more moral
> than Beethoven's Symphonies[1].

What next? We are in danger of becoming popular! It is true
that the *New Age* put the last sentence in a column which it
calls "current cant," but then is it not in the *New Age* where
one may read of the "changeless laws of morality?" However,
to Mr. Hatfield. Mr. Hatfield's query in substance is: "What
compensating values does the egoist offer to the moralist in
exchange for the depreciated values of social authority?" We
offer nothing and suggest no such exchange.

Let us be clear. We do not conceive ourselves as offering
egoist-vests in exchange for popular moralists-overcoats. We
would not willingly make a convert of one who found comfort
in moral wrappings, which wrappings we conceive to be of the
nature of skins rather than garments: the outer layers of which
drop off only when the new skin is ready grown underneath.
Whenever an amoralist argument is addressed to the moralist
crowd it is purely in self-defence: its intent is to splinter the
fangs of their watch-dogs on the hard bone of derision where
they expected to bury them deep into flesh: quite different
from its intent when addressed to friends where it is merely

---

[1] ≠ 1914.

for amusement and the pleasure of common understanding. That it is necessary to be able to state one's creed upon occasion to the herd: to be able to oppose a single lightning stroke as a fit reply to innumerable pin-pricks and wasp-bites, the fate of the author of *Dorian Gray* makes clear. For a dazzling intelligence to suffer itself to be shamed to death by the rabble is a shocking and offensive thing. Yet a brilliantly audacious and adventurous life, only half-self-conscious, and consequently only half-expressed, must of its very nature invite it, and—almost as hard a thing—allow of one's friends perpetuating the unintelligent grounds of attack even after the event. (Here anent a recent trial in the courts bearing somewhat on this issue we might point out that Oscar Wilde spoke with the inaccuracy of impatience when he said that books were neither moral nor immoral. As a matter of fact they tend either one way or the other: one would be sorry to be accused of writing a book with a moral tendency. And by a friend, too!) However, again coming back to the subject, apart from the putting of oneself in such a position that, should the herd presume to issue a challenge, the cost shall be theirs, the amoralist has no message for the moralist. In any case, such a message would not arrive, and for the only valid egoistical reason: that if "true," it would not serve his purpose. It is therefore, for him, not true: the skin is still alive and sticks. And for the rest, what does it matter? The situation is met when the amoralist has succeeded in making the moralist realise that it will be well with him only if he minds his manners. [...]

19. Authority: Conscience and the Offences

"The verbal virtue begins where the living strength ends."

I do not remember which of Matthew Arnold's commentators it was—though all my readers doubtless will—who made the observation that the poet in the lyric lines "Meeting," addressed "To Marguerite," is unconsciously confused by a mistake as to identity among his *dramatis personæ*. Says Arnold:

> I spring to make my choice,
> Again in tones of ire
> I hear a God's tremendous voice:
> "Be counsell'd and retire[1]."

Of course, says the critic, Arnold had confused God with Mrs. Grundy. The remark shows how completely an earnest critic may gaze with blind eye upon the most pronounced characteristics of his subject. The critic has failed to see that there is in those four lines the unmistakable cachet of the epicure in blended emotions. Perhaps it is in part due to the unseeing visions of such commentaries that Arnold is not much read now, which is a pity, because he is the cultured choice flower of that superabundant species which at present threatens to cover the earth, but which is found only in its meaner varieties.

With Arnold, the knowledge how to treat the thin and febrile among emotions was a consummated instinct. Just where the strength of emotions ended, he made actual his opportunity as confectioner and played the artist with them as a good cook will with an insipid vegetable, the insipidity

---

[1] ≠ *The Poems of Matthew Arnold 1840 to 1866* (London: J. M. Dent & Sons, 1908).

of which occasions the opportunity to work in the foreign flavours.

Where the strength of emotion equates into the fear of discomfort and the clacking tongues of–

> All the rest.
> Eight parents and the children, seven aunts.
> And sixteen uncles and a grandmother...
> besides a few real friends.
> And the decencies of life[1],

which (in Mr. Aldington's opinion) worked up such "extraordinary emotional intensity" in Mr. Hueffer's new poem "On Heaven" for instance: just here, right in the nick of time, he works his God into the scheme.

The raucous squealing of the parlour cockatoos first melts then swells into the organ tones of a "God's tremendous voice": the angry screams of the horde waiting to pick the flesh off your bones merges into the voice of the Almighty Lord stooping to counsel you in gentleness and give you a tip for your own good. Call these compelling tones the voice of Mrs. Grundy, Mr. Critic, and you reassemble the entire harping brood: the act of an unseeing crude man unversed in the game of life! A child might do it, as it might break a watch to look at its insides, but not an arch-priest of Culture. Not Mr. Arnold at any rate, nor millions of others less finished in sleight of hand, but with an equally sure instinct for the value of White Magic.

We are told that some of the sweetest scents are distilled from origins of very evil odour: but this whether or no, certain

---

[1] ≠ "On Heaven" by Ford Madox Ford (née "Mr. Hueffer") (1914).

it is that all the powers of the gods and smaller authorities are distilled from the lack of power in their creators. Men begin to "acquire merit" at the point where they are unable to exercise strength: the verbal virtue begins where the living strength ends. Authorities conveniently "forbid" where "I can't" or "I daren't." And it is reasonable enough. Gods and other authorities are soft cushions of words placed near the vague rim where power fringes off into limitation. They are creations designed to protect us from a too particular view of our own limitations. They cover our fears and save our vanity. The recognition of their limitations is the vision which men can least tolerably bear: that is why whenever it becomes necessary to reveal them in actual fact, men are most particular in words to make them the basis of edification: a proceeding very explicable, though in its effects in no small degree, misleading.

The *bouleversement* of values thus brought about has however managed to turn the chagrin of ineffectualness into a possibility of deep-seated delight. Under the shelter of its expressed form in human speech (of which it is the masterpiece); it has provided men with a second nature, which almost invariably they keep in more constant practice than the original. So does the human become the coy one amongst the animals; most coquettish and playful: serious only when bent on make-believe; and very adorable indeed when he mimes well–like Arnold. To make necessity's compulsions wear the graceful air of a conceded virtue is really exceedingly clever: too clever indeed to be conscious; as is proved by the fact that it is seen to perfection only among the coxcombs. Conscious intelligence acts on it like a sharp frost; conscious humour eats it up like an acid. To be able to say of one's ineffectual love affairs:

> A God, a God, their severance ruled.
> And bade betwixt their shores to be
> The unplumb'd salt estranging sea[1]

requires a triple-plated vanity as well as a trusting, playful nature.

It is because the vanity of this is so unconsciously complete that it is so extremely engaging. And certainly it is very comprehensible. The desire to feel oneself so important that the gods are called upon to interfere in our affairs, even if only to boggle them: to feel that one is cutting the deuce of a fine figure in the eyes of the cosmos distils a subtler delight for the epicure in slender emotions than the satisfaction of any one thin and timorous desire. Yet it only becomes really essential to feel something encouraging of this sort when one is obviously playing a losing game. Only when we have conducted our mundane affairs with such a degree of ineffectualness that our original way of assessing values would lead us almost to apologist for our existence, does it become comforting to feel that our modest matters are so important as to draw gods to earth to interfere. Let our affairs make it clear to us that we are feeble, impotent, ignorant, timid, fearful, and let us be vain: above all things, vain—and we must either conceive and bring forth the omnipotent omniscient admiring god or prepare for a bad quarter of an hour with ourselves. It is the feeling that one is small that makes us look round

---

[1] ≠ "To Margurite–Continued" by Matthew Arnold. *Poems*.

for stilts, as it is our meagreness which provokes us to swell out into that exiguous extensiveness which we call vanity.

It is because Mr. Arnold would have found it an indignity as well as a misfortune to appear to be afraid of his aunts that he works gods—the external authority—into his canvasses. That is why it is likely we shall always have authorities with us. What one has not the desire strong enough to obtain, but would like to appear as strongly desiring; what one's verbal education tells us we should admire desiring, but deprecates the venturesomeness necessary to obtain it becomes artistically the "forbidden of the authority." Which explains why authorities are so secure: impotence and fear compounded with vanity make so exceedingly strong an amalgam; and also why against them none need to fight or cry. One has effected the uttermost against an authority when one has understood it. Whether thereafter it can be overcome depends upon other and more absolute factors, but the cement which holds it together can be dissolved by understanding merely.

Authority is like opportunity: not something given and fixed, but adjusting itself from moment to moment. All seeming to the contrary notwithstanding, the seats of authority can never be occupied by a usurper. None can sit there without first being duly installed. The first essential for the creation of sitters-in-authority is the existence of such as are desirous that authority should be exercised over them. Authority takes shape and form on a principle like to that on which the solids and liquids and gases take on the characteristic which make them such: upon lines carved out by the limitations of those to whom they seem what they seem. A solid is that which we cannot easily penetrate; they are the points at which we feel resisted to such an extent that our power falls short. If our power were more the resistance would be less, and by as much as our power is more that characteristic which makes the impression of a solid would be less. Or our powers might be different; then the resistance would appear different. To a fish, doubtless, the atmosphere will have all the appearance of a solid. To men the essential difference between a granite wall and a block of glass is that our power as departmentalised in sight penetrates easily the second and with almost insuperable difficulty the first. To the being whose eyes had some of the qualities of the Röntgen rays the difference must be considerable. So the appearance of solids and other substances are the reverse side of the impress, beaten into form by the dead pressure of our impotence. So, too, are the authorities over us. And just as a craftsman creates his wares by niggling at the resistance, forcing it by this and that increase of his own power to give way in some degree after the manner of his desire, we, by the exercise and constant increase of our power, penetrate authority, of which the changes which subsequently appear as the reverse side have first been operated on the hither side. So those in authority represent not those who know and are powerful, but those who as we loosely argue "must" know and "must" be powerful because we don't, and aren't. They symbolise our negative qualities. It is not the positive qualities of the great which ensure their instalment in office, but the negative quality of those who permit them there. The stretch of authority in any sphere expands or shrinks automatically with the impotence or power of those who recognise it. The spheres in which we recognise no one's authority are those of which we know ourselves what there is in them to be known. But where we are timid and lack knowledge, where we desire to save ourselves the risk of experimentation as well as a realisation of the limitedness of our knowledge: we set up an authority. One may be ignorant and yet have a desire to know and have courage enough to be ready to pay the price for coming by knowledge. Such a one is not a creator nor a respecter of authorities. The fruitful creators of authorities are those who, being without knowledge, elect to remain without, and in lieu of it espouse—Belief.

Belief is thereafter accepted as knowledge, whereas belief is essentially one with doubt. Belief and doubt are two names for a particular process in a particular condition, *i.e.*, of thinking as an unfinished product; of thinking, not carried to the issue where the process of thought (which necessarily retains uncertainty as its moving factor until it is finished) finishes; where thought being dissolved knowledge is born in its place. Whether this state of ignorance as to the facts involved in the issue one has in mind shall be called by the name of doubt or its other name, belief, depends upon several things, but in the main upon a difference of tension in the mind. If the mind is tight-braced, strung up and alert, it is likely to recognise its condition for what it is; of being only partially aware. It bluntly says "As to this issue I do not know; my thinking has proceeded thus and thus far, I have a vague feeling that the next stage of thinking will reveal so and so, but actually of the ultimate issue I am still in doubt." But let it be a slacker mind which speaks, one less braced for effort, and such a mind will shrink from the realisation of uncertainty which the word doubt expresses and which is in itself a challenge to think to a finish. Such a mind will say: "I think I know" (a colloquial contradiction in terms) or "I believe"; the latter would serve well enough were what the words say accepted at their nominal value; but belief, owing to the false associations which authorities have cunningly caused

218

it to have with knowledge, has lost its exact connotation, *i.e.*, that of decision left open. The derivation of belief is from *lyfan*, to leave, which serves to throw a bright gleam of light on the bemused psychology of believers. To believe a thing is not only to be in doubt about it; it is a resolve of the mind to leave it so, and to this extent is unlike doubt, which implies that the debate proceeds and the enquiry is going on. It also makes clear why it is the mind which doubts rather than that which believes which leads in the way towards knowledge. Why, too, the voices of authority echo one to another all the world round with the cry of "Believe, believe." They mean, "Leave decision, leave it, leave it to us," in effect, asserting that knowledge is a spurious form, a degraded type of the ideal which is lack-of-knowledge. The excessive unction with which authorities invest the word "sacred" reveals its purpose, *i.e.*, the guaranteeing that vexed questions shall be left untouched; left whole and unquestioned. The sacred is indeed the first weapon of defence against the prying questions of intelligence. Raise any issue which touches upon the fundamentals of the word-games, as distinguished from moves made within them, and the authorities encompass themselves about with the label "sacred," as promptly as a threatened city would hasten to ensure the integrity of its walls. Very naturally, therefore, all that one believes is by the acquiescence of belief made sacred. "My beliefs are sacred"; they would be no doubt, were the decision left with the believers, but the believer, as the history of belief shows, is encompassed about with enemies: both from within and without, he is hard pressed. Not only do those who know and those who doubt alike beset him; every spark which flashes from every gleam of his own stirring intelligence are as so many maggots gnawing into the fabrics of his beliefs. Spontaneously bursts from him the cry: "I believe, help thou my unbelief. I have abandoned the quest: do thou (namely, sluggishness, comfort, whatnot) smother this itch I have to return to pry and poke[1]."

❦

Of course, the seats of the authorities have been occupied too long for the sitters therein not to have realised the necessity of guarding against a potential danger that even the stupidest may develop towards intelligence; so in the game full provision of language to carry off the overflow is always made. Thus men will justify every step towards enlightenment with the remark, "I must follow my Conscience," and will permit themselves to be persuaded—*i.e.*, they will believe that Conscience upon occasion boldly bears the torch of defiant power through the darkness, in opposition to Authority. It is one of the neatest manœuvres, considering that the realms of Conscience and Authority are one. The pride which one occasionally appears to have in "following one's Conscience" is a subconscious pride not in Conscience, but in the intelligence which has been able to make Conscience fall back a degree and make Authority write down Duty less. We can only track the pride in the assertion "I must follow my Conscience" to its source when we invert it to read, "My Conscience must follow me," and always this path along which Conscience is compelled to follow "me"—*i.e.*, the ego—is that leading from less to greater intelligence and knowledge. Where the ego becomes more powerful and more aware, the Conscience shrinks by just so much as is this increase: just as, when the sun comes out, the mist retreats as far as the sunlight penetrates. If the sun, in glowing admiration of the bright sunshine, were to say, "I must follow the mist" instead of "To the limits

---

[1] ≠ Mark 9:24

220

where I have power to act I drive out the mists," it would provide an exact analogy to the person who says "I must follow my Conscience." Like the positive power of the sun, the "I" as far as it shines out consumes the Conscience, and where courage and knowledge are at the greatest the area governed by Conscience is at the least. And vice versa.

Just as the stretch of Authority, whether of knowledge or or action, in any sphere, expands or shrinks with the impotence or power respectively of those over whom it is exercised, so does the dominion of Conscience: which is Authority's ambassador. We have pointed out how men, since they learnt how to forge magic armour out of generalised speech, and so become endowed with the power to invert all values and meanings, have ceased to be serious save in the make-believe of the great word-games. Initiate the game, erect the word-pieces, and solemnity is invoked and at hand.

Accordingly, in treating of these generalised words, God, Authority, Conscience, Duty, Sin, Immorality, Crime, Belief, Doubt; we have recognised the conventions—*i.e.*, the piece names of the game. Aces, Jacks, and Kings, Pawns, Knights, and Castles, to each we have allowed its game value. To have done otherwise in this, their most solemnest sport, would have been to rouse more rage than is conducive to understanding: as if a visitant from Mars quite new to the game, say of chess, should interfere with the pieces, to criticise their labels during the progress of the play for the world's championship. It would not save him from the wrath of the players if he were to plead that the Kings and Castles did not greatly resemblef kings and castles. To the players they do: they are them, in fact. They have become so accepted in the game that if we would describe it we ourselves must for the moment accept its word conventions as well as its rules. Moreover, most of them are hearthstone generalities, unlike some others, Justice or Freedom, throned triumphantly because remotely eternal in the heavens. They hover about our dwellings: nearer than breathing, closer than hands and feet, some of them.

So at their game-value let us spread the pieces out—Conscience, Duty, Obedience, Immorality, Crime, Sin. Conscience, the Ambassador of all Authorities, Voice of God, Authority at its height, begets Duty—Poetic Duty. Not, of course, the simple and vulgarly limited form of duty which is recognised as debt, the wiping out of which is merely just in that secondary sense which we recently have defined as the keeping of a promise: Duty as debt which we disburse from motives like those which induce us to pay our gas bills because the owners otherwise would cut off the supply. This sort of duty is of too low an order to be admitted into the great poetic scheme built up on Authority and Conscience and Duty about which the parsons preach and poets sing. The poetic duty recognised by the make-believers—the believers, as they henceforward shall be called—is based on Belief in Authority. The Authorities we believe in, Conscience tells us we must obey. Such action is our Duty. What form the Duty will take the Authority decides. It is the Authority's business to make out the due-bill, as it is Conscience's to see that it is paid: that duty is done. Let Conscience be what you elect to term it the "Voice" of Authority, its Ambassador, its Bailiff, Procurer, Pimp, Master of Ceremonies. Duty shall be what Wordsworth called her "Stern daughter of the Voice of"—the Authorities[1]. Like its

---

[1] ≠ "Ode to Duty" by William Wordsworth.

parent and grandparents, it comes of the stock of the impotent, feeble, timid, fearful, ignorant. It, as they, takes birth where living virtue ends, and, as into theirs, an incursion is made into its territory with every degree of increase in power.

Just as Conscience has never been divorced from Authority it is never divorced from Obedience and Duty. Always it prompts obedience to whatever authority can impose itself. It is equally obliging to all authorities, no matter what their sphere. As the Master of Ceremonies in the Festival of the Impotent it calls the Conscience-dances. They vary in character and measure. Some are stately and solemn and others are the reverse; but they all have one characteristic in common: they are all movements to rhythm, and the rhythm is Obedience. If it is the legal authority Conscience calls the measure "Obedience to the law: which same dance is your Duty." Disobey or trip, and Conscience and the offended Authority in chorus pronounce your tripping: Crime. Or it is the Social Authority, and the dance Conscience call is "Obedience to the common custom," Trip here and it is: Immorality. Or perhaps it is a dance in obedience to a lesser Authority, so minor in the popular estimation that its ordinances dwindle down to mere rules: a schoolmaster's, or a railway company's by-laws. The dance Conscience in such case will announce will be a two-step: a polka: in which tripping is mere naughtiness, though there are schools, for instance, in which a rule by sedulous exaltation is raised to the awed height of a religious observance. And this brings us to the stateliest measure: the very minuet of the Conscience-dances. It is the religious Authority itself, the one built out of the vast blank stretch of the unknown from which all those fears that are the more fearsome because they are nameless, spring. The Authority which is the Holy Ghost is the shadowiest dweller in the unlit mists, and is built round with the Holy of Holies—a wall between men's souls and the vision of that which they fear most. And Conscience calls, "Obedience to God, to His Ministers and to His Church, to all its ordinances, and to the Holy Spirit." This is the dance in which you foot it with the solemnity of a Rite. Trip and fall short here, and: You Sin. The heavens themselves, the sun, moon and stars frown and scowl blackly upon you. Conscience, the Voice of God, the Ambassador of the offended Lord, then takes up his seat in your very heart, nestling snugly in your deepest fears; and to him you tender your heartstrings as faggots with which he may pile up and keep ever burning the consuming Wrath of God. Conscience convicting a man of sin is Conscience *in Excelsis*. It then fully lets itself go, becomes orgiacal and reveals that Feast of Conscience which, viewed from the human side, men have called Hell.

And thus the play goes on. The gentle buffoon still clutches his magic mantle: his role is the tragic and comic both at once. They are matters of light and shade, and he is playing the one or the other according to the angle from which the observer views him. His life has its full compensations. His pleasures are real if his pains are formidable. And he has all the thrills of the gamble. Though to-day he writhes in Hell, to-morrow he may become reconciled and, like Browning's believer, full-fed, beatified, he may find himself smiling on the breast of God. A good game and a spirited competition, anyway[1].

---

[1] "... For in God's breast, my own abode, / Those shoals of dazzling glory, passed [...] For as I lie, smiled on, full-fed / By unexhausted power to bless..." from *Johannes Agricola in Meditation* (1836) by Robert Browning (1812-1889).

There are some interesting fictions called duties to ourselves. They do not, however, share in the High Game, and would best be deferred to a sequel.

20. Constitutions

"The 'price' of 'freedom' is to produce the individuals with the power to risk and fight, to assert and reassert: which is not a price at all, but a simple sequence of cause and effect."

[. . .] THE cry that the Constitution is in danger sounds as though it ought to be impressive, but now, as ever, it isn't, for the simple reason that there is no Constitution. It is a mistaken notion that there exists a growing body of "guaranteed permissions," automatically increasing, lumped together and called "freedom," which "constitute the Constitution." It is this feeling of doubt as to the *bona fide* existence of the Constitution which is half-expressed in the phrase, "The price of freedom is eternal watchfulness." But even watchfulness does not equate into "freedom"—*i.e.*, the "effects of power"! To get these effects we must furnish the power. It is not to guard the Constitution–the mythical "body" of rights—which will perpetuate them. No amount of watchfulness will avail to make secure the exercise of privileges the continuance of which those who enjoy them have not the power to enforce. The only negotiable "price" for the enjoyment of power is to continue to produce the powerful stock. So the "price" of "freedom" is to produce the individuals with the power to risk and fight, to assert and reassert: which is not a price at all, but a simple sequence of cause and effect. "Rights" and "privileges" are never permanently won: that we slowly add strength of precedent to strength of precedent is a delusion. Not merely is there no written Constitution, but the nature of that body of precedents to which is given grandiloquently the name of "Unwritten Constitution" is such as to make a steady accretion of powers unrealisable, precedents

being what they are—the acts and words of certain person-
alities noted because caught in the limelight–and because
noted–precedents! There could be no emptier opposition to
any actions than the cry "There is no precedent." It is the
cry of the deluded. If there is no precedent for the doing of
something a person of ability–a statesman or other—wants
to do: he does it, and then there is. And that is all there
is to precedents. What distinguishes men from muffs is the
inevitable addition which they make to this elastic body. To
this extent the King in calling a conference of an unprece-
dented nature is proving himself something of a character. He
will find, of course, that he would have had far fewer enemies
had he elected to continue to appear as a muff and played
for safety, for not even Kings can have things both ways. All
initiatory action belongs essentially to the spirit of fight, and
is full of risks because it rouses antagonisms: a fact which
the humanitarian, egalitarian, peace-loving fraternal spirit of
democracy plays upon when in its systematised attempt to
eliminate exceptional power in the spirit of fight it tries to
put force into the moral cry, "There is no precedent."

The belief in the ultimate success of the entire democratic
schemata is based on the assumption that men prefer the
safe and placid joys of peace to the spirited risks of war: an
assumption which is refuted hourly, in spite of the fact that
all the accredited mouthpieces dub the one the "lofty" and
the other the "degrading." The people continue to enjoy
disporting themselves on this lower plane, if only by proxy.
The continued popularity of boxing in spite of the preachers and teachers is an instance. It is the dumb but direct
repudiation of the doctrine which would hold the human

person "sacred," which would regard personal violence as a desecration of "divine humanity." This fear of personal violence which we all have, and which is in no need of augmentation, has been sedulously worked upon in the interests of humanitarian democracy. Yet it is clear that all power in the long run is tested by its possessor's willingness and ability to risk encountering personal violence, and the horse-sense of the crowd which backs the boxing-ring and neglects Mr. F. B. Meyer, if it fails in daring in this particular respect, itself proves that at least it admires those who do not so fail. Even women you begin to find repudiating the humanitarian softness: as indeed they must when men preach to men the adoption of women's feebleness as a proposed improvement of men's virtue. They must in self-defence. Women can only afford to be weak and finicking when they belong to men who are not: a fact which women have formerly understood. It is merely this modern inverting of values—the outcome of humanitarian democracy, with its attempted substitution of words for action and strength, which has sent the more wordy and feeble-minded out in search of a verbal utopia.

And democracy, which is the idealisation of the spirit of stick-in-the-mud, will find it will never fail to be repudiated, even if in faint, ineffectual fashion, by those who are in the mud. The jingoes, the crowds of spectators at football-matches, boxing contests, bull fights, cock-pits, are saying in the feeble way of proxy that they know where honour is due: that pity is like the arsenic in the medicine: it must exist only in very small doses if it is to be reckoned to have virtue: that if only they dared they would like always to treat it as insult. [...]

228

It is another of the feeble word tricks of the democratic movement that an effort is made to slide over class-distinctions. Democrats may of course keep silent about these: they may even deny them; but, what they cannot do is to efface them. There will always be classes, and the power of initiation which a man has will always be the index to the class to which he belongs. As for the workers in the mass, they possess relatively and in relation to the work by which they subsist none whatever. They have not even the amount of initiative which is implied in the assertion commonly made: that they "sell their labour as a commodity." For they do not so much "sell" as the employers "buy." The transaction only takes place when the employer has a job on. The trade union movement is indeed a movement set in the direction of showing initiation thus far: to appear as a seller; but even as an appearance it is only in the mass: it represents the initiative of the few who keep the organisation alive: the majority of the workers are induced to join their respective unions only with the greatest difficulty. On the other hand, such a movement as that known by the name the "Right to Work," far from being one towards responsibility and working-class enterprise, is indeed a desperate throwing-up of the sponge. It is an attempt of the "servers" to free themselves altogether from the responsibility for initiative by endeavouring to induce the State to become Initiators-in-Chief for the passive ones.

As for the difference between slave and wage-earner: it is simply one of degree—in amount of initiative. The emancipation movement was an attempt to prove that by kicking-out of the nest those that could not fly out, "reformers" could force high-fliers. The present, industrial situation is an answer to that: some have flown high, most have remained in secret communication with the nest, while the rest, the down-and-outs, are rapidly being reabsorbed into the nest of irresponsibility by a steady multiplication of statutes in the direction of making them the "wards," otherwise the "properties," of the State. The proposed scientific treatment of vagrants, of feeble-minded, of the poor and destitute, are the measures of Governments which propose to reassume that responsibility for subsistence which formerly was borne by the slave-owner.

It takes many phases to make a world, and it is not necessary to become inarticulate with indignation in describing any of them. Enough has been done when the phases have been made sufficiently clear to remove the danger of giving the palm to the devitalising instead of to the vitalising tendency: to that which accepts instead of that which originates: to fear and the playing for safety instead of to the hazard and the new precedents: to the democratic and peaceful rather than the autocratic and belligerent.

21. Quid Pro Quo

*"The depressing yet indicative feature of modern 'life'
is that it has so little to say for individual fighting."*

To such as are fascinated by the interplay of motives in
human action, the unravelling of the strands which combined to give the thrill of pleasure the adventure into war was
welcomed with, is as attractive as the war-lure itself. The
feeling of the people while waiting for England to throw herself wholeheartedly into war, was not that of mere approval
or disapproval; rather it was a sense of pleasure and veiled
enjoyment in the prospect of war itself. This was as much
the case with those who realise definitely that its prosecution
will mean inevitable material loss, as with those who are
vaguely aware that war is high-priced, and that we shall all
be implicated in the paying of it. Each man has been in fact
something of a revelation to his neighbour. The silent hope
which each was fostering that the issue would be war, they
would have been afraid of acknowledging even to themselves;
and certainly too afraid of owning to its existence to a neighbour. Then a sudden shock: an unpremeditated expression
of opinion, and each betrays himself to the rest: and, lo and
behold, all are alike: the secret sin against the spirit of peace
is universal, and can be proclaimed from the housetops.

The protests that were thereafter made were more in the
spirit of pious concessions to former utterances than sponta-
neous expressions of existing feelings, and they evaporated
almost before they were well uttered. Old phrases moved *en
bloc* on to the scene, disinterred from speeches made when war
was sour because hung too high for reach for the moment, did
appear wearing the look of ancient survivals. An orator might

232

say that the only gain accruing from this war would be the profits of the armament-makers, and writers might enlarge on the "working-classes," "the inevitable victims," "the poor souls for whom this hungry war opens its vast jaws[1]," and press into details of the "gouged out eyes, and disembowelled entrails of the soldier," but the fact remains that the poor are at least as interested in the venture, and as enthusiastic for it as the rich, while entrails notwithstanding, none is keener than the soldier: and the thought that war can be materially profitable to anyone—armament-mongers or others—is something after the mariner of a mild solace to startled consciences: a comforting thought that the war is not so ill a wind, materially speaking, that it blows no one any good; they know well that even should it prove so, for the spiritual satisfaction which it gives, they would still wage it. In short none of the objections made against war in times of peace have the force it was calculated they would have in keeping the desires of the people weaned from war when an opportunity presents itself to wage a good one. The error which gave birth to objections which proved themselves no objections arose from a failure to realise the existence of imperative human instincts which only war can fully satisfy, and which have as much force with a pacifist as with any jingo.

The delicate tact of Mr. Asquith indeed in working a few "blessed words" into the drab fustian of Sir Edward Grey's statement of the case for war is more to his credit from a human point of view than any of his earlier strong-man shows. To be so exquisitely sensitive to the shyer because deeper

---

[1] ≠ This exact phrase from *War—What For?* by George R. Kirkpatrick (West La Fayette 1910), in turn paraphrasing *Henry V* by William Shakespeare.

human emotions, as to realise that the Sunday Congregations and Peace Societies must shout joyfully for the war or burst, makes a man genuinely attractive, and the Prime Minister knew well that while to shout for war would strain the pacifist's creeds, to shout against infamy would fit in easily; thoughtfully therefore he works it in; the Kaiser's proposals are "infamous."

That is enough for the promoters of the gospel of peace: they are not the friends of war but the enemies of infamy: the same thing with a delicate allowance made for a verbalist difference.

It becomes easily possible to understand the lure of a good war when the advocates of the two generalisations about war are viewed together. When the purplish flush of the jingo is set off against the white-drained countenance of the pacifist it becomes clear what has happened. Two abstractions have been torn piecemeal out of their genuine existence in *fact*, the nature of which is distorted until they are joined again, when two fads will dissolve in robust common sense. When a generalisation, *i.e.*, a false abstraction, is made out of sound instincts, it creates the fad, and out of the remnants left by the incomplete generalisation is created another: a fad has always a twin. So to a gospel of Peace there must be a gospel of War. Whenever a sudden lull in the Structure of Words allows instinct to speak, it becomes clear that the purpose of Peace is War, and that when War is tired it seeks Peace: or rather, putting the generalisation of Peace and War aside, instinct reveals that we utilise the opportunity of the times when we are not fighting to make us ready for the test of a fight. The results of the test declared, we set towards peace to prepare for the test again: which explains why the kind of conduct which Christian propaganda seeks to make customary never becomes customary: never becomes any deeper. Constantly it advances and recedes—pendulum-like. In the shape of reaction from strife it gets a hearing now and again; to allow of recuperation for farther strife: not for its own sake. When the recuperative work is established: when men have got over their sick turn it is thrown aside as healed limbs throw off their bandages. The gist of the gospel of Peace is not so much the inculcation of a "slave morality" as it is the custom, *i.e.*, the morals, of the sick, the wounded, the uncertain of powers, of all those who are in *the process* of making good. When the period of peace is wearing to a close, always it becomes wistful with the longing for other things. The wilfulness of peace is the pause of the pendulum as it turns on the return swing towards war.

A fight is merely putting to the test activities of any kind. Like a test in any other sphere it is of the nature of an examination, and its object is to ascertain status, by trial of strength. It is the pivot upon which turns the balance of what is elementarily just and exact. In peace we muster the strength which in war we put to the best show possible. To remain too long at peace is dulling and disappointing for ability as it would be for a young singer or violinist to practise scales and exercises interminably, without the hope of one day putting their powers of strength to receive the verdict of the world. It is for instance because of the increase in strength which the Kaiser believes his country has made in the years of peace that he forces the putting of it to the test. Test and preparation, war and peace go together: they are two stages of one process, each as necessary to the other as is the obverse to the reverse of a coin. Wisdom lies in choosing the kind of test which one may calculate one's preparations and increase of strength has fitted one, for it is the probabilities of success which make the joys or woes of the contest.

This is why people who are not filled with the belief that their forces have a chance of being successful refrain from fighting, much as they would love the exhilaration of it. The exhilaration of fighting which is an elemental need thus recedes from many men's grasp—necessary though it is: which explains why such men will fight for sides while they refuse to fight for themselves: why for instance imperial warfare nourishes while the industrial war faints.

When a force is in a poor condition it is shy of fights: it seeks safety: let it improve or increase and fighting comes within measurable distance; fighting is in fact nothing other than the violation of boundaries which heavier forces have laid upon the less weighty on the calculation that the force is such and such.

The depressing yet indicative feature of modern "life" is that it has so little to say for individual fighting: that it deprecates it in fact. Verbal education has fitted itself to social customs which already place safety foremost, and back up a state of affairs which in themselves are sufficiently emphatic. The small boy with washed face and a volume on the "Worthy Citizen" under his arm, bent on doing good to his neighbour, not merely replaces but does so with official applause, the unsavoury ragamuffin who would invite the fellow of the biggest size which will allow of an outside chance of a win, to come and have a scrap round the corner. It is small wonder that in this anæmic atmosphere we fall back perforce on the second best: on fighting for a side: on praise of *esprit de corps*: on composite games of all sorts of which the biggest is a big war.

The steady pressure which latterly has been put upon the young (the old matter less) to substitute without questioning *l'esprit de corps* for the egoistic spirit is, as a precaution, curiously redundant. The tendency to do so is working strongly enough before education takes a hand in it. Timidity suggests it, and its advantages from the safety point of view are obvious: pleasurable too. It gives scope to one's constructive tendency to an extent beyond anything to which the abilities of the mediocre person could run. One can admire vicariously in the members of a side all those qualities which one lacks oneself. A side, a corps, a composite unity can moreover be constructed: built up by making good the deficiencies of each by the picked qualities of all. Then with this superlatively excellent thing one identifies oneself. The slenderest connection will furnish the *point d'appui*–the mark of identification: a common name school, county and nationality, and things far far less. And having assisted at the composition of the side, or oftener still having selected a ready-made one, one backs its fortunes and becomes identified with its interests. The "side" is the makeshift of the instinct to reach out into dominance, even if only at second-hand—or thousandth hand. It keeps alive a fainting self-respect, and lends the stimulus of the fight without its responsibility for risks and initiative.

This constructive sense which the cult of *esprit de corps* utilises with such wide-spreading effects is worth dwelling on since it is this which provides the underlying design of "Order," of which laws, regulations, the entire maintenance of the status quo, are but the subsequent steps taken to keep such orders permanent.

As has been pointed out in these pages many times, the establishment of any order is nothing more or less than the progressive development of a purpose. The detailed features of any order equate exactly into the purpose which ushers them into co-existence. All that is apart from, or unseen in, the planning of the proposed development is "chance." If such chance "chances" to accentuate the original purpose—if it can be utilised to further the purpose it is "luck"; if the opposite, it is "accident"; if it is thrown across the line of development of purpose by another willed purpose it is "opposition." Every living being represents purpose to the exact extent that it is alive. The husbanding of living strength effects itself by hanging on to its own purpose for what it is worth, for where the individual permits his power—(or purpose: they equate into the same thing)—to become scattered or unequally developed, a certain procedure works itself out. The individual failing to mind his own business becomes engrossed in others, because the spectacle of the others' more advanced development attracts him. Thus we find that those who can least afford to spare attention from their own development are the very ones who are devoting the bulk of their energy to the purposes of others, for the simple reason that they are more attractive. After a while, relying on a little trick of words, they will even claim the alien order as their own. It is their own, of course, for just so much as it is—that is a sense of being in touch, however remotely, with the dominant: a sense of which the reverse side is not a call to dominate but to serve. The humblest soldier in the Kaiser's service is allied with the Kaiser's highest purposes: the humblest little urchin in a London slum, brandishing his wooden sword bravely despite

238

his hungry stomach, is sharing in the glory of every British hero throughout British history. That the servers "serve" is their misfortune: the price they pay for receiving their joys at second-hand.

It is a mistake to imagine that the joys are any one whit less real than the yoke of service, and it is a fact open to even cursory observation that the way to make oneself thoroughly miserable is for such as are not competent to aspire to shine in a large and ambitious circle. Personal comfort, as well as success, requires a very nice and just estimate of one's powers and limitations, otherwise one is in danger of imagining that in accepting bestowed pleasures one will be requested to accept status to match the pleasures rather than the implications of bestowal: a very jarring mistake. Entry into ranks above one's capacity can be achieved only on an acceptance of the status of servant: terms, however, to accept which there is a willingness which is world-wide. To hobnob with one's betters on menial terms is the foible of the incompetent. The feeling that it is better to be a doorkeeper in the houses of one's betters than to reign monarch in the modest hut to which one's own individual powers run is nowadays almost universal. Is there not the common glory of the House, the State, the Empire: the common *esprit de corps*? To be the farthing dip in someone else's illumination-scheme is the "unity" ideal. The glory of Nelson, Drake, Raleigh, of Clive and the rest, of all the Empire builders, falls, as a mantle, on the shoulders of some underpaid seaman; in return he "serves" in the ranks. Napoleon quite accurately put it when he pointed out to his men that he lent them his glory: in return for which they— "served." Napoleon, of course, bathed in an effulgence of glory, and yet he did not serve: but that is the difference between being a Kaiser and being a unit in the iron battalions. Everything considered, it works out all square. The masses work to develop a Kaiser's personal scheme of order: he gives in return what glory an intimate acceptance of the *esprit de corps* reflects on them: he enables them, if they are not too wide-eyed, to flatter their self-respect, and enables them, of a certainty, to satisfy a starved desire for combat on terms which they can afford to pay. It is good enough for people who can do no better.

22. Promises

*"'Might' conditions 'Right.' Their variations are
in direct ratio, but 'Might' is primary. Challenge
'Right' and the appeal is to 'Might.'"*

IT would probably be paying English intelligence too great
a compliment to characterise the outcry which has been
made about the German Emperor's easy way with treaties, as
Cant. The outcry much likelier represents a genuine failure to
understand the function of treaties, compacts, or "Promises"
in the structure of human society.

To say that a Promise is not a sacred thing is not to
deny its importance as the cement of all society living on
a basis of non-violence. On such a basis the compact is
the substitute for the sword. It has the same compulsory
force, the same power of driving society's units into coherence;
and a challenge of its authority is visited with as prompt
a retort as a challenge of the authority of the sword would
be were the basis war. Whence it follows that just as it is
merely the hocus-pocus of the ignorant to regard promises as
"Sacred," it is not otherwise when their violation is regarded as
heinous and sacrilegious. Compact-breaking is not sacrilegious
but onerous: that is, if one breaks a compact one must be
prepared for serious consequences, whether social, legal, or
diplomatic. It is perhaps just because its consequences are
the least onerous in the field where a careless observer might
even believe them missing, *i.e.*, in the Social, that society
defends itself here by an appeal to supernatural disapproval,
such as is cloaked under the designation of sacrilegious.

The promise-breaker in the social sphere is the "bounder." Polite society being held together by an assumption that promises will be kept, the bounder can exploit it by utilising the assumption while failing to accord it respect. A society calls itself polite when violence is not included in its methods of reproof, and the bounder can therefore go far without hurting his skin. Upon such a one, polite society passes verdict to the extent of its powers by voting him unfit for society, and promptly shuts him out: he is ostracised. To characterise him as sacrilegious is a preliminary process of ostracism. The deficiency represented by the difference between this weight of punishment and the weight of disapproval is made good by invoking the force in the invisible wrath of God. Between the two the bounder has no easy time.

It is, however, what happens to promise-breakers outside the radius of polite society which really makes evident the function of the "Promise." Upon a scene where the sword has decided the issue—delineated the features of what is "just"—the fabric of Promises can be woven. Promises are the holders-in-fief for conclusions arrived at by the test of the sword.

It is, however, what happens to promise-breakers outside the radius of polite society which really makes evident the function of the "Promise." Upon a scene where the sword has decided the issue—delineated the features of what is "just"—the fabric of Promises can be woven. Promises are the holders-in-fief for conclusions arrived at by the test of the sword.

The might of the sword evaluates the forces, the weights of which will condition the Promises made by them. If, therefore, one comes to define the keeping of the terms of the promises as "Right," one can say that "Might" conditions "Right." Their variations are in direct ratio, but "Might" is primary.

Challenge "Right" and the appeal is to "Might": as can be illustrated afresh by a return of attention to the violation of compacts. If compacts whose sphere is outside the mere polite one of Social convention, and of which the violation comes within the legal sphere, are broken. Might is invoked to vindicate its offspring. Veiled though it is, the nature of the instruments which the penal code utilises are of the Sword: of Might: manacles, the bludgeon, the lash, the gallows. The primary and secondary characters of the Sword and of the Promise respectively, are made evident by the fact that the challenged Promise seeks its vindication in the Sword; but when the Sword is challenged, Promises are futile: they flee to the refuge of the future, and the Sword ultimately is absolute: it is blade against blade. Which brings us face to face with the spirit in which an emperor may tear up a treaty. Treaties are made on the computed strength of forces existent at the time, of their making: which forces, with time, vary: some increase in strength, others diminish, and that party to the treaty which has augmented its strength cannot feel itself bound by the old terms. Gently and tactfully they will be departed from, but if the augmented power is hindered from so doing, the Sword springs out of its sheath. Appeal has been made to it: a reputable, if often cocksure and foolhardy action, wholly straightforward and in no wise to be held akin to the underhand exploitings of the assumptions of polite Society which create a sphere for the "bounders," among whom, for instance, one would place the panic-mongers and price-inflaters of this our own patriotic population.

Under the heading of "War and Class War" the *Times* of Monday last had a column of observations upon the startling manner in which socialist propaganda has crumbled up at the touch of a really formidable contest[1]. It has disappeared as clean as a whistle—or smoke—without leaving a wrack behind. The phenomenon will, one hopes, be something for enthusiasts to remember and to give them pause when they are invited to swell the ranks of socialists in the future. For note what socialists—the individuals themselves—want: genuinely they desire that those who are poor and weak shall become somewhat richer and somewhat stronger; yet socialism: a manner of conduct which these individuals advocate, demands just the sort of temper which encourages the poor and weak to remain so relatively, permanently, at the same time filching from the unhappy situation just that "kick" which ordinarily it possesses within itself for its own recovery; the drive which makes poverty and weakness undesirable, *i.e.*, discomfort.

Perhaps the one answer which might be made to the *Times'* query as to why socialist propaganda has fizzled out almost in a night is that it has issued in success so complete that naturally a term has come to it. By placing side by side with the *Times'* utterance such an unintentionally expressed socialist defence as is contained, for instance, in a leading article in the *Daily News* of the same date (which paper has, by the way, latterly been pathetically extending its columns to Mr. and Mrs. Sydney Webb and to Mr. Bernard Shaw for dialetic assistance) on the "New Socialism," it is clear that there might be one reason at least to explain why socialists have left the field at this juncture without striking almost a single blow. It says,

> On Saturday the Government passed through
> all its stages in the House of Commons a Bill
> authorising the Board of Trade to requisition

---

[1] ≠ "War and Class War." *Times* (August 10th, 1914) p. 19.

foodstuffs in the same way as military and naval authorities. They also introduced a Bill authorising the immediate expenditure of £4,000,000 in promoting housing schemes throughout the country so as to mitigate unemployment. Both measures were received with acclamation by the Opposition, Mr. Chamberlain, Lord Robert Cecil and Mr. Bonar Law joining in the chorus of praise. They were scarcely discussed at all. Yet they mark two further important advances in the process of revolutionary change which has been going on with lighting-like rapidity before our eyes in the last week. The powers of the Government in the conditions in which we now are have been shown to be practically unlimited. The old social fabric has crashed down and a quite new and totally different structure has arisen as if by magic. A week ago cash payments were suspended for certain bills by proclamation. Last Tuesday the Government announced its intention of taking over the insurance of war risks at sea. On Wednesday the moratorium was made general for all debts but rent, wages, rates and taxes. On Thursday the Chancellor announced his intention of issuing new currency notes on a basis totally unknown in this country hitherto. Railway nationalisation has been effected at a single stroke without a word from Parliament. An aliens law of undreamt-of severity has been passed almost without a murmur. The Government have simply taken over the question of food supply and of unemployment, and no one doubts or grudges for a moment the vigour with which they will be handled. Society as we have known it has simply dissolved; and a new social organisation been set up in its place amid general acclamation.

No one dreams of blaming the Government for the steps it has taken; on the contrary, even its most bitter enemies applaud their vigour, and with reason. They are the sole alternative to anarchy now, and everybody knows it. They have been marvellously successful simply because they have the hearty support of the entire country... The new changes... are revolutionary, and they cannot be wholly temporary. The system which they superseded can never return in its entirety after the war, partly because the conditions in which that system was set will have vanished, partly because men's minds will have been so profoundly affected by the new experiment that they will not consent to return to the old conditions without modifications. The appeal from the Society of Friends which was published on Saturday called upon men of good will to prepare already for the great task of reconstructing society which will be imposed upon them after the war. There will not be wanting very new and very startling data on which to work for this end[1].

---

[1] ≠ *Daily News* (August 10th, 1914) p. 19.

The above, if socialists care to make a show of victory in words, will answer the *Times* fairly enough. "Why shout for a thing which willy-nilly is being thrust upon us?" they might ask. Yet they won't. It is to be borne in mind that it is not a socialist journal which pens the lines, but the mouthpiece of the socialist's arch-enemy of barely a month ago, of the wealthy humanitarian, pacifist liberal. One can feel safe in surmising that as soon as socialists can get their wind after this knock-out blow of having their utopias neatly parcelled up and presented to them out of hand, they will repudiate the above as spurious socialism, though to do so will leave the gibes of the Tories without retort. In the meantime, however, while socialists are dumbstruck by the present farcical situation, it may be possible to make a word penetrate through the hypnotising chant of words and shibboleths by which ordinarily they hold themselves separated from the onslaughts of common sense

The socialists know vaguely that they desire, and are willing to struggle for, a change in position of certain portions of the community. They are like people who sick of a disease which they cannot specify are persuaded by the glib assertions of quacks that the disease is so-and-so, and that the remedy must be their own special nostrum. The state of illness is in fact labelled to conform with the remedy. Because the quacks mean to insist that the remedy is socialism their pains are spent in persuading patients that they are socialists. That is why when the fortunes of quite other views of "social order" are for the moment fortuitously assisted by a spell of socialism, the wind is taken from the sails of the socialist "movement." The panacea for the withholding of which socialists have cursed their opponents as enemies of God and man, earth and sky, and as creators of all social woes is suddenly thrust on them; and the social complaint is unaffected. If there is a moiety of change at all it is all in favour of their powerful opponents. To those who already had much, more has been given as far as power goes. Far from power widening down from individual to individual as the hawkers predicted, power has folded itself up tighter into the central knot of the governing clique. Freedom of action, the means of life, individual lives themselves—are all at the disposal of the central group; under socialism.

It is an exceedingly happy accident for the elucidation of socialistic theory that the exigencies of the governing classes should have made it necessary to give a demonstration of socialism in practice just now. Upon the intelligence of people inocculated with shibboleths, argument is pointless. Hence an object lesson putting theory into practice is invaluable. On the face of it the experiment shows how little hostility there is between socialism and governments. The former is not merely innocuous as far as the latter is concerned; it is an enormous support to it; a very present help in time of danger. The reason the Government has thought it necessary to augment its ordinary great powers by the infinitely greater powers which accrue to it under socialism is for its own sake and not for the sake of those who will momentarily benefit by its action. Food for the people is as necessary for the successful prosecution of the war as rifles are for the Army. A starving discontented populace at home would be as disastrous to the Government's ambitions abroad as if one of the Allies went over to the side of the enemy. So out of the gush of warm feeling which the war has raised in all of us, the Government adds enormously to its powers and cuts down the individuals' proportionately; to the momentary accompaniment of the tune of the individuals' own satisfaction. For in a popular war it is as easy to disarm suspicion in regard to extraordinary measures as it is in love. Powers will even be given up voluntarily for the time being. A warm pink glow of sentiment veils everything.

Goodwill is at its height, so much so that the lie of the ground is hidden. As the *Times* heartily says, classes are forgotten. In the enthusiasm for the prosecution of an already successful "Order" just now presenting its Gala-show—it has brought out all its gew-gaws, its banners and its colour and music to allure us—it is really forgotten whose "Order" it is. For the moment, if we choose to call it so, it is ours, and we may as well accept this compensation considering that the pink mists of goodwill will soon fade; for last they won't and can't; even if they could we wouldn't have them; like sweet perfume half their charm lies in transitoriness. Then we should be able once more to reckon up how much of the great Empire belongs to us.

The communistic, collectivist tendency of thought upon which the socialist error is founded, is given rise to by the making of a permanent generalisation upon the basis of this transient, charming impulse. What merely serves its moment the socialists would make the basis of each day's humdrum living. Hence the usefulness of the Government's object lesson. The present socialistic conditions will last as long as the Government needs them. Should the politicians under popular pressure seek to perpetuate them beyond that period they will be faced by the opposition of the only persons who really count; those of initiative who, released from, or tired of the sport of the war, will be setting about their own individual business again. The dream that each is for all and all are for each will have passed, and each will be, for as much as he can be, for himself. Later, when the vaulting ambitions of the most powerful individual "orders" have, with the passing of time, again risen to their height, there will again be war, again the warm goodwill of the ordinary multitude, the spectacle of brotherly-love, socialism and... then back once more on the inevitable individual swing.

Accordingly, in this matter of socialism it is being revealed that a capitalist state can easily out-Cæsar Cæsar: as might have been expected, since capitalism commands, not only the means, but the capable men; as likewise, too, socialism does not seek to abrogate the powers of the State, but to augment them. Socialism is so pleased to image the State as a species of lucky-bag whereas, after all, it is nothing but an official recognition of the state of existent forces; and since socialism seeks to make the State all-powerful and the seat of all authority, the best and likeliest persons to carry out the job are, obviously, those who own the existent forces; certainly not those who are gaping powerlessly at their interplay from the outer fringe of their interaction: the socialists. It is really an interesting fact that the powerful ones have withheld their hand so long from this job of apotheosising the State, and have waited until it was genuinely necessary to them. Doubtless, had they not been too busy enjoying themselves, to fall under the influence of the "word-cult" they would have put it through long ago.

One is, of course, quite aware that the socialist would protest there exists all the difference in the world between an all-powerful Socialist State and an all-powerful Capitalist one: they would make the protest for a reason we have referred to above—that they never take the trouble to think what they are saying when they say "State." A State is the equilibrium of the orders which make up a community. The powerful orders are the interests and established purposes of the powerful people; and they inevitably, like oil in water, rise to the top. They will be there under socialism; perhaps, indeed, a little unpleasanter because of the lip-service they will be expected to pay to an over-ripe goodwill, by that time doubtless become a fine stench. The "workers" will be at the bottom, looking for their bit of excitement in a "call to serve" and "sacrifice" themselves for the State; for the whims of the people on the top. They will enjoy themselves very well for the moment, and, satisfied, they will sink back again—to their State.

It is plain why the egoist motive animating "tinker, tailor, soldier, sailor, rich man, poor man, beggar man, thief" is so carefully veiled. An egoistic explanation will always be confined to the very limited few who find their major interest in observing their fellows; and this for quite valid egoistic reasons. All the rest have interest to gain by flouting the notion with fine scorn. The aristocrat, the oligarchs who maintain their status by diligently prosecuting their notion of good order, *i.e.*, the continued establishment, of their own paramount one on unblushing egoistic lines, are prevented from acknowledging that they do so by the restraining thought that should they, others might be encouraged (so excellently does their condition commend their creed's efficacy) to mark and learn of them, and follow suit. Which would spoil matters entirely. For their projects and purpose to mature to their full flower it is absolutely essential that there should be a crowd of persons with nothing better to do than to serve them. The number of persons with initiative and willingness to accept individual responsibility must be small if those spacious schemes which give such light-headed enjoyment to the servers are to maintain their momentum. As Mr. W. S. Gilbert puts it: "When everyone is somebody then no one's anybody[1]." Whence, therefore, the Somebody must maintain that egoism is good for the classes but bad for the masses: carry the situation off blatantly and remember his place—on the top: as he did in the times when it was an achievement to curse like a lord—times when a lord was well loved by the people. When Somebodies take to dust-throwing as they do more and more nowadays, they appear less pleasant. They should regard high sentiments on brotherly love as the perquisite of the masses. For Somebodies it should lie regarded as sufficing if occasionally they feel it.

And if the oligarchic view of ruling "Orders" can only accommodate a few the anarchistic will tolerate none: except of course its own fad that there should be none. The anarchist looking round the affairs of the world sees that men are unequal in power: a condition the effects of which are that the less powerful fall into servitude to the great: he promptly leaps to the theory that the development of more powerful orders should be frustrated by a voluntary inhibition of will and initiative on the part of the greater ones. "Because *all*

---

[1] ≠ Gilbert and Sullivan, *The Gondoliers* (1889).

cannot equally establish such a 'Rule of Order' as each might desire, *none* therefore should attempt to establish any 'Rule of Order' at all," is the spirit beneath the doctrine of non-violation of individual liberty—the creed of the doctrinaire anarchist. It means in practice the non-utilisation of the limited character of the power of others. Naturally, such a doctrine of voluntarily applied embargoes has point only inasmuch as it is addressed to the powerful, and as it turns out the latters' care in this regard are very deaf: the first instinct of power is for room to grow, and whenever such growth requires it, the power creates its own opportunities to exploit whatever helps it on its path. All this explains why we find the genuine anarchist so utterly the reverse of what popular imagination paints him. Gentle, if ineffectual, he would put himself to unlimited pains in order to make world-room for a weed or a fly.

A syndicalist is an anarchist crossed with a mild egoist strain. He represents a first faint inarticulate prescience of the working-classes that if oligarchy suits them but little, anarchism suits them nothing at all. In "sabotage," or in the conception of the general strike, there is a faint realisation that to win large shares in the world's spoils working men must be ready to string their hearts and consciences up to the pitch of being despoilers. To hold one's own purposes so much in esteem as to be prepared to push others to the rear in their interest is a first sign of power. Other signs must be forthcoming in addition, but without this—nothing. It is because syndicalism has raised its lip, and revealed this sharp gleaming egoist tooth, that it has earned such hearty execration as offending both God and Man.

The measure of hatred which this very mild syndicalism has aroused, and the spectacle of the strength of a challenge armed force is sufficient to prove to the "workers" the kind of foe they can expect to rouse should they bring the "capitalist state" to the test of force. The answer to the query why the brave protestations of the industrial warriors upon the approach of an Imperial conflict have fallen so flat as to justify the phrase of the *Times* concerning "artificial conflicts" which are "dispersed at the touch of a real one" is that relatively speaking the characterisation is true. The workers do not care about their interests as imperialists care about theirs—though in peace times they may use terms as big. It is to this extent that their conflict is artificial. "Workers" are notoriously concerned about their balance of power. They do not really understand what the possession of power means or entails, nor do they desire to, very ardently. Had they desired it they would not have been misled as they have been by socialism for half a century. The track to anything we definitely want, we scent; and though we might not be able to advance rapidly along it, we should not be misled very far in a contrary direction.

In the case of socialism, misdirection had the advantage, it is true, of leading away from the genuine struggle which pursuing the path to real power would have entailed, and will entail, but for which the "workers" are neither fitted nor prepared. If they want to be prepared and fit, the present situation, in addition to providing the sport of a good fight, can otherwise effectively subserve their purpose. In the first place it can make plain that force is a primary fact, not to be blown away with windy words on paper. It can further make them familiar with arms and their uses: with the hardening of fibre which will stiffen for attack: it can settle for all time that we may not expect miracles of a sort: men who have been obedient for generations do not select the hour of war to make a first experiment in disobedience. On the contrary, they are likelier to achieve a new respect for obedience. And in secondary ways we shall very willingly—some of us, that is, learn that we have fallen into a habit of expecting, accepting, and making necessary to our selves, things which we could well forego if requiring them lessens our ability to garner our power. As we are all in a chastened and teachable mood, perhaps we as "workers" shall emerge at the far side of this crisis capable of waging a conflict to which the term "artificial" can be less justifiably applied.

23. Culture

*"A life joyously, richly, alluringly lived, is the fullest
and finest gift to his fellows a great genius can give."*

CULTURE has been for so long a figure of fun: among the
concepts that its recent hard-worked service in the interest of the solemnities is disconcerting. Clearly, culture may
mean various things according to necessity, and we propose
to suspend it in brackets and call it "Culture" until what
it stands for is clearer. Its recent citation in opposition to
militarism—which presumably is jingoism with a dash of stiff-
ening—seems to point to an identification between "culture"
and civilisation in the minds of our modern "fine" writers.
It could easily be explained how such identification might
arise. All modern English writers take it as granted that the
development of civilisation, of the process which seeks to fix
the nexus of society by means of words to the exclusion of
any tests of violence and force, is a sign of steadily augmented
vitality among men. From this point of view "culture" is the
conscious recognition and abetance of the process: a means
to an end whose excellence it proclaims and affirms at each
step of the way.

"Culture," so viewed, becomes at least arguable, and this
explains why "culture" has suddenly been provided with a
platform by the "civilisation-school" in a moment of panic.
Perhaps it is its very uncertainty and unworldliness which
have stood it in good stead. Civilisation which prides itself on
its fine tone is just beginning to look a trifle fat and gross in
its need for a little toning. Civilisation which exercises strong
egoistic pulls of the more pedestrian order finds itself being
abandoned in favour of different egoist pulls which are not

simply less gross, less commercial, less bent on five per cents., but are actually stronger. If, therefore, civilisation has special graces it is willing to sport them now. Hence: Culture, hard worked and solemn for the nonce. But "Culture," apart from momentary associations and special pleadings, has a meaning of its own. Culture stands for something among plants; and it stands for something on the stock-farm. First it stands for a High Interferer who lifts the struggles of competition as between species and species out of the sphere of their own decision as cultured and uncultured; from being a contest waged according to their own merits it becomes a selection fixed according to the pleasure of the High Culturist. They compete not as they could, but as He wills, and fall into places as Weeds or Choice Blooms according to His requirements. The Elect of the Gardener grow and increase because He in this omnipotence makes bid for earth-room for them. He makes His Chosen the Favoured People, and lays an embargo on any attempts at encroachment on the part of the rejected Weeds.

Now human "Culture" is the verbalist attempt to carry out a human selection on an exact analogy with the sub-human one. There is one missing factor, however, and this being the potent one, it falls to "Culture's" part to supply it. There is lacking a High Gardener; hence the ushering of the Gods into the game. Since the game is earth-made we must all play in it; since only the Chosen may prosper, we all elect to choose ourselves and create our Gods to prove the authenticity of our Choice. All our Gods we create on one principle: we create them in our own image, and give them proportions to match our own; then "culture" sits in judgment and gives to the largest God the palm. Culture's function thereafter is to compose paeans of praise to the great Gods, and build a system of embargos—the codes of behaviour—for the small persons whose Gods are of such trifling proportions as to confer on their creators nothing more than the status of weeds. Those persons of "culture," who, as we said at the outset, have made "culture" a figure of fun, are the possessors of the imbibing minds which still chant the old paeans of gods who are deposed. For the pagans last long after the gods are gone. Powers pass and gods decay, but words are well-nigh everlasting. The daring of genius once wrote: "In the beginning was the Word, and the Word was God[1]." How could the origin of "culture" be better put. The "Words" have survived and accumulated, but the Gods have changed times innumerably often. It is because the culturists have had to stretch the old words to suit the new Gods and their systems, that culture has attained to the rank of the Grotesque.

That human culture was plainly an impossibility for lack of a culturist to make the selection, was no reason whatsoever why it should not be put forward as admirable and practicable in words; rather it was a reason why it should. For false analogy is an instinctive dodge with the human intelligence which has established its position of superiority rather by means of cunning than by sheer strength. Tricks with a foe are human intelligence's masterpiece. Hence with the development of words, the culture-analogy, false as it is, had everything in its favour. The earlier human dodge of overcoming sub-human enemies by hurling weapons at them from a distance was an effort to protect themselves from the damage which results from an intimate trial of strength. Later, when men found their enemies among themselves, the more intelligent of them

[1] ≠ John 1:1.

sought to overcome their feebler fellows without the trouble of a trial by strength, and invented "culture," whose essential function it was to furnish a super-gardener, who by his mysteriously intimate communications should persuade these that they are Weeds in the interests of those—His Elect. The Gods always play the gardener, making a bid for earth-room for their chosen by demanding that the non-chosen shall fall back to give them place. The disadvantage at which they are placed by comparison with mundane horticulturists in not being able to pull up the mean weeds by the scruff of the neck they make up for by installing conscience as their ambassador in each mean one's breast to ensure that his giving way to the chosen should be no whit less effectual. Conscience is looked to to lay on the embargo. And ordinarily it manages it. The Divine-Gardener though an absentee, protects his Chosen Ones exceedingly well, whether they be of the Church or of the State, or of some powerfully predominant Order. "Culture," then, is an instilling of information as to the great Culturist's good pleasure, where He would have the "hands off" order of the embargo principle specifically act; also it inculcates the properly submissive state of mind in which the rejected should carry it into effect.

So it becomes still clearer why the civilisation-school should at a pinch identify its interests with those of "Culture." Civilisation, as its name implies, entails the laying of an embargo upon all those individual ways of taking possession and of making attack or reprisals which go beyond the spoken and written word. The individual's resources under civilisation in these respects are exceedingly limited, and these limits, from time to time are only defended by the administering of liberal doses of culture. Culture says, "Thus far and no farther." Asked why, she replies, "Because you 'ought,'" or, "You 'ought' not"—the only effective opposition to the "we can" and "we can't" of individuals. It is inevitable here in England now, that civilisation and culture should join hands. The English are the Chosen People of the present time; of course, they would prefer not to risk their possessions to a trial of strength, much as they are looking forward (vicariously most of them) to the fun of a fight. Being the ones in power and possession they naturally set much store on the showing of a properly respectful attitude by the rest of the world towards the embargo-principle. The feasibility of these recognising their "rightful" position as Weeds, and of being duly fearful of trespassing within the confines of the Elect is obvious. Praise of culture accordingly sits well on us. The gospel of remaining respectfully content with that area of territory whereunto we are all now "entitled": the gospel that all differences about "titles" should be settled in words after the civilised manner we can whole-heartedly endorse: is a proud pleasure indeed even to make war for these very loftiest concepts of the cultural scheme. To acknowledge that "culture" only works well with such inferiors as acknowledge their inferiority: that it breaks impotently against the self-willed: that the Gods themselves change sides without a qualm since they must always be on the side of the wilful battalions which scorn every embargo not imposed by the limits of their own strength, would be an error of frankness from which sound English cant keeps us inviolably immune. England is "Mistress of the Sea," the "World Empire," and some other things beside: all the present Weeds that are Weedily-inclined—that is, all with Consciences—among the nations accept her at that, but such as have plucked out the weed-principle of conscience—the first conscious act of a living power feeling its strength on the increase—just bide their time: when ready they will challenge the Elect: so Germany now! So England in her time! Succession in the line of the Elect proceeds by self-election. The normal "principle" of possession is audacity to take hold and to stick fast, of which "principle" England in her prime has given brilliant demonstrations. But having "arrived," it suits her well to keep the veil of "culture" lowered until it is forcibly torn away. Happily for those who realise most how the mighty are made and kept, and how thin is the "veneer of civilisation"—and are accordingly the more anxious to be prepared for other than "civilised" eventualities, there is a happy release from the obnoxious if useful task of belauding the culture-trick: those whose tricked intelligence ordinarily they despise will scream its praises aloud: the "believers" in Civilisation and Culture are joined.

There are, of course, those who say that castes, noble, kingly, or priestly, and Empires are one thing, but that Culture is something other and apart: something great, eternal; something to do with mind and the soul of man. Culture is Thought. Well and good: one has merely to distinguish afresh a difference many times indicated: the difference between Thinking and Thought. The function of Thinking is: destruction of Thought. Defective thinking, of course, will breed thoughts: but good thinking destroys them. Thinking might be compared with a system of drainage: bad thinking is like a bad drain, besides which the complete absence of drainage is relatively innocuous. The function of thinking is to end Doubt; Thought (in the sense in which we speak of the History of Thought, *i.e.*, as it is a synonym of "culture") is Embalmed Doubt. To receive a liberal education is to be made acquainted not with knowledge but with the

Doubts of the Ages: the Miscarriages of the thinking process, now petrified in a gruesome misshapen collection as Culture. Scholars, indeed, ordinarily are quite mummified on account of their extended intercourse with decayed thinking. It is their aspect which happily has put "culture" at a discount. All that is virile is at war with thought. A virile thinker feels a nauseated disgust at first contact with "culture."

It is certain that any who have been hypnotised with the decadent fascination of Thought have never given any vigorous consideration to what the thinking process, the intellectual, the reasoning process, really is. Yet it is a first necessity for making any headway in philosophic knowledge. It is as necessary to know the limitations of thinking as to know its powers. A modern philosophy tending to establish a fundamental distinction between intellect and instinct for instance, seems to show that there is still confusion as to what intellection is; consequently as to what it is capable of doing. Intellection is a process of treatment of images. It scrutinises, sifts, compares, collates and combines—images. Feeling, that is, life, defines itself into images: they are thinking's raw material without which to work upon the intellectual process is meaningless, as the process of a cotton-weaving would be meaningless apart from cotton. The existence of definite images is the precondition of all intellection, and whether feeling results in such images or not depends on the power of life which feels. The ineffectual efforts of literary-culture in the sphere of knowledge inasmuch as they have not been directed to definitely practical ends of popular deception interested to uphold some paramount, priestly, or secular Caste, have been efforts to make silk purses from sows' ears: or rather out of vigorous and ingenious passes made with the knitting-needles. Such "Culturists" have attempted to make a substantial fabric from a raw material so inadequate that it breaks into furze at the first touch of the machine; there has been no fabric, only a fluff-choked atmosphere thickly enveloping the thinker with his futile thinking faculty still forlorn of knowledge groping through a cloud of mystery, to set the reasoning machine afresh on the same shoddy stuff merely raises the cloud a little higher. It will all settle later to the old dead level. What philosophy requires is a bigger power of life inside the philosopher. What the philosopher requires is images which only he himself can provide. A man who feels powerfully will find that his intellectual faculty will work with certainty and power to that extent. Peasants, for instance, or wholly illiterate persons will speak with the shrewdest discrimination and certainty on deep human matters about which they have actually felt, where some University professor who has been reasoning the matter for a lifetime will sound empty like a rattle. In short, the image is the thing: the "problem" is, how to increase the power of human feeling and make human power grow and throb until it emerges from the obscure diffusion of vague feeling into the definite lines, sound, colour, movement of the clear image.

It is doubtless this unspoken consideration which is in the minds of those few who being neither knaves nor nincompoops have recently joined in the loud talk of "culture" and civilisation and the profits of peace. They believe that the security of civilisation is the milieu in which the quiet weavings of the mind proceed best, and believe that in affirming this they are affirming something quite otherwise: that the stuff over which the shuttle of the mind passes is at its best under civilisation's security. It is a conclusion to which they have abandoned themselves over-quickly and without due warrant. Security, whenever removed far from the struggle which has won it, is a deadening influence: risk is the stimulus of living. A willingness to risk one's life to the uttermost is as regular a feature with men above a certain modicum of soul-power, as eyes are usual features in the head. Risk is as necessary as water and bread. Not because a man does not value his life, but because his life has imperative needs which he is at pains to satisfy, and of these the excitement of risk is one. Failing to get it he becomes bored: soul-sick. Boredom and monotony are the premier sicknesses of life: more deadly than privation and physical pain: they make the soul faint: they are more repugnant than the fear of death. To keep alive long is a less thing than to live vividly and swiftly, if briefly. All martyrdoms and high adventures are proof of it. These are espoused not for the sake of a "cause" or for "duty," but for fun: heightened life. This absence of risk, this monotony of service in our fat, rich, and peaceful civilisation, cannot even enforce itself under such advantageous conditions. The spiritually-starved people construct risks for themselves, and paltry enough they appear. Lotteries, gambling of all sort, backing of sides in our vicarious national sports, are the mean-looking equivalents of the risks suppressed by the suppression of individual combat. Intoxicants, drugs, even militant suffragism, are the attempts of the over-civilised to come by the more vivid images which a life of less security and less monotony gives. Because civilisation does not produce adequate equivalents for these it is undermining life and weakening feeling to the vague blur of the imageless. And unfurnished with images intellect weaves the empty air; thinking is arrested, becomes barren, and degrades into thought. Feeling runs thin and Culture flourishes: sham artistry and tortured forms, fantastic wild dashes at wild theories replace honest Art, which is nothing more mystical or obscure than the expression of images sure, vivid, and sincere, seeing which men know that the images have lived in reality in the soul of their creators before ever attempt was made to make them live for others in the line, word, colour, or sound in which they take form. Art-expression of images whose stimuli come from the soul-thought inevitable to a strongly-strung race is a secondary matter: the primary affair is the strong life lived which means that images have come to birth. Power of life is the thing, and quite possibly this may find its full expression in the energising of an active and vivid existence. If so, though Art may seem poorer, the community will be as rich, perhaps richer. Quite possibly a life joyously, richly, alluringly lived, is the fullest and finest gift to his fellows a great genius can give. It is so easy to bruise the joyousness out of life in crushing life's essences to distil Art.

However that may be, it is certain that the profounder knowledge of the human heart which should be the burden of genuine philosophy, must pause until stronger feeling is at its service, and it will be all to the good when the hypnotism of security which relying on the steady return of five per cents on the one hand, and the deadly monotony of mechanical labour on the other gives, shall have given way to something more "wasteful" and adventurous. "Wasteful," since all is well-wasted if the power to feel may grow. It is true that in the fat times of peace knowledge of images of which the stimuli is eternal and maniable, and can be produced and reproduced at will may, can, and actually does, grow. Science prospers in peace, but knowledge of images which are furnished by heightened heart-beats must needs wait until thinkers' own hearts beat high. Great philosophies can come only from lives greatly lived.

24. Humanitarians

*"A virile people feels securely at peace
when it is safe on the top."*

[...] IT is possible that the humanitarians' distressingly confused mental muddle is due to a mistaken identification of "humane" conduct with just ordinary human kindness. What this mistake entails becomes clear when the differences of meaning between "human" and "humane" are brought out. "Human conduct" is men's conduct as it is; "humane" conduct is what men's conduct "ought" to be. Into this "ought" is pressed every sort of fad the humanitarian cares to patronise. Thus the humane one says you should eat no meat, because you ought not: that you are strong and powerful, and therefore ought not to do this, that, and the other; or you are weak, and he tells you you are lord of the earth, and ought to consider yourself the origin of power which the strong merely "derive" from you; that you ought to be protected therefore: and they propose to undertake your protection. Incidently they propose that you ought to allow them to take any and every liberty with you which may come into their heads: all of course for your greater protection. The humane one, in short, had made it his fad to espouse the "Cause of the Weak"—often, it is cheerful to note, to the disgust of the weak— and his crusade consists in directing a multitude of words, reproachful and very "oughtful" against those who are trying to do the best they can for themselves to the best of their ability. Humanitarians are embargoists: they endeavour to lay the weight of their "ought" across other peoples' fads, and endeavour to inhibit them by an appeal to the conscience: their own fad they call the "protection of the poor"—to which they give such free rein that they are fast becoming the apostles of perpetual gaol for the poor. They call it supervision; they are the friends—on a scientific basis of course—of the poor; looking at their ways one might think that they cherished malice against the poor, but one would be wrong. It is not malice but applied Social Science.

That the "humane" writers have an enormous influence on the temper of the wage-earning workers cannot be denied: to such an extent in fact that from the emotional—the most important—side the workers view their situation precisely upside down.

They are the under-dogs—they and the humane ones agree in that—and yet they are crying out about peace. But the cry of peace is seemly only in the mouths of the top-dogs. England can, for instance, blandly enlarge on the beauties of peace and feel at ease in the role, but the Germans, for instance, have no illusions about the blessings of peace. A virile people feels securely at peace when it is safe on the top: a virile people when it is not on the top will cry peace only when shown absolutely that excellent though it believes itself there is a power more excellent still. Why, then, are the "workers" so enamoured of peace?

And they call for disarmament: call, that is, upon those who are more powerful than they to lay down the weapons which make them so. And it is the most devastating stroke of humanitarianism that it has succeeded in persuading the industrial under-dogs that their demand will be acceded to. As though a powerful order will not always see to its defences: the only way to meet a powerful order is to oppose it with another powerfully defended order. That is why the Germans are so inspiriting. A worthy foe is as inspiring as a worthy friend. It is those who mistake the quality of both friendship and enemity who are depressing. They necessitate cuffing not combat.

Very probably the humanitarian ideal has been encouraged by an unwarrantable extension of the "family" analogy. Liberty, equality, and fraternity are the kind of flowers which might be expected to flourish in the close circle of the family with its basis fixed in intimate affection. To believe that they will flourish equally in the social "family" is to ignore the unique characteristic which creates the family. It is just because there is not much love to be relied upon abroad which makes the love in the home noteworthy. The vitiating effects of the "womanising" influences now working in the social temper are due to an untenable presumption that a frame of mind which women can calculate to find in men towards themselves will be forthcoming from men towards men. Women are, of course, in normal cases even more physically defenceless than the male civilian: but in the attraction which they wield over men they possess a physical competence for the acquisition of power and status which does not come in a man's category. Women are self-protected by a competence which belongs to themselves; because they can neglect certain powers of self-defence it by no means follows that men can do likewise. Yet the humanitarian ideal is to rely for men's safety upon a softness of dealing which is only available for women. It involves a positively deadly miscalculation.

❧

We had thought that the funniest thing appearing in print since the outbreak of the war would have been the suggestion of Mr. and Mrs. Sydney Webb in the *Daily News*, that when we have rooted up and eaten our last carrot the Distress Committee will fatten us on rations of beer and cakes—the amount to vary according to our progress in executing on the flute and doing fancy crochet-stitches; or perhaps it was in mathematics. Anyway, whatever it was, the Webbs are completely outshone—by the *Spectator*. Not in the course of a long vivid life have I read anything so inspiriting as the *Spectator*'s "Advice to Italy[1]." These articles have positively clicked with wickedness. How they must have set the fresh mountain air blowing through the dry bones sheltering in English rectories. "Clean pure hands" indeed! And "Reasons for War!" The *Spectator* informs Italy that the sound reason for war is the chance of a good one: as for the occasion meet for war: the traditional form of defiance of the street gamin—for which hands are always clean enough—will serve when the time is ripe. Honest, selfish, shameless, the *Spectator* failed to be dull. When the journal resettles comfortably into its best clergyman manner, "Italy" shall be remembered to its credit. What a blight it is on life, to be sure, that honest speech is almost non-existent. One might even make terms with a life without war if speech were a little oftener stripped of its deception, its veilings, its cant. Sound words unsheathed might make as clean war as good swords. Perhaps! Perhaps for a first round: for the second the sword might have become imperative.

---

[1] ≠ circa July 16th, 1914.

25. The Illusion of Anarchism

*"A good fight will justify any cause: a good fight
being one which is aggressive and WINS."*

ANARCHISTS are an interesting body of people whom governments take too seriously and who, unfortunately, do not take themselves seriously enough. Governments fear them as hostile, bent on mischief: whereas they are harmless, after the disconcerting harmless manner of infants. For the People indeed: for Humanity, they conceive themselves filled with an ardent passion: but towards the ways of humans—when they, as men, emerge from out the blurred composite mass of: "Humanity"—they are averse in the thorough-going implacable way possible only to people who frame their dislikes on principle. Doubtless, if one were to search the world over for the bitterest-sounding opponents of the theory that we are all "born in sin" with our natural bent inherently set towards "evil," one would fix upon the anarchists: but this is their idiosyncrasy: a foil to contrast with their main tenets. Their opposition penetrates no deeper than a dislike for the phrase, because perhaps more commonplace persons than themselves have espoused it. In substance it forms the body of anarchism, and anarchists are not separated in any way from kinship with the devout. They belong to the Christians' Church and should be recognised as Christianity's picked children. Only quality distinguishes them from the orthodox: a distinction in which the advantage is theirs. As priests administering the sacraments they would not be ill-placed.

272

At the birth of every unit of life, there is ushered into existence—an Archist. An Archist is one who seeks to establish, maintain, and protect by the strongest weapons at his disposal, the law of his own interests; while the purpose of every church—institutions all teaching anarchism as the correct spirit in conduct—is to make men willing to assert, that though they are born and inclined archists, they OUGHT to be anarchists. This is the true meaning of the spirit of renunciation—the rock on which the Church is built. The "OUGHT" represents the installation of Conscience, that inner spiritual police set in authority by the will and the skill of the preacher. Its business is to bind the Archistic desires which would maintain and press further their own purposes in favour of the purposes of whomsoever the preacher pleases: God: or Right: or the People: or the Anointed: or those set in Office. Whether the preacher or the individual's desires will prevail will pivot about the strength of the man's individual vitality. If the man is alive, his own interests are alive, and their importance stands to him with an intense assertiveness which corresponds with the level of his own vitality, of which the strength of his own interests alone can provide a sure index. Being alive, the first living instinct is to intensify the consciousness of life, and pressing an interest is just this process of intensifying consciousness. All growing life-forms are aggressive: "aggressive" is what growing means. Each fights for its own place, and to enlarge it, and enlarging it is growth. And because life-forms are gregarious there are myriads of claims to lay exclusive hold upon any place. The claimants are myriad: bird, beast, plant, insect, vermin—each will assert its own sole claim on any place as long as it is permitted: as witness the pugnacity of gnat, weed, and flea: the scant economy of the housewife's broom, the axe which makes a clearing, the scythe, the fisherman's net, the slaughter-house bludgeon: all assertions of aggressive interests promptly countered by more powerful interests! The world falls to him who can take it, if instinctive action can tell us anything.

It is into this colossal encounter of interests, *i.e.*, of lives, that the anarchist breaks in with his "Thus far and no farther. Lower interests may be vetoed without question, or with a regretful sigh, but MAN must be immune. MAN as MAN must be protected: his Manhood is his shield: to immunity his Manhood creates and confers his Right. The lower creation stands and falls by its might or lack of it: but Manhood confers a protection of its own." Who guarantees the protection? "The conscience of him who can infringe it. If that fails, then the outraged consciences of other men, jealous for the dignity of 'Man.' Such an one as does not hold in awe the Rights of Man, who does not bow down to the worth of Man as Man, and not merely as a living being, and hold it Sacred and Holy, he shall be held to be not of the community of Man but a monster preying upon the human fold, fit only to be flung out, and to foregather with his familiars—wolves and strange monsters." That is the creed of an Anarchist, whose other name is "Humanitarian." His creed explains why he loves humanity but disapproves of men whose ways please him not. For men do not act after the anarchistic fashion one towards another. They are friendly and affectionate animals in the main: but interests are as imperative with them as with the tiger and the ape, and they press them forward, deterred only by the calculation of the hostility they may arouse by disturbing the interests which they cross, as cross they must, since by extending the tentacles of interest is their way of growth. That this is so would be plainer to see if men had single interests (as some men have, and then it is all plain enough). But men have many, and what might be expected to be a straight course is a zigzaged line. And interests lead not only by way of oppositions: by wrestling for possessions: in love, for instance, they lead to a seeming commingling of interest. It is only seeming: the love interest is as archistic as any other. Into this stimulating clash of powers the anarchist introduces his "law" of "the inviolability of individual liberty." "It is feasible to push," he would say, "the line of satisfaction of men's wants—since being born into life and sin they will not wholly renounce them—but only to the lengths where it can be squared with the wants of everyone else. Such wants will work out perhaps, and probably merely to the satisfaction of certain elementary needs: of earth-room, of sustenance and clothing: a title to which are the indefeasible Rights of Man. Only when these have been assumed to all may the interests of any be pushed further. To wealth, according to his necessities, each has a *right*; in return each must serve as he can." It must be acknowledged that it is a creed which lends itself exceeding well to eloquence carrying the correct noble ring with it; it makes converts increasingly; and when it wears thin in one garb it readily rehabilitates itself in changed raiment; as Christianity, as Humanitarianism, anarchism successfully and continually seduces Public Opinion.

Why it should have no difficulty in drawing Public Opinion to its side the nature of Public Opinion makes evident. Public Opinion intrinsically is—bellowing. It is the Guardian of the *Status quo*: its purpose is to frighten off any invader who would disturb established interests: it is always, in its first stage, on the side of good faith, the maintenance of contracts, and fixed arrangements: it is like a watch-dog barking at all new-comers, be these friendly or hostile. Its bark is worse than its bite, however, and flouted or ignored, it will always arrive at a temporary halt. The halt is to gain time to see what measure of strength the disturbing force has. Public Opinion, it is to be noted, is the affair of non-combatants, and is supposed, therefore, to be also Disinterested Opinion. Which does not in any way follow. Public Opinion is in fact the calculation of the self-interest of non-combatants. Its primary and involuntary bellowing function is its first instinct with intent to warn off disturbers: but if the aggressor perseveres unmoved and proves to be more powerful than the member of the settled order whom he is attacking, Public Opinion, *i.e.*, the interests of the non-fighters, gets ready to come to terms. It gets ready to live at ease with a force which apparently has come to stay. It has poised the merits of the two claimants: and peace—the maintenance of the *Status quo*—first weighted the side of the defenders: but the aggressor having won success, success becomes his defence, and proves an adequate makeweight. Which is why success succeeds. It is easy to defend the defensive side: to hold him "in the right" at the outset: the defensive is the defendable: it would have been difficult to do otherwise: since to defend the aggressor is an anomaly in terms: the aggressor can only be "justified": and only success can justify him. But let the aggressor fail, and for Public Opinion he at once appears diabolical. For instance, if Germany is successful now, the German Emperor will command the admiration of the world, and will get it. Should Germany lose there will be none so poor as to pay him reverence. His reputation, as far as Public Opinion goes now, lies in the womb of time: a matter of accidental forces more or less. The heinous offence for which the world will hold him a demoniacal monster is a miscalculated judgment; that which will make him the Hero of his Age—its Master—will be just—a verified judgment.

Which explains why a good fight will justify any cause: a good fight being one which is aggressive and WINS. Thus forces, on any pretext whatsoever, having been mustered for a test, the question of public repute will pivot about a nice estimation of the strength of those forces. Execration is not meted out to the despoilers of art treasures as such only if the despoiler likewise shows signs of being the vanquished. Louvain will be a trifle, regrettable but necessary, if the German hosts are victorious. So contrariwise: any schoolboy may lightly hold the reputation of Napoleon as to "Right" at his caprice—*because of Waterloo*. It is Waterloo which separates Napoleon from Alexander and Julius Cæsar: not the bloodstained plains of Europe; as it is Naseby and Marston Moor which pales the memory of Wexford and Drogheda, and makes Cromwell a Kingly Hero instead of a villainous knave and murderous assassin. On like counts, too, was George Washington a Hero and "right," while President Kruger was a scheming seditionist, and "wrong."

Public Opinion, therefore, is nothing more than a loose form of alliance founded among non-principals, based on a momentarily felt community of interests on the defensive. The initial shock of invasion having been parried, the passage of time, and especially the course of events, will begin to make clear to what extent this first apparent community of interest with the defensive was due to mere alarm, and how far it represented something more permanent. Moreover, in the account of the development of Public Opinion it is to be recognised that the very dash and daring and picturesqueness of the aggressive may actually give birth to an interest in which the non-combatants will find themselves involved by sheer fascination: to such an extent even it may be that to be permitted to share in the general risk of the fight will appear a high privilege. A great aggressor will find he can always count on this. The conquerors have been the well-beloved. Napoleon had the adoration of the men whose lives he was "wasting." *They* would have called it a glorious opportunity enabling them to spend themselves lavishly with a correspondingly lavish return in pleasure. It is indeed a most ludicrous error to assume that interests are all "material." There are interests that are of pleasure, interests of spiritual expansion, interests of heightened status, quite as compelling as those of material profit; it is indeed doubtful, even among the meaner sort, whether the "material" interests have so strong a pull as the others. Moreover, *kinds* of interests are very unstable, and will develop from one form to another with extreme rapidity under the influence of threat or challenge. So, at the appearance of a great personality who can give body to more spacious interests, even the most intimate interests–those of nationality and kinship—will suffer a sea-change:—

If my children want, let them beg for bread,
My Emperor, my Emperor is taken[1].

There is bespoken the influence of one Emperor: a second has welded spirited, jealous and antagonistic States—even indeed the younger generations of the subdued provinces into a homogeneous unit under the influence of a fantastically adventurous yet living dream. By interests of a different sort England soothed Scotland into unanimity as she is engaged in soothing the Dutch in South Africa. Other interests—those of status and prestige—are the forces which have won for England at this present moment the loose alliance which is implied in a friendly American Opinion. That Americans

---

[1] ≠ "*Lass sie betteln gehn, wenn sie hungrig sind / Mein Kaiser, mein Kaiser gefangen!*" Heinrich Heine: *Die beiden Grenadiere* from *Romanzen und Balladen*, 1884.

share a common language and in a measure all the prestige of the English tradition, literary and military, implicates the status of Americans with the maintenance of British Status: they would have hated England readily enough had she given indication just now that she was on the point of lowering it.

At the present time, it is true, England is blushing with the embarrassment of the unfamiliar, by allowing a parrot-like press and pulpit to persuade the world that she is now a disinterested fighter in a great and holy Cause. She appears to be beginning to feel herself infected with the preacher's own liquid emotions as she listens how she is going forth—not for her own sake but—TO RIGHT THE WRONG, to avenge the weak, to champion civilisation, to suppress the Vandal and the Hun, a Bayard, a Galahad, the Armed Messenger of Peace, waging a spiritual warfare. There is one consolation indeed—the "Tommies" are too far off, and too busy to hear any of it. And there is this excuse for the preachers: that they have looked round carefully and have not yet set eyes on any of those likely and tempting bits of territory which hitherto have always been hanging as bait when England has gone to war: it hasn't occurred to them that this war, far from requiring excuse in poetic babble, was necessary to save England's soul from the devastating unconfidence bred in these years of peace. To please their souls let them call it a spiritual war: at any rate it answers a spiritual need, and in the nick of time: Englishman's need, not Belgium's, or culture's, or civilisation's, democracy's, and the rest. Twenty years hence the conflict probably would have been too late; as it now seems likely to prove twenty years too soon for Germany. The cause of the war is German disparagement of English spirit: both as to its fire and its intelligence. The Germans believed that, average for average, they were better quality: that English prestige was an anachronism, an heritage already sunk to a relic bequeathed from a spiritual past, from whose strength modern England has fallen off: that the nation was devitalised, and as interests can only be held in proportion to the vitality of those who forward them, they could be torn away if seriously challenged by their naturally ordained successors. And they had plenty of evidence to support them. The spiritual fire glows out not merely in one direction: it is all-pervading: and German philosophy, German Science, German inventiveness, energy, daring, and pushfulness, provided evidence which all the world might see and compare. By that comparison, Germans had convinced themselves, and were convincing the world—*and us.* They were undermining English confidence, not by their boasts but by their deeds: and naturally, if they excelled in the arts of peace why not in the art of war, where prestige registers an accurate level? They were wearing down our spiritual resilience: the subtle thing of the spirit which, once lost, is never recaptured. A people which feels this subtle thing departing from it will strike instantly for its preservation, or know itself lost before a blow has been struck. It has seemed a puzzle, and to none more than to England herself, why she has suddenly found herself in such abnormally good odour. It is an unusual situation for her—in these latter days. The explanation is the promptness—haste almost—with which she entered into the war. It was because she seized the first suggestion of an opportunity to vindicate herself, that she instantly stood up—vindicated, rehabilitated with the respect that had in latter days been given her with a questioning grudge. Had she hesitated it would have been the sufficing sign of weakness, of the insensitive lack of pride which the world was more than half expecting, and was more than a little shocked not to find. The "friendliness" of which she has been the recipient since is the outcome. The explanation applies as much to feeling within the limits of the Empire and to malcontents at home, as in the world outside. And the result immediately to follow, one can safely trust, will be equally in her favour: that is, the brilliant vindication of British spirit on the seas and the battlefields will speedily have a counterpart in British laboratories: in renewed and confident strength of spirit in English philosophy, literature and art (where it is needed, God wot!). Confidence, which dare look at plain fact without latent undermining fear, confidence and deeply stirred emotions are the materials which inspire a new spirit in the Arts. After the war, because of the war—the Renascence!

So, to return to our anarchists, embargoists, humanitarians, culturists, Christians, and any other brand of verbalists: the world is to the Archists: it is a bundle of interests, and falls to those who can push their own furthest. The sweep of each interest is the vital index of him who presses it. And interests have this in common: the richness of the fruit they bear grows as they push outwards: the passions they excite are then stronger; the images called up—the throb, the colour, vividness—intenser. For this, a man has the evidence of his fellows to add to the weight of his own: men will even desert their own greyer interests: greyer because less matured: when lured by the fascinating vividness of another's interests far-thrown: the great lord can always count on having doorkeepers in abundance. To keep the door has become their primary interest: because so, they live in the vicinity of a bright-glowing strength. Neglect to analyse the meaning of friendly Public Opinion has misled anarchists as to its real nature and as to what attitudes towards their fellows, men can be persuaded to adopt. Combination of interests against a powerful aggressive interest, which is the first stage of Public Opinion, is a momentary affair, intended to parry the attack of a force which is feared because its strength is unknown. The reverse side to this temporary hostility of Public Opinion towards the aggressor is the favourable acceptance of the doctrine of non-pushfulness: of anarchism proper. But the friendliness is as shortlived as the hostility: since fear of the unknown is not a permanent feature of the public temper: rather is an accommodating adjustment to strong forces emerging out of the unknown, its permanent characteristic. Friendliness to, and admiration for, strong interests is the permanent attitude of this world's children: only varied by some direct antagonism born of an opposition to one's own particular personal and private interest. Hence the reason why anarchism—embargoism in all its many forms—never penetrates more than skin deep. It is always encouraged by great promise of adherents: always it finds itself abandoned by men in earnest with their powers about them: always the world is for the Archists, who disperse and establish "States" according as their powers enable them.

So, opposition to the "State" because it is the "State" is futile: a negative, unending fruitless labour. "What *I* want is *my* state: if I am not able to establish that, it is not my concern *whose* State is established: my business was and still remains the establishing of *my* own. The world should be moulded to my desire if I could so mould it: failing in that, I am not to imagine that there is to be no world at all: others more powerful than I will see to that. If I do make such an error it will fall to me to correct it and pay for it." Thus the Archist. When the curtain rings down on one State automatically it rises upon another. "The State is fallen, long live the State"—the furthest-going revolutionary anarchist cannot get away from that. On the morrow of his successful revolution he would need to set about finding means to protect his "anarchistic" notions: and would find himself protecting his own interests with all the powers he could command, like a vulgar Archist: formulating his Laws and maintaining his State, until some franker Archist arrived to displace and supersede him.

The process seems so obvious, and the sequence is so unfailing, that one wonders how the humanitarian fallacies gain the hearing they do, though the wonder diminishes when one reflects how the major proportion of the human species holds it a just grievance that we walk upon our feet and not upon our heads, and that the tendency of falling objects is down and not up. According, one might argue, it is *because* it is the human way for men to push their interests outwards that humanitarians step forward and modestly suggest that they should direct them backwards. Object that outwards is the human way and the retort is that inwards is the divine one and better, higher. And there may be something too in a customary confusing of an attitude which refuses to hold laws and interests sacred (*i.e.*, whole, unquestioned, untouched), and that which refuses to respect the existence of forces, of which Laws are merely the outward visible index. It is a very general error, but the anarchist is especially the victim of it; the greater intelligence of the Archist will understand that though laws considered as sacred are foolishness, respect to any and every law is due for just the amount of retaliatory force there may be involved in it if it be flouted. Respect for "sanctity" and respect for "power" stand at opposite poles: the respecter of the one is the verbalist, of the other—the Archist: the egoist.

And there are the illusions about the ways of love: where one seems to desire not one's own interests but another's. Again it is mere seeming: the lover is a tyrant kept within bounds by the salutary fear that the substance of his desire will slip from his grasp: whereas his paramount interest is to retain his hold on it. The "exploitation" is nevertheless as sure and as certain as that of the sorriest old rascal who ever coined wealth out of misery. Mother-love, sex-love, with friendship even, it is one and the same.

But whatever may be the illusions which lead him on, the anarchist's hopes are vain. Water will take to running uphill before men take seriously towards anarchism and humanitarianism. The forces of their being are set the other way. The will to create, to construct, to set the pattern of their will on the world of events will never be restrained by any spiritual embargo, save with those whose will would count for little anyway. There is some substance, indeed, in the old market-place cry about levelling "down" instead of "up." The embargoists, the anarchists, and all the saviours, are bent on levelling-down: they are worrying about the few desiring too much: whereas none can desire enough. The "problems" of the world—which are no problems—will be solved by the "down-and-outs" themselves: by a self-assertion which will scatter their present all too apparent anarchism. When it becomes clear to them that it is only seemly to want the earth, they will feel the stirrings of a power sufficient at least for the acquisition of a few acres.

26. Disaster

"Life is for fun. Only when we are thoroughly browbeaten by the solemnities do we seriously affect that it is otherwise."

[...] A. G. G. in the *Daily News* reflects musingly how a disaster makes evident that all things tend for their solution towards Communism[1], and in a Communistic anarchist journal—*Freedom*, P. K. discourses triumphantly on precisely the same subject[2]. He says that prophetic anarchist dogma, in contrast to the bourgeois economist teaching of "To everyone according to his services," has been all these years "To each according to his needs," and that at long last Time has given verdict in the Communist favour. He illustrates by quotation thus:—

> Let any great city be visited to-morrow by a calamity—a siege, or the like—and you will see that, immediately the Communist idea will come to affirm itself in life. The question of "bread," of food for all, will impose itself upon the community, while the question as to the remuneration of the services rendered by this or that member of society will be thrust into the background. Every one's *needs* will be every one's *right* to his share in the common store of available food.

[1] ≠ Possibly Alfred George Gardiner.
[2] ≠ "Communist Kitchens" by P. K. *Freedom* Volume XXVIII Number 305 (September 1914).

He comments:—

> Now, Western Europe is living through a period
> of calamity, and we see how the idea of Commu-
> nist kitchens is rapidly spreading everywhere,
> as a first small step towards a Communistic
> conception of organisation.

He winds up with:—

> Many comrades are quite right in seeing in such
> kitchens the means to prove to the working
> men that in constructive work Anarchists can
> be *practical*, and even more so than those who
> pretend to be practical, simply because the
> latter stifle every revolutionary thought. A
> good propaganda of the Communist idea is
> already being made by this supply of food, and
> the communalisation of housing and clothing
> may follow very soon,

which shows how even anarchists when they can will work up
the speed for their hobbies. Well: to smooth the crease from
A. G. G.'s puzzled brow, and to slacken Prince Kropotkin's
Communistic pace (if the writer of the *Freedom* leader be
indeed that ardent anarchist). The first thing to note about all
this evidence flattering to Collectivity provided by disaster,
is that it is provided by disaster. Circumstances are not
ordinary, fear is all around, and under the influence of fear,
it will be noticed all animals, from highest to lowest, tend
to herd. During a thunderstorm the lady newly-settled in
the house across the way—a stranger—presents herself on
my doorstep and literally shoves her way in. She is afraid of
thunder—that is all—but sufficient apparently completely to

reverse her normal conduct, and there is no need to pucker one's brow and foresee the necessity of creating a brand-new social polity because of it.

To herd is the normal defensive instinct: Communism is defensive—the social impulse which seizes on individuals affected by fear. The impulse passes with the passing of the exceptional danger. As far as present measures give evidence, the observation will not need emphasising that the activity of the collectivist direction has lent itself almost exclusively to restrictions. The purpose of the moratorium, for instance, was to prevent individuals pressing for payments; again, a measure to prevent them offering produce for sale at prices beyond a certain figure; or, one may not pass a sentry without replying to his challenge. The collective Government has tabulated very many things which may not be done: it has had practically nothing to say about what one may do, beyond giving generous advice to get about one's own business, and not expect too much from it, even in the way of restrictions. What the situation amounts to is this: we are all lying low because faced with a common danger, the danger to trade, and means of livelihood, being as common to employers, and those called "independent," as much as to "workers." Like outdoor life before a storm, all have taken to shelter. It is not an active time: "Nothing doing" is the commonest phrase that is going.

Adventure has been paralysed by fear and its consequences. Even Amundsen has abandoned his trip to the Pole, one hears. Things are shaky enough: the financial measures taken by the Government are to prevent them from being made worse by panic. These measures represent no triumph of the human spirit: they are the make-shifts of the moment, made use of, *faute de mieux*. Nothing worth while is ever done under the influence of fear: the best to which energy can aspire in such circumstances is to keep things from becoming precipitate while awaiting a more favourable period. Achievement means adventure, and adventure needs confidence: at present things are paralysed, more or less. When the first shock has passed off we shall begin to sally forth again like insects after rain, units, each bent on prosecuting his individual ambitions. Communists should not allow the fact that people have appeared to enjoy the little communist interlude to blind them to the actual origin of that enjoyment: it was not the communistic measures, whether in the form of communist kitchens, or otherwise (there are communist kitchens in every prison and workhouse which do not appear to be very exhilarating affairs) but the pleasure of excitement at the prospect of change: it was the outcome of the excitement, and not of the kitchens, though in their huggermugger moments, when tired and worried, they would doubtless allow that such kitchens were a boon indeed. At heart men are all children: not "statesmen." Life is for fun. Only when we are thoroughly browbeaten by the solemnities do we seriously affect that it is otherwise.

[...] A note on some correspondence in the last issue of *The Egoist*—A correspondent protests against the validity of recognition of "classes," and says "For the true egoist there are no classes[1]." He might just as well say there are no orange-boxes or pigeon-holes, or deny that there exists any system of nomenclature and identification. Classification is an inevitable proceeding with the potentiality of vast usefulness: a thing is "classed," for instance, merely by naming

---

[1]≠ Apparently an unpublished letter in response to 'Views and Comments' from Volume I Number 17 (September 1st, 1914).

it, which process places it under a certain recognised division—an obviously necessary proceeding in a multiple world. Classification has fallen into contempt because of bad classifying, *i.e.*, making one certain feature the classifying criterion, and then proceeding to swear that all things coming under the division are possessed of a thousand and one features which were never indicated or intended in the grouping of the class. If, for instance, one were to make a "class" of "men acceptable for service" out of all able-bodied males of ages ranging from 18 to 30, and then were to proceed to press in for active service all the old women and children because these latter speak English, as do the able-bodied men aforementioned, one would get a partial hang of the trick which has made "classification" a suspected mental activity. "One-eyed" men is a sound classification: the nature of the odious process which has brought classing into contempt is that which would insinuate into the class the assumption that "they are all therefore treacherously inclined." So: the classification of wage-earners is as sound as that of "apples" or "one-eyed men": it brings under a division all such as work for an arbitrary return upon enterprises for whose initiation and direction the responsibility has been assumed by others prior to their engagement on them. The descriptive-label of "defective initiative" attached to wage-earners is as pertinent and essential to their designation as the description of a certain kind of fruit is to the designation of the class "Apple." In short: a wage-earner is one who labours on a job not initiated by himself. The remark of the correspondent to the effect that a particular wage-earner shows initiative by entering the correspondence columns of this paper, while it may be true, is yet wholly beside the point. The defective initiative implied in the classification of wage-earner extends no further

than the area of his activity of wage-earning: which is quite
sufficient to make clear the fact we intended to make clear,
i.e., the difference of status—of class—between an "employer"
and those whom he "employs."

27. Women's "Rights"

*"Every form of self-responsible power demands
—not last, but first—capable physical self-defence."*

THE War—still the War—has brought the wordy contest
about Women's Rights to an abrupt finish, and only a
few sympathetic words remain to be spoken over the feminist
corpse. Two parties were quarrelling about the validity of
the one party's claims to "rights," and without any warning preliminaries both parties, with the rest of the world,
stand spectators at a demonstration in the natural history
of "rights." To "rights" in their maturity we have all been
accustomed. Men as well as women had become so implicated
in their matured existence that all were inclined to forget
that "rights" had an era of birth and consolidation, as well
as a period of maturity. The "Women's Rights" agitation
was working industriously on the assumption that rights were
conferred by ordination, and could be allowed by goodwill
and favour, when the War arrived to shatter it. Incidentally
it clears up a confusion between "absolute rights" and "courtesy rights": a confusion which has already addled not only
the "Women's Rights" agitation, but also the proletarian
agitation, and was within measuring distance of placing the
German Emperor in the position of schoolmaster, authorised
by divine right to enlighten the world as to the difference.
The confusion has arisen out of an assumption that ultimate
authority lies in words; that every difference can be settled
amicably if only it is argued earnestly enough; that courts of
arbitration are final; that the legislature is the fount of power.
The Legislature, as merely the *channel* of power, has seemed
a contradictory, illogical, perversely inclined institution to

the vast body of opinion which starts out on its reasonings from the base that "In the beginning was the Word[1]." Accordingly the "rights-claiming" women were only one band of a company of humanitarian, pacifist, proletarian, Christian believers, to whom the regarding of words as secondary phenomena, addenda attaching to forces with function merely to describe, assist, disguise and defend such, as circumstances might require, was simple blasphemy. As they now stand spectator to the birth-throes of a revised order of rights, horror at the blasphemy is the substance of their mutterings against the forces which have compelled the revision. Their curses do not spare their eyes the spectacle all the same; the forces take their course, leaving the verbalists to put what interpretation they please on them, since interpretations are as little germane to the forces as straws are to the force of a torrent which sweeps them along. What *would* be germane to the forces would be an exercise of force like their own; short of such exercise, words have the value—and no more—of the detonation of the combatants' guns: they have effects which impress the timid and the simple.

At present, in the greater part of four continents, all "rights" are suspended, and if, owing to favourable situation of locality, and the force of long habit, the effect of possessing rights still continues, it can be regarded only as an accidental escape. In the countries at war the inhabitants are entitled to the rights of the inhabitants of Louvain, or to those of two aviators fighting in the air—*i.e.*, to what they can get. Civil rights, as well as courtesy rights, circumstances have called in, pending a settlement of fundamental rights, the rights which tally

---

[1] ≠ John 1:1

with the arbitrament of might when exhaustion compels one body of combatants to ask for terms. Those terms will be the "absolute right" at the moment of settlement, and will be the foundation and the ultimate authorisation of all subsequent civil or permitted courtesy rights, both of which species of right those who control the armed forces of a community can abrogate whenever they see fit. The granting of civil rights, in the main, follows a tendency dictated by the nature of settlement with absolute rights: those in control granting rights to those who appear capable of making serious trouble if they are not granted. Might even in these deluding times still forms nine parts of most laws; the tenth part is the "scrap of paper" to correspond: the ocular evidence of might constituting a "right." Should the nine parts vary the tenth will rapidly vary to correspond, the flux of rights being only the outer evidence of the inner spiritual flux of might. Might is spirit: there is no doubt of that. All great military commanders, and the commonest observations of ordinary men, agree in that. Spirit translates itself as might—physical superiority–a simple phenomenon of the spirit which verbalists seek to cover by labelling—in a hybrid lingo—spirit as *morale*. The great charters embodying new rights have all been given in response to actual or threatened insurrections in might–*i.e.*, in spirit—of those who desired them, and as such they fall into harmony with the spirit of the absolute rights actually established at the sword's point. Between such rights and the courtesy rights which men have conferred on women there is a swing almost to an opposite; a sweep of difference, bridged to a certain degree by what may be called "bluffed rights"—rights conferred by astute politicians with an eye to popular favour in response to agitations too utterly feeble ever to put their issue to the test of any tribunal other than that of words and intrigue. It is a highly pernicious process, because it misleads and subdues spirit, and it is to this increasing vogue of ultra-modern political institutions that the "Woman's Rights" agitation is largely due. Such a vogue existing, women, naturally, who have to obtain most of their material requirements by "courtesy" means—by request and persuasion—could not be expected to believe that there existed anything obtainable on terms of talk which men might obtain but which women might not. Hence a "movement" founded in confusion: a confusion which women may truly say they became immersed in only when men themselves had become lost in it, and out of which, intellectually speaking, it has been left to the women themselves to make clear a way.

Women's ready acquiescence in the humanitarian belief that, back of all things, stands the "Word" (translated into practice that means that all powers flow from laws), led them to make the request—adulated later into a demand—that they should be allowed to participate in the making of the laws. The request's refusal led to the reviewing of woman's status in the community, and it was the evidence brought to light in the reviewing which became in its turn accountable for an increasing acridity in the "request." For the first time women became aware in a general way of their secondary position—a realisation which, unaccountably as it may seem to men, came as a genuine shock to their pride, the reason for the surprise being that women, since men became artic-ulate, have been the pleasedly persuaded victims of men's flattery. Women's actions, of course, flattered men; they were not sufficiently articulate to flatter than in words. Men, on the other hand, flattered mainly by words and women, be-lieved in the superiority which men ascribed to them. The women who have an unshaken faith in the actuality of the lofty status ascribed to "woman" by the penny novellette far exceed in numbers those who have, at any time, followed the banner of the "Rebel Women." Hence the unpalatableness of the "facts," and the determination to alter their character at the first opportunity: hence the determination of "advanced" women to ladle out to themselves "rights" from their primary source—as they imagine, the legislature. Hence the "Votes for Women" agitation.

A slightly increased power of observation in women made them aware that, while they were competent to secure for themselves every kind of material advantage, there existed a species of initiatory power, over and above all material wealth–and in fact the source of it—into touch with which their existent competence seemed powerless to bring them. They had the power to draw to themselves the results of the initiatory power where they found themselves belonging to men whose initiatory activity was satisfactory: they had no difficulty in securing their own aggrandising with every form of wealth and comfort. They were the passive recipients on whom men—the active members—heaped their spoils. Physically weak, their men protected them as valuable property, mentally slow and unimaginative, men could win them by the evidence and results of their own mental alertness and imaginativeness, as they could keep them pleased and content with the flattering interpretation they placed upon the relationship. Men called them their "property" only when annoyed—their "own" was the more passionate and poetic—they were the masculine complement, and the better half at that; the stable passive element which was always reliable—and always there like the house and the farm-stock. In short, women found that the only thing which put men out was, not extravagance or graspingness, but a desire for activity beyond a circumscribed limit. Women's extravagance and irresponsibility has been regarded, in fact, always with indulgent eye as a very venal foible: but any enlarging to the sphere of activity was frowned down as "dewomanising," shewing a break-down in fundamental womanly instinct. The whole weight of man's imagination, his "idealism," his pictured desire as to what women could mean for him was, is, set directly against it. Women imagined that "an appeal to reason" would win them their point (such as they vaguely conceived it). Off-hand they soothed themselves that their powers had failed in the particular direction for lack of insistence: lack of laying claim to it. Later, they found that by claiming it they had put themselves further off from its attainment than they would have been by quiet requesting and patient waiting for its conferment. The more they sought to strengthen their claims with reasons, the easier it became to frame opposition against it. They failed to appreciate that the appeal was silenced in advance by the counter-assault on vanity and pride; and where women are concerned vanity is man's main feature. It is the pride of possession which has made it a comparatively easy task for women to turn men into toiling, hard-pressed, monotonous money-grubbers; and it is a most delicately ironical fate that confused observation should have led women into an attempt to carry the assault against men's vanity, when at the same time they proposed increasing the pressure on men's responsibility.

Confused observation is the only explanation of the trend which has been set to the "Woman's Movement" during the century and more which constitute its first stage, and to which the war has now affixed the term. For instance, only confusion could account for women's umbrage at being "property," while at the same time they insist on retaining and augmenting those protective advantages they are possessed of, just because they are property. Property is that which, being a non-initiatory body, can offer no self-defence, and becomes, automatically, the possession of those who can best defend it. This does not mean to say it has no value:—its value increases with the power of its owner; one may not cast a glance awry at the smallest possession of the very powerful, but its value is to its possessor, not to itself. "Property rights" is a misnomer: accurately they are "property-*owners'* rights," just as it is "property-*owners'* responsibility." The property itself can have neither rights nor responsibilities. The rights of the owners work out at an agreed claim to accord and receive neighbourly assistance in the work of protecting the hold over one's property, and are based on reciprocal claims that each owner shall prevent his property from becoming a nuisance, either from allowing it to "run wild" or fall into such decay as to affect the well-being of his neighbours. Thus women, being property, have no rights beyond "courtesy" permitted ones: but their owners have responsibilities towards them, which at their minimum they must fulfil because of the demands of their fellow-owners, and at their maximum in order to gratify vanity in the pride of possession, and to increase that attraction between women and their owners, which is at the root-cause of men's assumption of responsibility.

The stronger, therefore, the call for protection, the stronger is the implication that the responsible one is the owner and the protected one the property; and as it is the "advanced women"

who have pushed the claims of masculine responsibility to hitherto undreamed of lengths, the fact that it is they also who make the outcry against women being "property" invests the movement with the element of uproarious farce: the more so because they themselves remain sublimely unconscious of any element of humour. This explains why, by comparison with the "advanced women," the "womanly" women *look* the more intelligent. Actually there is, at present, no difference between the main objectives of either: they both seek to augment their status through the obliging acquiescence of their mankind, but they differ as to the means. Both want advantage in material affairs by civil means: that is, by avoidance of an appeal to physical force to which a male subject class would have to resort if it wished to carry an insurrectionary point, but the "womanly" women have the sense to see that such a procedure can only be put through by "courtesy" means. The desire for heightened status which is embodied in the "advanced" women's *demands* to share in initiatory power, of course puts the "courtesy" attitude for them out of the question: they feel they must needs *demand* because power is their *right*. A vague instinct that power must be self-bestowed is perhaps behind their "fight" for parliamentary enfranchisement. They imagine when they have laid hands on voting-power they will be at the source of initiatory power: that they will then be "free" (*i.e.*, powerful) to help themselves. While this struggle for voting power has been proceeding, there has been too much heat engendered for the women to become aware that the reviewing of their position, which has revealed so much to them, has likewise been bringing into full consciousness in men's mind a realisation of women's position which was only subconsciously realised before. It is ceasing to be regarded as an unquestionable, divinely-ordained law of the universe that men should be "responsible" for their women kind: it is apparent that if responsibilities are undertaken they are so only in consideration of privileges in lieu. The day when women can invoke the responsibility, while denying the privilege, draws to a close after a brief noon. It is becoming clearer what, in the way of freedom of activity, women must needs renounce if they proceed with the one species of feminist propaganda, *i.e.*, unrestricted entry into the labour markets, payment of wives, and the like; and equally clear, on the other hand, what responsibilities they must be prepared to take on their own shoulders if they press the opposing feminist shibboleths: "free" love, equal claims to divorce, and so on, is becoming clear. The two brands of the propaganda, though springing from the one source, are heading in opposite directions; but neither is aimless. One is the instinct towards the emoluments and conferred status which goes with "property": the other is towards the self-responsibilities of "freedom" which, being interpreted in its only useful sense, means "power." The question is whether women have the power, the genuine self-supplying power, and not the bogus counterfeit of conferred power. Because, if they have not, by assuming heavy and unaccustomed responsibilities, their ambitions are leading them towards disaster, just as inevitably as every Englishman believes that German ambitions, backed by over-rated powers, are leading their nation to disaster. For instance, every form of self-responsible power demands—not last, but first—capable physical self-defence. One might venture to say it would be impossible to find in these islands any "advanced" woman who has not felt herself made into something of a fool by the unequivocal evidence as to the position of women presented by the war—not merely in the countries actually devastated by the war—but here in England. They find that they may busy themselves with efforts to assist their less "protected" sisters towards maintenance: they may form an admiring audience: they may have the honour of being allowed to share in their country's defence by dint of knitting socks: or "serve," as one ungallant soldier put it, by providing one of the "horrors of war" as a Red Cross Nurse. In the war-area itself, they form part, along with the rest of the property, of the spoils of the conquered. One cannot easily refrain from the inference that, though they have weakened the pull of the old-womanly competence, the "advanced women" have done very little in the way of furnishing the necessary foundations for its successor.

Whichever path one takes in considering this question of womanly complementariness or secondariness, if one so chooses to call it, always the same conclusion is arrived at: an effectual assertion of *physical force* is the first essential to any successful digression from the normal womanly protected sphere. It is a blunt fact, with a none too attractive sound, and there will be few women who will care to give voice to it: which silence, by the way, is more telling evidence of the amount of distance which the "movement" has travelled than fifty years of platform oratory. Poor Mrs. Pankhurst, to her bewilderment, found herself driven irresistibly against the fact only to gib at it each time she came up with it. She could not avoid it, still less could she go through with it. "Militancy" in its infancy and "Militancy" now, in its decrepitude, are the translations into practical effect of her realisation of and her revolt from it.

❦

Whether the "revolting" women will ever move on to the point of acquiring the elements of self-defensive and aggressive force depends on the extent to which the ardour of ambition can survive the depressing effects of the present too realistic presentation of their actual position. In any case, the set of circumstance and environment are against it. *For* it, there is nothing but pride of temper; the same ferment, however, which has been responsible for the rising of every subordinate race and class. If Englishwomen elected to, there exists nothing in themselves to prevent them from being as good a fighting force as the Japanese, for instance: and that would do to be getting along with. What does prevent them is *lack of desire*, and therefore lack of initiative; consequently there is no apparent necessity to make a drive through that heavy inertia which the substantial triumphs of passive womanliness have fostered. They are accustomed to win success almost solely through well-utilised inertia, and the better they succeed as "females," the more encouraged they are to remain inert. The spur of necessity, occasionally, will overcome it; but, lacking that, there is nothing to urge them on, and everything to pull them back. Even status—*women's* status—lies that way. Ninety-nine out of every hundred women can better hope to improve their status by looking to their marriage chances than by "carving a career." Only a personal pride (out of the ordinary), and intelligence, and the unique something which sets straight for individual power, remains to count on. Their possession is rare enough, and even when possessed are to be exercised only if something quite as vital to women can be fitted in alongside. In exchanging the old competence for the new, no women can afford to forego that end which was the main objective of the old competence, and which this earlier proved so superlatively successful in attaining.

28. Cant

"Might is not mocked: it is the one sphere where here the genuine is winnowed from the sham."

"LET us rid our mind of cant": in which sentiment witness the hustle of the popular philosopher. Why rid ourselves of cant? Who knows anything about its uses? May not cant be a necessary utility like clothing: why, then, should we allow ourselves to be hustled into casting it off merely to live up to the exigencies of dramatic oratory? Rather let us dissect: the one safe course to follow in doubling popular heroics back upon popular philosophy. *To chant* is to sing: To cant is to make—anything you please—into a song. The difference between the two is that each directs its emphasis towards a particular and different stage of the vocal process. To chant, *i.e.*, to sing, is to have regard to the actual execution of the arranged harmony. To cant, *i.e.*, the making of a song, concerns itself with the process antecedent to the singing: it is concerned with the construction of the song. Joy in the actual performance is the main attraction of the chant, and the substance and arrangement of the song subserves that. In canting the pleasure is in the substance and arrangement (selective interpretation!) and it is this which the pleasure of canting subserves. The difference between our local "philharmonic" letting itself go on the Hallelujah chorus and Mr. Lloyd George or any other statesman letting themselves go on the causes of the war can be rendered down to this difference.

No one dreams of saying "let us rid ourselves of song!" Why then the difference in acquiescence when one says, "let us rid ourselves of song-making!" It is due to a recognition of the reversal in motive: it is due to suspicion: in a song the words are intended to heighten and increase the pleasure of the singing: in cant, the pleasure of singing is to further and enforce the substance embodied in the words. In the song the expression of emotion is the end. In cant the emotion embodied in the expression is utilised to serve the interests embodied in the words: with intent of making that interest paramount over all other interests. To heighten the importance of a matter by emphasis and reiteration is, in fact, just what the man in the street has always meant when he observed that someone is "making a song" about a matter. "Making a song" is a design to make one aspect of an affair all-absorbing by means of repetition, lilt, rhyme, rhythm: but above all by repetition. The song and cant (motives apart) are identical in this. Consider the common church anthem as an instance: a tag is taken: it is told once or twenty times over in the treble: it is told over again in the bass, and again and yet again in the tenor and contralto: then in twos, then the quartette, then the full chorus: a most pleasurable diversion altogether. And one does not forget that tag in a hurry: it "runs in the head" to the exclusion of all other tags, for days. Cant does the same thing, and is *intended* to. Atrocities, German atrocities, more atrocities, always atrocities, always German, bombs, cathedral-fronts, stained glass, women, prisoners, and so on without end. Cant! The journalists and mob-orators have considered it necessary to "make a song" about these things in order to impress permanently on the British mind the connection between atrocious deeds and a German. Evidently they consider it necessary in order to keep English rage up to the fighting point. Others may think it unnecessary, and only a very poor compliment to boot, but that for the present is a matter of opinion. One might, nevertheless, point out that with all songs at a certain stage there arises such a phenomenon as surfeit, when revulsion does the work of poetic justice and corrects the balance. We seem to be hearing it! Journalists and orators might note.

But to rid ourselves of cant, how can we? And why should we? We can try to be clever at canting and not to allow a possibly useful weapon to be turned to our own disadvantage. Because cant is not the attribute of anyone in particular: everybody cants. Any particular man's cant is his emphasis of his own point of view, which inevitably he seeks to press home by all the agencies within his power, and of which words have become the chief. Consequently, it is open to everyone to accuse any rival of canting. The Kaiser with his deity cants like chanticler: but he is lost besides our shrill roosters at home. The essence of cant is to fill the bill so completely and continuously with the statement of one's own case that the other side's case fails to reach the ear of the populace. We English have no "case" in Germany and Germany has no "case" here. In each country, however, there should be those in power who recognise the scope of cant: that it is only a preliminary defence. *They* assuredly should have heard to the last syllable the whole of their opponent's case in order to gauge the force of egoistic temper behind the force that will further it. It is essential to know the temper of the opposition they will be called upon to meet. Cant is not out of place with the multitude, if it were, it would not go down so well. In truth, it keeps them in good temper with themselves: but it would be fraught with the direst effects if it had influence with those who have to take stock and make plans. For the "masses"

of the stout-heart but unbraced intelligence cant evolves a "battle-cry." It gives consistency to a possibly doubtful faith in the efficacy of the sword: it warms and expands the spirit like an intoxicant: those who fear to lose a point for hocus-pocus by using plain English would say it strengthened the morale. Undoubtedly the war-whoop is cant's primitive and undeveloped ancestor, as the ear-splitting detonation of the big guns is its modern offspring. The intent of both is to put the foe to confusion by bluster to one's own advantage. There is no cause for alarm, therefore, in that the parsonic hosts are placing their pulpits in the market-place, and filling them with cantatists of all orders, exhorting us to mend any small rent which we may have tolerated in our robes of thick British cant. This vigorous species with the bell-like tones may continue to assault the heavens, unique as ever in its lack of guile, too stupid and unselfconscious to be insincere. It would serve if, in the prosecution of their solid business, men are able to put cant in its proper place, and if in national affairs those who are charged with responsibility know at what point its good uses end: limited to fortify one's own spirits, to depressing one's opponents, to winning the applause of the onlookers, and—above all—furnishing our spiritless shibboleths with their natural antidote. In the timid, if piping times of peace, men having created a verbal "Wrong" which they hold to have an existence independent of the weakening of Might, *i.e.*, of Spirit, it behoves them that at times when at all costs that error must be corrected they shall have at hand always a verbal means of escape. Cant enables them to dodge the "Wrong" label and holds it firmly affixed to the brows of their opponents. They *cant* themselves into the right by making a song about it: incidentally drowning for their own side the sound of their opponent's cant, which, be assured, is engaged in the same heartening business in its own behalf. So cant remains a thing of words always, an affair intended for the gallery: useful in its sphere. Its baleful effects begin when it is taken for something fundamental: when it convinces its victims that it seriously affects the issue. When men get into the temper which can sing:

> For Right is Right, since God is God,
> And Right the day must win[1],

cant looks likely to be dangerous. Men are so liable to overlook the subtlety of such a sentiment. "Right" always, as the hymn says, wins the day: that is, Might wins it, and having won it, is automatically invested with its new title of Right. Cant tends to antedate the birth-hour of Right: that is why it proves a snare if its influence spreads into the quarters that matter: into the initiatory quarters. Cant may not, with impunity, penetrate into serious business. There men must look facts squarely in the face if they are to prevent being hit in the face by them. The rough-and-ready effects of cant are out of order here, where success and precise observation belong to each other. In business as in affairs of state, of course, it is quite in the way to attempt to confuse one's rival with cant, if one can safely; but in reviewing ones own case for serious purposes, no.

How far, therefore, men who are seeking to direct affairs on a large scale can manage to utilise the potentialities of cant, and yet keep themselves unspotted from it, becomes a nice question. Certainly by a sort of horse-sense even with

---

[1] ≠ *The Right Must Win* by Frederick William Faber. *Selected Hymns from Faber* (London: W. Isbister & Co. 1874).

the crowd, the man who has least to say carries most weight: certainly with the weighty: but there appears to be no end of good fun in exercising one's power to send thrills down the spines of audiences of thousands by audacious tickling of their vanity: in oratory that is, which orators a bit shame-facedly, it must be confessed, have railed the exercising of a sense of power. Yet there is always a certain feeling of contempt for it: a feeling of the second-rate, and should be left for those "on the climb." Probably it is the uneasy realisation that out of an audience of ten thousand there will be five men who are chuckling under their breath at the spectacle: the five who stand for more than the remaining thousands. One cannot help feeling that, if the itinerant Ministers, now on the rant, had decided to forgo the exhibition of their eloquence, British prestige would have been none the worse, but better rather, and more meriting the onlooker's respect.

Mr. Lloyd George's flamboyant rhetoric about "scraps of paper" (over which effort, by the way, *The Times* gurgled a gleeful half-column of applause), would have come with undiminished dignity only from parsons, ecstatic novelists, and journalists. Coming from a responsible person it flecks the brilliance of feats of arms with the dimness of unintelligence. Yet from beginning to end it is a triumph in the art of covering up one's opponent's point: it is first-rate cant in fact, glowing with the speaking, forming, and colour of the picturesque. "Have you any Bank-notes? What are they? Scraps of paper! Made from rags! Tear them up! Burn them!" subserves exquisitely the arranged anti-climax that these have the "credit of the British Empire behind them!" It is in the choice of the anti-climax that the full artistry of cant is revealed: for does not the opponents' whole case turn upon the fact that it is just the credit of the Empire that is being questioned? If the *Might* of the British Empire failed to be reasserted on the spot the "credit of the Empire" would be rapidly run down to the level of rags and scraps of paper. Let a German government establish itself in London, and Mr. George's enraptured audience will swiftly apprehend the connection between "armed force" and "the credit of the Empire"—this or any other.

The Times, which on the eve of war was a valuable national asset, is now disporting itself in ungainly fashion trying to win the favours of the verbalist host whose influence it was mainly instrumental in overcoming two months ago. One must see in it another of the multitudinous uses of cant it is to be supposed! Having broken the pacifist temper from its moorings in the first place, it seeks now by a gentle impersonal chiding of pacifism subtly combined with encouragement and judicious personal flattery of pacifists, to manœuvre them past the impending danger of making an outcry for an early peace. In keeping with its present tactics, it has delivered itself afresh on the "meaning of the war." The war is, it says, "when reduced to its simplest expression—a struggle between false and true standards of life." It piously proceeds, "We stand for a principle that no might can, in the long run, maintain itself, unless it be founded on some moral law." The "some" is delicious: it is so safe: so safe that the leader-writer concludes that here he can do no better than leave it. If he developed his point he needs would require to enlarge on the "ethical law," and doubtless he has a strong premonition that, when formulated, his ethical law would bluntly run

"Might is right." At least we gather as much when a little further on he plaintively—or is it satirically—delivers himself thus: "The people of this country have hitherto lived in the touching faith that, sooner or later, it is truth that tells. They have not only neglected," ... etc., etc.—neglected, that is, to keep their powder dry by matching German "News" agencies with similar British "News" agencies, and out of his own text it is easy to double back on the pious sentiment of his first paragraph, and adapt its phrases to fit the model of "Ye perfect English." "Prussianised Germany," he says, "has staked her existence upon the claim that might is right, with the corollary that Prussian might gives the measure of others' right." Adapted, this would run, "England has had, reluctantly, and in spite, of mumbo-jumbo, to confess that her 'right' to existence as foremost nation is staked upon her ability to refurnish the 'might' to prove it. Having proved it, the corollary follows that English might will give the measure of others right." It is a curious historical phenomenon to find two paramount nations with such completely identical characteristics. In their ambitions, their cant, they are one. Only the difference in their *Might* will define and divide them.

There are arguments used, however, which it would perhaps be paying too great a compliment to describe as cant. They are too obviously just erroneous observations. If one said that two and two made three, it would not be cant: but just a silly mistake. Of such is the orators' argument that we oppose "material force" with "spiritual might." All directed forces are the outcome of the spiritual: that is, animated by the living spirit. A gun, an airship, all the material appurtenances of war are aggressive evidence that spirit has been previously at work. The army of the veriest tyrant is all composed of the workings of mastering *spirit*. It is not the material which has made and makes them formidable, but *spirit*. Those who look contemptously on the material forces of armies, and call them material, have the eyes which see not. A big dream, shared and toiled for by millions, is embodied in those devised means of aggression. The Might of a force is indeed the measure of the amount of spirit, just as submission and unwilling preparations are the measure of the lack of it. If we are subdued by the German host it will be because *their* spirit has been greater than our own. It is because of the great spirit of the German that he animates material with which to measure himself against the world. It is a great-souled thing to do: not lightly to be undertaken because not lightly to be abandoned. The world should see to that: as it will if it has the spirit. Which is why talk of peace, before events have revealed unmistakably the victors and the conquered, is childish. To challenge the world to a test of might is not a matter to be regarded airily, but a matter of life and death: as much so to the nation as to the individual. To know that this is so, is to hold the automatic check on irresponsibility and foolhardiness. Might is not mocked: it is the one sphere where the genuine is winnowed from the sham.

Nearer to the spirit of good cant is the surmise of the orator that the struggle is to espouse the "ideals of freedom against the oppression of the Iron Heel"—Iron Heel presumably meaning, "armed force." A politician, or any professional deceiver can always count on doing good cant-business if he flourishes the word "freedom" well enough. That is because there is an utter lack of comprehension as to the meaning of the word "free." The word "free," in fact, charming as to sound as it is, for explicitness is a word too many: it is the redundancy responsible for abortive attempts without number in social aspirations. The "free" and the "powerful" are one. When one has the power to encompass a certain end, one is "free" to do it: not before. To be free means no more than that—to be powerful in any particular direction specified: but the aspect which needs engraving on the human consciousness is that it means no less: the spurious "freedoms"—"liberties" graciously allowed, without the *power* to enforce them if withheld: all that long list of "rights" held by powerless, enfranchised masses: these are the poor things, the winning of which makes the history of centuries: they are the liberties of sheep, of domestic beasts of burden: they have little or nothing to do with free men—men of power—capable of self-defence, forces to be reckoned with.

29. Tempo

"The only kind of revolt which is worth while: an individual's revolt against his own failure to exploit the nature of things."

PURSUANT on the notes on "cant" in the last issue[1]: it is not merely repetition reduced to a harmony which secures the effects: not merely what one says but the way one says it. Tempo and distribution of emphasis have effects equal to that of the prominence given to the substance of the tag. For instance, how a few months ago the "best minds in England" would not have been able to offer you any more scathing epithet to apply to the "disciplinary forces of order" than "Cossacks." They would hurl it with a tense-drawn face and with all the belief in the efficacy of its sibilants of the villain of melodrama. That was before the Cossacks became our interests' very good friends: now that this damaging force is for us we say "Cossacks!" in that tone of deferential admiration which recognises in them the finest mounted force in Europe. The consideration which has transformed this brickbat into a bouquet is the sense that now it serves our interests: the unfailing criterion according to which we decide to label distinction, fame or notoriety. Now add tempo to selectiveness, repetition, harmony, intonation, and emphasis and you possess the recipe for concocting the impressive presentment of the orator, which is cant. Tempo is the most important ingredient of the "Impressive," as might be illustrated by the case of the church organist who was in the habit of working up his congregation to the highest pitch of awe and devotion by effects achieved from the voluntary *Pop Goes the Weasel*

---

[1] ≠ Volume I Number 19 (October 1st, 1914).

taken at slow tempo. The slow and measured diction of the Impressive is not an accident: it is part of its substance.

The ordinary human animal, as a matter of fact, is not as obvious as at first sight he appears. He has left his soul naked neither to his enemies nor to his neighbours. The cheap and handy means of cant he has converted into the bricks, laths and plaster with which he builds himself a house of refuge. If his spiritual house is even more ramshackle and jerry-built than the one in which he shelters his person, it nevertheless often serves him a very good turn as a protection: of which form of protection Public Opinion is not the least. Its protective effects carry just as far as it can continue to produce the impressive, i.e., the illusion of weight; with those, however, who go beyond the impression and take to measuring its weight by force, it proves to be something less of a protection than a house of lath and plaster: it reveals itself an affair of wind and words shot with the lurid flashes of atmosphere which oratory can create. It proves a mirage. At the approach of those who are primed for violence it vanishes. Cant—the haven of the feeble has this defect: it attracts those who are least in a position to rely on it. It has this advantage: it screens the eyes of the feeble from the danger which impends: it gives the comfort of safety in the midst of the perilous: it also allows to the strong, relief from the former's prying questioning as to the intent and possible effects of the latter's activities. It is potent to comfort and to inflate confidence for a period, to deceive for a period, to attract into alliance a few impressed ones may be; and when real business is on foot, where strong and genuine interest meet, it knows better than to intrude: it does not hamper the ground; it vanishes like a spent breath.

It is like those accommodating people who recognise their "place": they are great guns in the kitchen, but shrink to suitable dimensions in the presence of their betters.

❦

It is in virtue of the vast extensions it has made in the realms of cant that the period through which we are living is called "The Verbal Age." It has accepted the given pieces as valid material for building purposes with the unquestioning acceptance of a child of its toys. It has sought to "specialise" as the "Constructive" age, and in the diverting task of manipulating its ready-made materials it has drugged its adventurous energy into a tamely pleasant submission.

Delineation of the "ways of men," delineation without comment, is out of the question: the constructive ideal interposes itself between observers and what they would observe. When the ways "ought" and "ought not" to be such and such it addles the mind of the observer to be confronted with what they actually are. So they dispense with things as they are and soar loftily into the "ideal!" Psychology is a farce because it must be "constructive" too: mental scheme-spinning is the limit to which psychology aspires or can hope to aspire as long as words pass non-suspect. Minds clogged up with the cheap and all too handy set-systems of words cannot generate the steady force which emotional analysis requires. What view must a mind take, of forces—their origin, course or tendency, when it is withering with rage against them, not because they are hostile, but because they are "wrong." If they are "wrong" the inference waits to follow: that being wrong they are not there: the "should not" promptly is made more valid than the "are." Forces accordingly burst in upon this verbal plane as disruptive forces—all uncalculated for and sinning blasphemously against the Holy Ghost, because they have grown athwart the spirit of the scheme: unconcernedly spoilt the mosaic.

It cannot be expected to be otherwise: a matter-of- fact statement as to existent forces could be listened to only as the out-pourings of the children of Beelzebub: the mental currents which carry in them the momentum of habits of thinking of generations cannot be doubled back on themselves and set in an opposing direction without giving rise to a troubling of the waters. The solvent acid of analysis cannot be set working in this age of "Causes" and "Movements" without causing heart-burnings, and causes and movements are as far as this age attempts to go. The two run together: a cause is a form of activity energised by a slogan: which ensures it going thus far and no farther, the slogan being the form of speech which is intended to dam up thinking, while a movement mentally necessitates a standing still: a pause before the fixed idea. Analysis would gobble up the war-cry and the inhibited mental processes would flow on, overwhelm the stationary idea, and put an end to the "Cause." War-cries exist only because they are protected from analysis: as ice exists only by being protected from heat. Slogans and analysis require to be kept apart: an analysed war-cry is a contradiction. The workings of an analytic spirit in this pretty-pretty age of "problems" and catch-words would mean devastation. It would produce only such a solution of the "problems" as fire would with the problems set out on the chess-board: solve them by destroying them: the last thing to be desired by the posers of problems. Only by keeping the catch-word intact can the problem with its accompanying "cause" be made permanent, and the to-do about verbalities kept up. And failing verbalities only forces remain, and force is too violent, unmanageable, unimpressible by oratory, to hold anything save horror for a delicate age.

Turned, for instance, on that problem of "emancipation," analysis reveals this alluring seducer of the energies of centuries with a clarity which the lovers of liberty—the friends of freedom—can ill brook. It appears as yet one other of the screens of illusions by which cant veils the harder necessities: and emancipators as the comforting deceivers of the people. Yet many of the "saviours of the people" are earnest, and would learn, if they could, why the efforts of the freedom-winners result ever in a flow and ebb of achievement which mounts onward only to draw back. By seeking after a freedom which is not synonymous with powerdom, but which it is tacitly and otherwise implied to be, they encourage the unintelligent revolt against the "nature of things," but not the only kind of revolt which is worth while: an individual's revolt against his own failure to exploit the nature of things. They would appreciate the difference if they saw it, but between them and the vision stands the opaque Word.

30. Arms and Disarmament

"In order to fight greatly one needs must desire greatly."

[...] THE fact that civilised authorities discourage their peoples from having enemies except such as they themselves duly authorise, goes a long way towards revealing the actual nature of civilisation. We quoted above[1] a writer who believed that the common sense of the world opines there is something antagonistic between civilisation and gunpowder (by which latter is meant, we may assume, armaments on the modern enormous scale). Yet, as we pointed out, the big gun has the appearance of being the greatly prolific progenitor of just those forms of society which we call civilised. And inevitably, settled peace is the display of force so unmistakably irresistible that it is not within the limits of possibility for the conquered powers to gainsay it. Force—a force that is—asserts and establishes itself. It is now, therefore, in the ascendant: it makes known its will: which is now the sole dominant will: it delineates its own conception of the forms its expressed will desires to take; that is, it outlines its species of order. It lays this conception of its order on the conquered, demanding for its execution an unquestioning obedience and for guidance in carrying it into being effectively and smoothly it frames laws. A law is a command accompanied by a threat, in case of refusal, to use all or any of the forces of compulsion which it is known or assumed are at the disposal of the framers. It can be taken for granted that a community in which the laws are accepted without

---

[1] ≠ "Disarmament has been apparently just, the slogan of a 'cause' intending to imply no more than the pious application to international affairs of Mr. Watts' sentiment in regard to little children—little nations should agree and keep their angry passions down." *The Egoist* Vol. I No. 21 (November 2nd 1914).

question—which is highly civilised, that is—has its forces of compulsion in effective condition and well under the influence of those at whose inspiration the laws are made. To say that "the individual does not suffer in honour or interest because law has replaced violence in his social relationship," is to give evidence of complete incomprehension of the question at issue: law does not replace violence: it merely gives information detailing the manner in which violence will be directed. If one can manage to square one's honour and interest with the incidence of violence, well and good: if not, *tant pis*: one meets the violence. On this wise is the only authorised enemy of civilised society discovered to us, *i.e.*, the flouter and disturber of the "Law and Order" ordained by the paramount: disturbers of the peace, which has been commanded by the force which commands the most effective gunpowder. The gentle ways and modes of civilised society take rise in precisely the same manner as similar phenomena appear among children of a stern parent who likes an ordered peace in his house and is powerful enough to see that he gets it. The children do not quarrel among themselves because "Father" finds it a confusion and an annoyance. Quarrelling upsets his "Order": the rebellious child is the domestic criminal.

It is, therefore, easy to trace how the possession of forceful and successful arms affords to a great power (particularly in these modern times of enormous armaments, whose very enormity puts them beyond the possession of the people, and makes the State the obvious custodian) the basis upon which it can begin to build its particular brand of civilisation. Freed by its power from gainsaying both from without and within, such a State has leisure and authority to call into being an "Ordered

Society," to become civilised that is. An ordered society means precisely what it says—a society which shapes itself in conformity with the orders given by the manipulators of the armed forces in its midst: orders which, described as laws, perforce the people must obey. For no large body of people, apart from unusual moments of danger, obey orders unless the possibility to do otherwise does not lie in their possession. Such a condition of deficient power can only be effected by a body which is by comparison superiorly armed. A State possessing formidable and centrally-controlled armaments, with which the defensive weapons of those whose obedience is demanded cannot hope to compete, is precisely this body. Such a State commands just the conditions necessary to the laying down of orders which will effect peaceful submission between itself and its peoples, and if it so desires—and it usually does—peace among the individuals one with another, whose differences must be settled through its own appointed media. It can afford to take up the position that it will "stand no nonsense" in regard to disorder between individual and individual: can afford to insist on the regulation of social life by civil means, *i.e.*, by means of vicarious violence. Individuals may settle and arrange matters among themselves only within limits: by verbal or written means. Violence remains the prerogative of the State. Such is the basis of civilisation, and it explains what civilisation is the expression of: *i.e.*, enforcement by violent compulsion of ways of settlement among a governed people who have been deprived of any power of gainsaying such external settlement by a previous deprival of arms. It is this settling of intra-individual affairs by civil means which is called Justice. "Civilisation must rest not upon gunpowder but upon Justice." Well, well: it amounts very much to the same thing! "I rest not upon this planet but upon this couch." Though civilisation depends upon Justice, Justice depends upon gunpowder, and civilisation therefore depends upon gunpowder ultimately. It is, as a matter of fact, however, a favour allowed in charity to the rhetoricians to admit that civilisation rests upon Justice: Justice and civilisation—abstractions both at best—are not two things but one. Civilisation is rather related to Justice as a special case. It is Justice in limited and secondary application. Basic Justice is coincident with gunpowder.

If, then, Justice fails the would-be disarmers: if Justice be not some transcendant and archetypal figure enthroned in the heavens before Earth or Time was, but, as far as civilisation is concerned, merely the internexus of guarantees for contracts of which the nature is conditioned by the arbitrament of arms, on what other supports may disarmament fall back? Two for their support have been furnished: a rationalist and a theocratic: the authority of "The World" and of "God." Both are passionately espoused, and naturally, for support for a task stupendous and baffling cannot be lightly foregone. Note what the task is on which the disarmers have set their hearts: it is the acquiring of supreme instruments of compulsion in order to overcome compulsion while yet anathematising compulsory instruments. They would themselves compel all men else to believe that compulsion is "wrong." Hitherto compulsion has always led to armaments, but what now when compulsion would compel towards disarmaments? If all others are to be compelled not to arm at all, some authority must arm itself very efficiently. The power which undertakes to abolish Napoleonism will need to be very greatly and grandly Napoleonic. So this thing runs in a circle: Napoleonism is ever under the curse yet ever triumphant, ever to be brought under the heel yet ever on the heights. Hence the attempt to create a Napoleonic power which need fear no rival: The World. It is odd how at every great crisis "reason" reverts to this fetish of "The World versus The Recalcitrant": odd because in every attempt to apply it "The World" itself furnishes the subversive elements which make the rebel triumphant; "The World," in fact, cannot be the Super-Napoleon because "The World" cannot hang together. Napoleonism represents a progressive cohesion, while "The World" is the loose and disparate sum-total of disintegrating differences. It is unable to cohere: a poor opponent, therefore, for even a lilliputian Napoleon. One is compelled to realise that "The World" does not mean what it would imply, but relies for its impressiveness upon its good comprehensive, sound. On a closer scrutiny "The World" appears one of those all inclusive generalisations which mean nothing because they aspire to mean everything. What does "The World" mean to any of us? Who stands for "The World?" One could almost as readily develop a partisan ardour in favour of a constellation as become enthusiastic over "The World." Even the religions which were founded to "save" "The World" in order to wake an interest were compelled to split it up to furnish a portion which could be assigned to damnation. In fact, interest can live only upon difference, and those who have argued that because out of "The World" many States have been carved they can, therefore, by a simple process of addition, collect the States together and obtain for "The World" the united coercive power of all the States' "virtues" in order to annihilate in each all their particular vices, and all to the glory of the unified creation called "The World," have strayed lamentably in their reckoning. States are States (nationalities if one prefers so to call them), not because they are alike but because they are different. They exist not to accommodate what their neighbours consider their virtues, but the traits they consider their vices. All splits take place in order to allow the vices of the secessionists a better run. Adding secessionists (*i.e.*, States) together to make a unified "World" can only be expected to produce effects procurable by mixing together, say, saltpetre with sulphur and charcoal: a nasty explosion. A nation acquires its dominant characteristics far more by what it excludes than by what it includes, and to this extent it is the embodied expression of the motive which is common to any other form of grouping. A group is formed in order to keep out the crowd: as in the case of club membership, of which it is precisely its powers of exclusion which distinguishes it from the fair-ground or the street.

The rationalist notion of an all-coercing "world-power" affords an excellent example of the floundering of cantatists. With all their desire to hit upon a fine-sounding justification for this strange new passion of great States for small ones, their wits seize upon all the fakes and omit the sole genuine one, *i.e.*, that their lives in human nature an instinct which renders involuntary admiration to the small power putting its fortunes to the risk in order to rise: that there exists in men an involuntary admiration for the signs of growth. While it is a misleading folly to encourage small States to believe that they have any justification except such as they can assert at the sword's point, it is an equal folly not to calculate that a small State putting up a likely fight to ease its growing pains will exercise an enormous pull on the affections of the onlooker: not, of course, so much with the elderly party in authority whose interests its insurrectionary activity is flouting—but with the bystanders. Otherwise there is no justification for small States apart from the fact that their existence serves the interests of a greater by whose will alone they are enabled to live.

Small States might, indeed, be considered as the women in international polity. As with women, their status is not defined at first hand by their own intrinsic strength: they find their value in the fact that their existence chances to be useful to some other power who on this account accords them a courtesy status. Their "rights" are in virtue of the needs of the mightier, and are enjoyed by permission until such changes take place in the hang of things as may make their continued existence unnecessary: whereupon their "rights" shrivel to the dimensions of their virtual merits: to their might. For instance, the right of Denmark, Belgium, and Holland to exist lies in the fact that their existence as buffers is very useful to England. Their "rights" will dwindle very materially should Germany–to whom their existence is the reverse of a necessity—become the superior power: a fact which the King of the Belgians is doubtless very well aware.

Accordingly, this creation of the "World" as supreme authority possesses little with which to attract men who have not the itch for airing theories in newspapers. They do not incline towards investing it with coercive powers strong enough to reduce all other powers to a state of feebleness at which resistance becomes impossible. With a man of Mr. Roosevelt's temperament matters will appear different. Mr. Roosevelt elects to put the nostrum "The World versus the Recalcitrant" under his patronage, and it is ill-luck that contemporary history should so blatantly thrust forward its refuting commentary.

Mr. Roosevelt calls for a world-police which shall secure the peace of the world... to supplement and make effectual "a world agreement among all civilised and military powers to back righteousness by force." It should be "solemnly covenanted that if any nation refused to abide by the decision of such a court the others would draw the sword on behalf of peace and justice, and would unitedly coerce the recalcitrant nation[1]." Now, what save the adhesion of the United States to the side of the Allies is missing from this picture of a world-agreement backing "righteousness by force" in the state of affairs existant to-day. The "World" minus the United States is coercing recalcitrant Germany: with what ultimate effect it still lies too far within the veil of the future to see. But if Mr. Roosevelt imagines that the stepping in of the United States would make the desired difference and change the existing bloody spectacle into one of friendly peace one would make bold to say that he is enormously mistaken, for the reason that though he calculates the number of heads he miscalculates human nature. The spectacle of Germany to-day facing her enemies—Belgium under her foot, France held with her teeth, her right arm holding Russia and her left England, while from far beyond she can catch the swelling sound of foes trooping from every continent, Japan, Canada, Australia, India, South Africa, New Zealand—is tolerably

---

[1] ≠ 'The World War: Its Tragedies and Its Lessons' by Theodore Roosevelt. *The New Outlook* (September 23rd, 1914).

heroic. Should the United States ally itself with Germany's enemies (if for the sake of illustration such a combination may be contemplated), then whether because of the fact that "Germany against the World" is too heroic a figure for human pride to tolerate her annihilation without a suffering from its own self-contempt; or whether because of a certain sympathy which always lurks in the under-world for the bravely beaten; or because of a new-born jealousy of the world-power itself when freed of its most serious rival—on account of some or all of these causes "Germany against the World" will prove that the World is a less formidable foe for Germany than the present combination of the Allies. The Alliance swollen with the adhesion of the United States would be far more likely to tip over on the right side for Germany than the existent Alliance. The disintegrating forces of the enormous collectivity—The World—would begin to dissolve out of it, and to its own detriment.

The concept of the "World" in addition to that of "Justice" both proving illusory as forces towering high above national and Imperial gunpower, what is there existent over and above the State powerful enough to compel the pugnacious ones to fall back in contented mediocrity and love? Nothing save the guns of one State to silence the other. The query presents a problem for human ingenuity, and this latter has not failed of a solution for lack of making attempts of which the conception of the theocratic State, the State coerced by Moral Suasion: by the Ghostly Police: by the Inner Voice: by the God over All, remains alive and paramount.

The vision of the King of Kings, whose vice-regent is Conscience, whose Ambassador is the Inner Voice, and whose ordinances are "Right," is the most audacious as well as the most subtle effort of human ingenuity: it is so ingenious that one might say "ought" to "work." It does work exquisitely and impressively in rhetoric. There is one voice only against it: that of experience. Unfortunately that voice is decisive: because it is in experience that the scheme is required to work. And therein the Omnipotent One is quite notably powerless. All experience has to tell of how the Omnipotent is worsted. His incursion into practical matters is therefore limited to an invocation of the "Great Name." He can scarcely attain even to the establishment of an identity. Men commandeer their enemies' God as their own devil, while in complementary return they may see their own similarly installed among the enemy and Jehovah interchanges with Baal. A like impotence is to be observed of the Omnipotent's Ambassador—the Inner Voice. It fails to make sound just where in its own interests its self-assertion is vital. It makes itself heard just where it can matter little whether it speaks or remains silent. Its purpose being to restrain the Napoleons, it yet flourishes only in the non-Napoleons: a Napoleon being by definition one constitutionally incapable of hearing an Inner Voice. The spell of two thousand years of Christianity has its testimony to add to the evidence of other theocracies: *i.e.*, that its gospel is powerful as a working principle with the powerless.

Christians are not, however, to be dismayed because their creed works only by opposite in experience: if experience fails to embody the theocracy, so much the worse for experience.

Experience, *i.e.*, the tale of the world, the flesh and the devil—must be repudiated: ignored by a World-authority established in a Kingdom beyond the World[1]. Christianity sets forward with undiminished energies to win the "World" for Christ. Intelligently it makes a bid for men's hearts, intelligently, because there the egoistic desires which cause all wars are born. The Christ is for peace and desires born of hearts that are Christ's must faint at birth. By negating desire the rivalry born of the struggle to satisfy desire, is forestalled. In order to fight greatly one needs must desire greatly. At that low-toned level at which one has little enough of desire as to be ready to suffer all violence and yet to offer none, one has arrived at the crux of the disarmament question. A theocracy, therefore, of the Christian cast accepted by all the world is undoubtedly its one solution. Since Christianity beseiges and seeks to conquer the Force whose power is above the State, prior to it, and has the shaping of all States and all secessions from States which make up "the World," Christ conquers the World: He silences the desires of men in which lurks the power which towers high above all States. These, silenced, the warring cries which accompany the ever fluctuating struggle of men with men and State with State will be hushed. The peace which indeed passeth all human understanding since it is the peace of the grave holds sway: a Thought without a thinker reigns silently over Nothingness[2]. Disarmament more drastic than that which starts from the socket is accomplished: it has started from the heart. When the heart has been drugged no need remains for lopping off the arm. The dilemma has been evaded and all other dilemmas with it...

---

[1] ≠ "*Tria autem sunt quae nos tentant, caro, mundus, diabolus.*" Pierre Abélard *Opera hactenus seorsim edita nunc primum in unum collegit textum*, 1849.
[2] ≠ Philippians 4:7.

Otherwise Napoleonism reigns supreme: its efficient moderator is a world of Napoleons with whom desire is great and rampant.

31. From Gunpowder to Politeness

"The cloak of civilisation, to secure to its wearers
its advantages and yet to prove innocuous to them,
must perforce carry a 'barbarian' lining."

IT may seem a long way from gunpowder to politeness, which, for most people, is a synonym for civilised dealing. To explain civilisation without explaining politeness is, for them, to leave civilisation unexplained: as though one should consider the art of the sculptor to finish with the blasting of the block-marble, without concern for the chisel-work which actually constitutes its distinctive character. Yet blasting and chiselling are parts of the one process, though the one is prior to the other: and gunpowder and politeness stand in a like relation to civilisation. Before men become material suitable for polishing, for civilising, they needs must be reduced to maniable conditions by harsher methods of treatment: and it is primarily this prior reduction which separates the civilised from the barbarian.

The barbarian is the outsider: the one which has not begun to be submitted to the polishing process of a specific order. Thus, there is nothing absolute about barbarian or civilised: always it is a matter of point of view: it is the outsider which is the "barbarian" from the outsider's point of view. No race can appear barbarians to themselves, because, from their point of view, they are insiders: that is, they have been submitted to the particular dominating power which governs them.

❦

Accordingly, it is not an accident which makes politeness an accompaniment of any strongly established class, and boorishness a trait found, if found, in the dominated. Politeness is the progressive utilisation of the subjected material in the manner to which the nature of subjected material most readily lends itself. It is an intelligent, adaptation of means to ends, once the great assumption of subjection has been accepted as a fact. Politeness is the smooth gloss which disguises precisely this fact: boorishness is its painful obtrusion through the smoothly-spread veneer. "To bury the hatchet," "to let sleeping dogs lie," is the sentiment which animates politeness and civility. The intent being to secure smooth working for the dominant and a soothed complacence in the dominated. It serves so well that it always achieves good repute among those who create good reputations, *i.e.*, among the dominant, and so manages to get an overwhelming amount of prestige behind it. According as the sense of class remains sound among the dominant, its observance towards inferiors is regarded as *de rigueur*. The sentiment of *noblesse oblige* is one of the exigences of healthy dominant-class interests. Among equals politeness is merely a convenience of variable utility. For the dominated it presents a different aspect. Its exercise is based upon a soother complacence, an instinct for safety, whereas boorishness is a kicking against the pricks. It is disliked by the dominant because of its inconvenience, while it is despised by the dominated because of its futility. It is the harping on the existence of a sore which cannot be healed, but which may be forgotten or ignored: it is a refusal to accept with grace what cannot be resisted with effect: it is the attribute of the "grouser" and "kill-joy," achieving all the pains but not the joys of the rebellious. The "little less," by which the boorish fall short of effectual reassertion, makes him just something less than even an unsuccessful rebel: it is merely a satisfaction of temper to no purpose, and it looks unintelligent because it succeeds only in defeating itself and proclaiming its defeat. President Kruger represents one thing: but General Beyers, might one say, represents something considerably less: they are the rebel and the boor. The difference is constituted by the difference in their chances of success.

"Civilised dealing" with the dominated then is the extended application of the fact that every condition of things has a better and a worse side according to the spirit in which one accepts it: the spirit which seeks to find in all things—compensations. With the dominant, on the other hand, it is the realisation that compensation for the dominated must be emphasised at all costs. For both, it is the utilisation of that dual aspect of appearances which makes them appear the right side upwards which ever way they fall. On this same duality, "good" manners are based as well as diplomacy and sound policy. For, if there are "Overs" there must be "Unders": and each will distil from its condition its own comfort: diplomacy is the sensitive touch which feels for the fitting one to be brought into relief at the apposite time.

It is a limited intelligence which can "tell the tale" only in one way. An intelligence has not grasped the simple elements of any situation until it can tell it forth in at least two; even the dual-telling process itself must be described dually as Duplicity or Diplomacy as the case needs. It is part of the weight of stupidity which seems to settle upon civilised States when they become afraid of the sound of the words "duplicity" and "diplomacy" while yet enlarging on the merits of civilisation. Such fear plainly argues that they have become the victims of the particular form of duplicity which constitutes civilisation—have lost their way, in fact, between one story and another. It seems that the cloak of civilisation, to secure to its wearers its advantages and yet to prove innocuous to them, must perforce carry a "barbarian" lining. The outcry for frankness from the upholders of civilisation is like the plaint of one who thinks he is bent on a good game of cards though he clamour for a preliminary exposure of the players' hands. Polite, civilised society means a society which tacitly disavows frankness. Civilisation deals in superficialities only, but is none the less important for that. Nine-tenths of the experiences of life work their course out along a surface of superficialities, and it is as absurd to depreciate superficialities as it would be to despise the surface of the earth: one can appreciate the value of the external crust and yet remain cheerfully aware that a few thousand miles within the crust conditions are distinctly different, and that if one is going to have to do with these interior conditions quite other preparations will need to be taken from those which are necessary for activities on the surface. So, politeness—the methods of civilisation—fare well enough within the limits of a fixed and accepted status: within the orbits that is of recognised State Orders, but where these themselves are in question the cry for "civil" methods is simply absurd.

The evidence of the stupidity's existence among our over-civilised of to-day–the stupidity which is innocuous only when limited to the claque, but quite seriously undermining when it spreads to the dominant-class, is not confined to such *ni-aiseries* as "equal rights" as between the civil and military castes, or between men and women; it emerges, unconscious and unfaked, in complete unmistakability in the democratic demand for an "open" Foreign Policy: for a complete diplomatic explicitness. "Diplomatic explicitness" is an amusing combination if it is examined well enough: a direct contradiction, in fact, being an "unfolded folding-together." A paramount Imperial foreign policy, of necessity, is diplomatic, duplex, making great show of one set of cards in order to keep rival suspicions asleep as to the existence of those on which she actually relies for success. A "frank" statement of what an Imperial Foreign Office seeks to establish and maintain in its foreign relations would prick into activity just that sleeping pride of foreign nations which it has been the burden of its labours to lull. Imperial "frankness," far from avoiding war, would bring an Empire's rival buzzing about its ears with the animus of a disturbed nest of wasps. On the other hand, diplomatic "frankness" on the part of an ambitious "rising" State would find its analogy in, and would receive the treatment accorded to, the boorishness of the private individual. A rising nation requires to be actually "risen" before it can be diplomatically frank (*i.e.*, dispense with diplomacy) with safety. Unless a nation is in a position to fight so irresistibly as to command a frankness to match its own, it must needs match guile with guile. Otherwise it is likely to find half the world arrayed against it: which is not a healthy sign, but one which argues crudeness and unfamiliarity with the ways of dominating power. In short, a nation's policy can safely be "frank" only when it is practically certain of the issue in reverting to that "extension of policy" which is an appeal to force, and there exist grounds for so many miscalculations in regard to the issues of force that even then diplomacy can be laid aside only with reserve. The susceptibilities of the stupid making up nine-tenths of Public Opinion: the diplomacy of those who own even the biggest battalions will need to keep a reverting eye to that. In these days of a world-extended Press particularly, though in war the sword is still supreme arbiter, the number of times it must strike can be enormously increased by effects due to scratches of the pen. If, for instance, Napoleon had been proclaimed world-ruler in advance of his insidious growth, his warned and alarmed foes would have scotched his career before Napoleonism had the chance to work itself out. But it became established long before the world was half aware what a Napoleon was. A pre-acclaimed Napoleon has a task before him infinitely larger than ever was Napoleon's.

32. Freedom

"Strictly, 'I am free to' means 'My power is able to.'"

NOW that one may hear "freedom" applauded loudly in high places, one may speak a few words in mild reason about it and its friends—those loquacious "wee frees." The world is composed of these, plus the freedom resisters: The difference by which one may know them is that while both may shout "Freedom" on the ecstatic note, the resister will say "'Freedom!' *and we are it*," while the friends of freedom can merely say "Freedom! Ah, would that it were ours." Resisters keep their references to freedom for rare occasions when stirred to emotion by their own greatness, goodness and general self-satisfaction—as now. The friends of freedom, however, never cease from their crying: the wail after that freedom which is not theirs, is their meat by day and night: if one may be generous and call a smell of a roast meat. Did one not know the sickening effects of satisfactions deferred, one could humorously jeer at these ineffectual desirers, who have come to regard the attitude of supplicants as a credit and an ornament. Instead of jeers, therefore, one accords them pity: whereon their pride is in being pitiful. Their relation to "Freedom" is like that of some humble admirer who adores from afar, endowing the unfamiliar one with all the charms of the unknown, though wholly unconscious of their character: even of the qualities which make their charm for those familiar with their ways.

It would not seem that the foregathering of supplicants would be able to offer many very great attractions: yet, oddly enough, the "cause of freedom" wins much capable youth to its flag. Misunderstanding must exist somewhere: a clamour which is the adult equivalent of the infantile howl, requiring no ability beyond lung-power and pertinacity, is not attractive in itself, yet "freedom" attracts, and nothing will suffice to shatter its attraction, until one can stand outside the "Cause" and weigh up its meaning. That alone, damages the veil. Strictly, "I am free to" means "My power is able to," and this meaning, in accuracy, is pertinent to every phase of "free" activity, whether of acquisition, domination, suppression or abandonment. "Being free" is a matter of possession of power, therefore: why then has the "cause of freedom" resolved itself into an onslaught—into endlessly reproachful tirades—against the iniquities of the possessors of power? A most wasteful expenditure of energy on fruitless means! For at what do they aim? They want power, and instead of husbanding carefully what they have, while it grows from little to more, they spend their all in a reproachful demand for the favours of those already in power: in making claims for favours which they call "Rights."

Hear one of their most spirited on the subject "All men *are entitled to* that equality of opportunity, which enables them to be masters of their own lives, and free from rule by others... all men are called on to resist invasion of their equal rights... ," and this, if duly carried out, we are told, "will kill monopoly." Doubtless! Here then is to be found the basis of reproach. Freedom lovers—those desiring a power, not theirs, believe they are "entitled" to the same. Probably the five virgins, whose lamps had no oil, thought they were entitled to the oil in their companions'[1]. This matter of entitlement is the subtlest delusion ever conceived for the confusion of ineffectuals. What

---

[1] ≠ Matthew 25:1-13

can entitle save power—competence? And what can others do to one's competence save ratify its relative effects by their acquiescence! The reproach of the advocates of freedom is that the powerful do not confer on them their power or use it in their interests. This, they believe themselves entitled to demand, and are injured when they are not gratified—these imaginary rights. Looking about for something to base them on, they have hit upon: Consensus of opinion, the opinion of the mob: that multitude of units with powers similar to their own. Consensus of opinion is a very useful thing: a good bludgeon in the hands of the simple, and an easy subject to exploit under the manipulation of the powerful. It frightens the already frightened: the frightful—those whom the freedom-lovers hope to scare off by it—know the very narrow limits of its horrific powers, since they are constantly making use of them for themselves. Consensus of opinion is not going to be of much service to the seekers after grounds of entitlement. On what then do they fall back? They fall back on bluster and the sentimental.

An infant tries to get what it wants by howling vociferously for it. The fuss and inconvenience which it is thus able to make constitute its power. This power is competent, however, only on account of a prior competence: its hold on the affections of its guardians. Howling would receive very short shrift without that: a howling dog would very soon be put out of the way. Now the friends of freedom make bold to raise their clamour, almost wholly on the strength of its inconvenience, unbacked by a corresponding hold on the affections of those who have to put up with it, and under these circumstances the lot of the emancipators, so-called, speaks volumes for the patience and forbearance of the empowered. Perhaps there is a modicum of caution in this too—a faint apprehension that in spite of the evidence to the contrary, the clamour may not limit itself merely to the aggravation of sound: the wailers may have a more adequate competence in process of evolving. Certain it is, however, that the latter have been permitted to clamour for so long, unmolested, that the recognition of their "right" to do so has become one of the main planks of their platform. Any infringement of the "rights" of "free speech," or free assembly is now regarded as sacrilege against freedom. At any attempt to interfere with them there is no end of bluster; yet it is obvious that the bluster must be patently empty. A man stands on a stump on a public place, anathematises the State, in so doing possibly rousing the wrath of most of his audience, as well as the suspicion of the officials of the State. Now his claim for "free" speech is this: the officials of the State against which he is haranguing, shall in the first place protect him from the anger of the populace, and in the second, shall refrain both from preventing him continuing his harangue, and from retaliating with any form of punishment on the count of its own vilification. It is, of course obvious bluster, though, if one carries it off with an air, as one usually can in these word-sodden days, who shall say a word against it? Not we at any rate. Merely, to youths who are interesting and earnest, one would point out that to rely on power of this sort is to rely on the fifth-rate variety, which will let them in at one point or another. Based on a clever word-trick it will succeed here and there, and particularly so when nothing of importance depends on it: but when anything really vital is at stake, the swagger will crumble out and it will shrink to its accurate dimensions. It will then reveal how illusory its former triumphs were.

For instance, when a State does allow the "right" of the various "frees," it is for reasons of interest—its own. Perhaps it realises that discontent, like a rash, is better out than in. It reveals its nature all the better. So, moreover, discontent is given the chance to run itself off in talk. And the stronger the State the more "liberty" it can allow: it need not shatter the first tiny little fist that shakes itself against it. To appear generous tactfully veils the fact how "just" it can be: and when a great State is just to its enemies they realise their lives are not their own: how little then their liberties. It would, therefore, ill accord with a body whose power is so overwhelming to be fussily sensitive in regard to the indiscretions of its wilder members. Free speech forsooth: *allowed* speech, and allowed on the balance of considerations which have nothing whatever to do with the fanciful "rights" of the permitted one. The only speech which could be "free," in the accurate sense, is that of the all-powerful ones: Napoleon might have spoken freely—but he had too much sense. The Kaiser might have accepted a tip in this direction with advantage. And any man who invested his entire interests in the "cause" could be quite "free" in one speech before he died—in his last. In brief: speech, press, assembly, love, all are "free" when they have power enough behind them to foot the bill when the consequences fall due.

Apart, however, from the deluding assumptions based on the word "free" in the popular instance cited in the foregoing, it remains to be pointed out that the word is one of which the actual meaning forbids its being allowed to roam at large. It is meaningless unless limited by a qualification. It is worth while detailing the main features existent in the attitude of mind which makes use of the word "free." Rhetoric apart, when it is used spontaneously, it is always in relation to certain specific spheres of activity in which one considers oneself "free." One is not "free" as regards the "universe," but free in relation to this and that: where this and that represent specific circumstances which can be regarded as potential obstacles. The notion of an obstacle is a salient feature in the state of mind which makes use of the term "free." In the second place, but constituting a still more salient feature, is the notion of possession of power in a degree competent to make the obstacle of non-effect. And in the third there is the element of comparison between the present actual condition where power more than equates obstructions and another condition remembered or imagined in which the powers possessed were not adequate to the effective degree. Now it is because of the fact that anyone of these features can be emphasised to the exclusion of the rest which explains the otherwise puzzling phenomenon which the presence of persons of spirit and intelligence in hopeless entanglement with one or other of the "Freedom" propagandas offers. It explains, moreover, the genesis of these highly differing propagandas. By the features which they chose to ignore or emphasise their relative spiritedness may be gauged. It is, for instance, by a rigorous ignoring of the first feature, *i.e.*, the particularity of application requisite to the meaning of "free," that the numerically strongest battalions of freedom-lovers are recruited. For, by ignoring it, they are enabled to make the meaningless abstraction of which the result is the concept "freedom" itself. They have poured out the precise meaning, and are left with any empty vessel constructed out of the mere label–Freedom: which, like Mesopotamia is a word of good sound.

The sentimental, the gushers, the rhetoricians, orators of all sorts, hypocrites, hangers-on, every brand of human, provided they run easily to slop, rally to augment this goodly lot.

By ignoring the second feature—the actual possession of power as the condition of the "free"—those who are rallied to freedom's cause by the aggrandisement of the "whine" are roped in. They are won by the prospect of apotheosizing "talky-talky": by the big sound of Inherent Rights. The democrats, socialists, humanitarians, anarchists—embargoists of all sorts— row in this galley. This ignoring of the second feature leads naturally to a special emphasising of the third: the emphasis on "conditions." Thus, the particularised character of obstacles which the first variety of freedom-lovers find it attractive to ignore, receives from this last class their entire attention.

A parentally-anxious removal of obstacles becomes the ideal of the modern saviours of society: in fact, the only articulate theory of modern social and political activity works out at just this. What are "democratic" leaders, the "emancipators," concerned with but with their lists of "obstacles to be removed," and the successful invoking of the assistance and assent of the more powerful in the job, for which the power of the masses is inadequate? The essential thing–power in oneself–is waved aside as tainted with the soulless harshness of feelingless drivers. These indulgent, freedom-loving, social grandmothers have not been satisfied with a mere sparing of the rod: they have persuaded the children that it is inhuman to use rods or harbour them. When, for instance, an effective rod appears—as now—in powerful hands, a mellow-tongued friend of freedom—that popular leader of popular causes, emancipator of the people, what not: Mr. Lloyd George tells the people how he has military authority for it that such a rod could only appear in the hands of one possessing the "Soul of the Devil": the retort to which is, of course, "Mind of a Midge!"—argument of kind with kind.

33. Why We are Moral

"Man is the vainest of the animals."

ALTHOUGH—and as we have many times explained—morals are modes of conduct which have become customary, and the intent of the passionate rage in support of the moral is to shield these customs from anything which may cause them to vary, this exposition does not explain why these modes, primarily special and particular, adapted to serve the interests not of All but of a Few should have become customary for All: so much so in fact that the guardianship of morals is in the safest hands when it is left to the fierce partisan feelings of the "Crowd." Before going into the psychology which explains this problem, so perplexing on the surface, it is advisable to indicate a nice distinction which has come to exist between kinds of conduct to which, in popular usage, is given the term "Custom," and conduct equally customary but to which the term morals ordinarily is given.

Custom is habitual conduct, but to the observance of which public opinion attaches small weight either by way of approval or disapproval. The emotion which failure to observe it calls up is, in the main, surprise, not the blind, passionate rage which the bulk of people show at the infringement of morals. Its observance or otherwise is left to individual whim; judgment as to its benefits or disadvantages is left to the caprice of private opinion. It is a habit which lies open and unprotected from vulgar inquiry and personal individual tests of its value. Its valuation is not fixed though its observance be wide-spread and general. What separates Morals from Custom (popular version) is the value which Authority (which commands public opinion) sets upon the habit's significance. If the reference is

to customary conduct of which the continuance is necessary
for the maintenance of the power which keeps the articulate
class in authority, such conduct is carefully extracted from
its association with mere customs and elevated by Authority
to the plane of the Sacred by the laying of the Taboo on
all discussions as to its origin and the fundamental nature
of its motives, so that in time it comes to be regarded as
the Mysterious, the Occult, the Supernatural, the Divine.
Whereas customs are exposed and open to valuation, their
ancestry apparent and their future the possible victim of
whim and caprice, morals are kept unsullied from the common and mundane touch and their origin and valuation one
may question only under pain of becoming impious and a
blasphemer. Naturally many customs are on the fringe between the status of Customs and that of Morals, a fact to
which elegant if delicate young intellectuals owe many hours
of exciting and dangerous sport. The debating clubs of the
Literary and Philosophic Societies and of the Young Men's
Mutual Improvement Society, of the Y.W.C.A.'s, not to mention the Smart Set and the Cranks: what violent intellectual
striving has given these birth if not the desire to settle points
of such cosmic significance as the Right and the Wrong of
church-going, theatre-going, gambling, racing; of those crimes
or larks for women: smokes, bicycles and bloomers, dyed hair
and paint? To decide whether these things belonged to the
go-as-you-please realm of Custom or to that realm which supports the Cosmos high above Chaos—Morals, has provided
occasion for the exercise of the strong and daring young wits
of the last half-century.

This popular distinction between Morals and Custom throws into relief the question which still awaits an answer as regards the genesis of morals.

If men *have* held to custom, common sense is ready to suggest that this is not due to accident, and if customs have been fostered it has been because—sheer ease apart—the results which come from doing so are such as seem to serve their interests best. Did they not, the custom would surely if not speedily have been abandoned. And if not from a prescience of this willingness of men to abandon a custom productive of disappointing results, what other motive would the authorities have had for taking measures to ensure such customs as they consider significant from the possibility of such a fate, by protecting them with that "Mystery" which results in their conversion into Morals. Customs are habits which *may* be kept up. Morals are customs which Authority insists *must* be kept up, good results or no. What, then, is the instinct, primary and fundamental as it must be to have held good for so long, which makes the great mass of people, the governed classes, not merely faithful to morals in face of their ill-effects, but faithful in an ardent and passionate spirit which does not seek to spare either themselves or those near and dear to them? The character and working of the inducements which are responsible for this seeming miracle, reveal how unerring is the instinct which leads men steadily to track down their major satisfactions through a whole complex tangle of conflicting considerations.

348

The basis of any scheme of morals is altruism. The moral claim that its observance, against or in conformity to inclination is for "Good," obviously is prepared to demand the over-riding of the private "good" of him whose inclination is against it in favour of the "good" of those "others" who constitute the All: in which remote good the thwarted one is vaguely enjoined to believe that he will once again refind his own.

An element of strong, if vague, distrust of the belief that one finds one's interest served best in the good of All, does not encourage a close observer to seek for the clue of unswerving moral action in the influence of this generalisation: the Unity of Humanity. One is tempted rather to look about for definite egoistic rewards in altruism itself than to believe there exists so much solid weight in flighty conceptual stretches for the popular intelligence. What, then, does Altruism offer to these egoists of not-too-intelligent an order? On its face value the theory of Altruism appears to be a tactful statement of the case for peaceful submission among the Dominated, and is made current by the powerful egoists who are the backbone of the dominant class what time it suits the latter's interests to remain at peace: that is, while refraining from those more violent forms of competition called war. It is the inculcation of the principle that it is wise to make peaceful terms with, and good friends of, those who have established a dominance by respecting their status, their interests and their wishes. That it is the *dominated* class which practises altruism whereas the dominant practise it only in so far as their necessities, *i.e.*, their interests, permit them, in no way detracts from the weight of evidence which goes to prove its origin among the dominant: it merely supplies additional testimony as to the fine quality of the tact employed in its inculcation. Thus morality, *i.e.*, the habitual practice of altruism made compulsory by Authority and Public Opinion, is part of the great game of egoistic war—the interplay of interests—which ebbs and flows ceaselessly wherever life is. In that warfare, however, morality represents such a distinction as to method that it is convenient to label it separately and allocate it to a niche of its own. Morality is the mode of warfare made use of during the "civil" periods, its *rôle* corresponding to the physical slaughter which is the mode when the warfare of civilisation gives place to a special kind of warfare ordinarily called war. The difference consists in the substitution of weapons—of Words in place of Armaments. The nature of moral warfare necessitates a sort of seige-action in place of the aggressive physical assaults of armed warfare. The moral concepts fence round the authoritarian class as effectually as, if not more than, concrete fortifications do a city; the action of these Sacred Words being not so much to withstand the savagery of an onslaught as to paralyse the forces of the enemy before he can lift up an arm against them.

Their effect, handled as Authority tactfully handles them, amounts to that of hypnotism: results not however due to a brilliantly conceived, conscious artifice or planned contrivance of means to purposed ends on the part of the dominant: but of a semi-conscious exploiting on their part of an elementary human instinct too obviously in existence for its possibilities to be ignored. On the other hand the practice of altruism as opposed to its theoretical exhortation, subserves urgent egoistic needs on the part of the second-rate egoistic powers. If its observance by the dominated serves the egoism of the dominant inasmuch as it spares their energies from the necessity of constant reassertion of superiority, it spares at the same time the vanity of the dominated. The "status quo" which at first blush was accepted through necessity and fear by the class which that "state" leaves subjected, is, thanks to morality, afterwards accepted in happy submission by dint of the tactful assaults which the moral concepts make on their vanity. Owing to the comforting hypnotism of "morality" and its "altruism" the submissively dominated are able to flatter themselves with the thought that the "Great" most scrupulously desire and strive after the formers' own special and particular "good": that these actually make themselves anxious on account of the state of their souls in addition to care for their temporal good; and later, in return for the adoption of the course of action enjoined by the conceptual scheme—action which always turns to the Good of the established, by the way—they are rendered happier still by the sound of the inflating "well done" of their betters. It all works extremely well. Man is the vainest of the animals, and individual men are vain in inverse ratio to the stoutness of their spiritual stamina. The "Crowd" the Non-distinctive, the Majority being the vainest, the appeal of Morality realises its own special hunting-ground in their midst. The "Crowd" provide the country's moral backbone. They even make a boast of it. And sensibly enough since such Conduct as we arrange to live by, we arrange also to praise if we value our own comfort. And the adoption of Morality is as much a piece of distinctive human ingenuity—a display of intelligence—as is the adoption of Arms. That it is more definitely connected with the swagger of the dominated, whereas prowess in Arms is the swagger of the Dominant, need not necessarily induce the former to misprise the solaces of their class.

❦

Tennyson somewhere sings, not without a gasp of surprise indeed at his unexpected discovery, of the speech which half reveals and half conceals the thought within[1]. As far as the speech, which moral concepts are wrapped in is concerned, the poet has gone wrong in his proportions. Their *whole* intent is to conceal: and the motive is as purposive with those who practice them as with those who teach. That both sides are inarticulate and only semi-conscious does not detract from the superlative skill with which the set purpose is achieved. It enhances it rather. Moral principles resting on altruism, by a skilful sleight of hand conceal the fact that altruism is an illusion created to subserve motives wholly egotistic; that the interchange can be effected without raising a breath of suspicion, is due to the suffusing influence of one of the most fundamental elements affecting human emotion: to the action of vanity.

Vanity skilfully played upon goes a long way towards confounding even the soundest human judgment. As palpably as heat expands a gas, flattery expands the human spirit beyond the normal. It is this sense of expansion which causes men to feel pleasure; it is the sensation of conscious life in actual being: it is in fact the sense we call power. A flouting of vanity depresses spirit, and creates despondency. Both actions—inflation and depression—tend to take place the more readily the flimsier the vital force on which repute acts, but it is probable that on no single intelligent human being can they fail to make some little variation. It is true that those who are concerned with their own self-initiated interests and with

---

[1] ≠ "I sometimes hold it half a sin / To put in words the grief I feel; / For words, like Nature, half reveal / And half conceal the Soul within." Alfred Lord Tennyson, "In Memoriam" Part Five (1845).

whom the powers which have play over their spirits are more self-centred and self-impelled, are less responsive to outside treatment. It happens however, that with the vast majority of men, obedience and imitation are the strongest springs of action. To be capable of acting from a self-interested motive is extremely rare. Hence it turns out that the balance of pleasure for most men must be come at by way of honour conferred by stronger and more definitely conscious egoistic powers. The balance of satisfaction when all has been counted in fear of failure, fear of envy, of punishment, hostility, fear of lonelissness, and a deadening sense of uncertainty—for the vast majority of men falls on the side of honour rather than on the other. Accordingly men's actions inevitably set towards Honour and the earning of Applause. Whereupon propitiation rather than aggression becomes their natural role. It becomes their virtue and all forces—men and things—which make little of propitiation—which is peace, love—are their natural enemies. All things propitiatory become thereupon "good": propitiatory proposals, offers of peace, civility, mildness of temper, and all species of intra-mediation are "good": and those who make them are "good": and it is "good" to fall in with them. "Good," that is, for those who love Honour, for Morality, for the reputation of Altruism. Hence the moral demands find in these second-rate egoists a mind and temper ready prepared for them: those who desire to be persuaded are already waiting for those who will persuade them: the two come together by an inevitable attraction: the outcome of a natural desire to make use of each other. United, they make a compound hard and resistant enough to baffle all attempts to break in upon it: a nugget to break one's teeth against rather than to crack. Between the ardour of each for the other there is nothing to choose.

❦

There are unobserving persons who imagine that human beings desire a commodity which they call Truth. How truth is a much-used word which may mean anything or nothing according as one is pleased to employ it: but allowing for the moment that it means what such persons imagine it to mean, *i.e.*, a faithful description of passions and motives and of the relative powers among the individuals of a community, it is the crassest stupidity to think that people desire truth or anything approaching it. You, dear reader, don't want such truth about yourself. I, dear reader, won't have it about myself. The maximum quantity of this species of truth which you and I can stand is just as much as we are compelled to swallow from our own disillusioning experiences; and even this amount we prefer not to discuss with any, particularly not with familiars–families and friends. But many of us are not averse from airing this truth as it relates to others: our rivals and acquaintances, though even here we must he content with a reasonable amount: penetration must not penetrate too far because instinctively we are aware that some short distance beneath its surface-layer the fabric of truth is in one piece: lower than a certain depth the same fabric covers us all; penetrate inwards too deeply and we all stand with our motives naked and exposed. And our motives are far more elegant clothed, as clothed they are. Men have clothed them partly, perhaps, on account of use and comfort, and partly because they have conceived a shame for them: a shame which is the reverse side of the cult of Honour in fact. Only the external motive—the altruistic motive–is kept in evidence: the motive which was the motive of the show of altruism is concealed: instinctively men know that it is of the egoistic and dishonourable kind, and a poor specimen at that. Men would never indeed have fallen into the attitude which makes them ashamed of it had they not been aware that it was poor. Altruism is egoism at the second and tenth rate, adopted because of one's inability to make headway in the best. If men do not feel themselves possessed of the power to make themselves respected on account of their skill in getting what they want they compound in a purely egoistic bargain and become Moral. And serviceably and comprehensibly enough. The pleasure they will get from applause is likely to exceed any satisfaction they expect to get from enterprises initiated by themselves: and on show of the balance their egoism makes choice-for a cloak of altruism. (The disadvantages they meet will form another story.) But because they are not proud of the necessity which forces them they conceive a quite sound detestation for the "Searchers for Truth": alongside their approval of the preachers of the Moral Ideal. They are suspicious of the evidences of "Truth": they are not suspicious of the Moralist's praise: they have no need to be, because praise to them is an end in itself: it is what they want: the *bona fide* exchange for the services they have rendered.

The Trojans were advised to be on their guard against the Greeks when they came offering gifts; and sensibly, because such gifts to the Trojans were of small concern: had these gifts been more to them than Troy itself what would there have been to fear in receiving them? So with the Moral and the Dominated's reception of the praise of the Moralists. Their praise is Honour and Honour they have made into the crown of life: how should they then allow the prying chatter of so-called "Searchers for Truth" to endanger that which can confer on them their most desired boon: allow the spoil-sports and kill-joys a free hand amongst their own selected "good." And a moral community is not going to welcome with a shout of glad surprise a too closely probing inquiry into the reasons of morals! They consider it is enough that they are moral because it suits them, *all things considered*. And they are not prepared to regard it as good manners to inquire beyond a point what those things are. Their elaborate altruistic make-believe: their artificial moralist construction is built round about what for them constitutes the charm of life: subtly flattered vanity. The fact that it is all on an "artificial" basis: a verbal basis does not affect them: indeed the fact is lost sight of until civilisation gives place to war: when this base proves to have been not only artificial but a trifle flimsy.

Men find morality none the worse, *i.e.*, it gives no less satisfaction because it is artificial than a picture or a novel does because it is artificial; the subtlest situations in life gather round just those things which are most frail at their foundations, assumptions which, by a tacit understanding are allowed for, but which are too perishable to be battered about in discussion. The artificialities of civilisations are not despicable because a sword may one day shatter all their delicate and subtle tracery; they are to be despised only when they fail in that which they set out to accomplish, *i.e.*, to provide satisfactions equal to or greater than those which they might have attained by a more natural, *i.e.*, a more frankly egoistic application of ability would have furnished. One would be for instance an ingrate, not to say a fool, to cavil at those aids to beauty which an ill-favoured human adopts to avert at least the repulsion of his fellows, just because they were artificial: if they serve their purpose. Very amusing, charming, important, and impressive are the things which are "artificial." Even a Krupp gun is artificial. In fact it is not artificiality which affects the question: it is utility. The measure of the value of artificialities like the measure of the value of everything else is gauged by the purpose to which they are set, and their efficacy in achieving that purpose. And purposes depend on the men who propose them: their spiritual size among other things. He is a sad and sorry man who seeks to frame a purpose bigger than he has the capacity to enjoy the achieving of. So a man with a passion for big schemes but without the capacity to effect them draws greater satisfaction from being a doorkeeper in the houses of the great than he could eating out his heart toiling at his own bench, the independence of which his taste cannot relish: it is, in fact, too independent for him. What he would gain in satisfaction, of course by so doing, he sacrifices in status: but then all satisfactions demand their price. When these are greater than our natural competence provides for we perforce let ourselves out into bondage if bent on securing them. Our too great wants and our too small abilities are the exploiter's opportunity.

One begins to understand why cranks and their works come to so little. They have the misfortune to witness an indiscretion: one little brick in the wall of pretence has fallen away and one thin shaft of light has revealed egoism and duplicity at some point in the scheme of things. And for the rest of their lives they live in wonder and uneasiness at their own discovery. They devote their energies to the blocking-out of that one gleam. They inaugurate a "propaganda." That it is but one thin pencil streak of an ever-shining sun-like orb does not occur to them. The world, to be sure, is heedless of their "discovery," and is in no way "upset" to meet their "exposure." Nor is it alarmed by those who cry out against "Cant." Though men do not clearly *know*, they instinctively *feel* that one who makes a fuss about "cant" does not understand cant. They feel it is not cant that is objectionable but poor cant: cant that is so badly sung that it fails in its purpose, *i.e.*, the complete deception of those whom it is intended to impress. The way to deal with him who objects to cant is to ignore him or soothe him as the case may demand, but never to follow up his argument. The Church of Rome has the prescient understanding which knows this: it does not make the mistake of thinking that doubts can be laid to rest piccemeal. It knows its business and promptly anathematises doubt. It knows that the correct answer to all the arguments of the Devil is to kill the Devil. Nor is the World greatly put about by those who make light of its morals on the big scale: it forgives its Napoleons as soon as their immediate disagreeableness is forgotten and withdrawn: while as for the immoral on a small scale, men content themselves with administering the usual and necessary severe rebuke and punishment. It is a different person for whom they reserve their full implacable rancour. Napoleon at the close of a single century after his death is already held in honour more or less: but four centuries have passed since Machiavelli wrote the *Prince*, and he still remains "Old Nick." In fact, the Devil is a symbolic generalisation of all the injuries done to the Altruistic Interpretation by those who dare to crumble the moral concepts, and lay bare their egoistic foundations: so robbing them of their popular title to Honour. The Devil is the common spirit of all Blasphemers everywhere: Blasphemers being those who speak injuriously against the Sacred Words. The Blasphemers are the figures drawn up in antithesis to those of the Heroes. A Hero is one who represents the sublimation-point of adhesion to the Divine: his distinguishing attribute is his close kinship with the Gods to whose greater glory his bold deeds minister: that is, he is one whose deeds establish the Word-System, the

Moral-Scheme, the Altruistic-Good, by providing them with a supremely hypnotising Crown of Honour.

Of course the Moral or Altruistic Scheme holds good only within the limits of the particular community which has conceived its own sum-total of the "All" as the single Organic Unit. Morality can only find a place in a community in which the various factions have tried their strength, and have more or less contentedly accepted the verdict and settled down in their suitable classes as Servers and Served, Dominant and Dominated. When two such moral communities are at logger-heads and proceed to violent war, moral blandishments are at a discount. As it is not the common people–the practisers of the altruistic and the moral—who make international wars, but rather the dominant and more strongly egoistic classes, the warring parties do not attempt to address each other in terms of morals save in so far as it is necessary to spare the moral susceptibilities of their own respective following—their respective crowds. Otherwise, in war, it is bluntly a struggle of Might against Might: and all the weapons of Might are pressed into service precisely in so far as they give promise of success, *i.e.*, of crushing the opponent. But articulate spokesman of neither side could say as much openly because of the attentive ears of their followers as was said above: They know that sooner or later this specific kind of warfare, fierce as for the moment it is, will cease for a period and no matter which side wins or loses each will have to settle down in their own communities and make good once more the Altruistic Tale among their fellows. A wise economy, therefore, teaches them that though war compels them to stand face to face with all verbal veils withdrawn before the eyes of an acknowledged enemy, it is not necessary to destroy these veils. If they have no place in war they have a place of extreme importance among subjected peoples as long as ever the Dominant seek to perpetuate submission by dint of the artifices of peace: by Words in preference to the Sword.

Dora Marsden
(1882 – 1960)

The Gospel of Power Concentrated

Dora Marsden Quotations
Selected and Arranged
by
Trevor Blake

p. 270
p. 231

W HAT a blight it is on life, to be sure, that honest speech is almost non-existent. Lo and behold, all are alike: the secret sin against the spirit of peace is universal, and can be proclaimed from the housetops.

p. 110
p. 181
p. 189
p. 110

The "poor" man is the one who lacks the power to get what he wants. If he had had the "might," the "competence" to cover the wide expanse of these "rights," he would not be in the position of a beggar asking for the favour of a job from a master: he would have set about being his own master: the one thing which to this day the ordinary wage earner steadily refuses to be. "Reformers" have tried to get a comprehensive view of the "world's work"—which does not exist save in their own imagination—and they have come to neglect and hold lightly work viewed from its only real aspect—the personal satisfying of needs and wants as they rise up spontaneously from each varying individual. Social rebels will get no way until they acquiesce willingly in men and women being what they are: accept their oddities and wayward differences and then make the best and most of them to serve their individual ends.

p. 199
p. 273

The egalitarian would have men treated as they imagine some ideal person called "Man," whom they have in mind, should be treated; but as men are unlike this "Man" as cheese is unlike chalk, the treatment is not forthcoming. A person who is a shuffling hanger-on will not be treated as though he were a strong independent self-reliant individual. He will be treated, i.e., used; i.e., exploited for what he is, just as the strong man will be exploited for what *he* is. Men do not act after the anarchistic fashion one towards another. They are friendly and affectionate animals in the main: but interests are as imperative with them as with the tiger and the ape, and they press them forward.

p. 27
p. 226
p. 248
p. 250
Democracy represented the increase in the number of people who are prepared to take liberties (*i.e.* persuade by personal violence), with the people who refuse assistance in the furthering of the audacious ones' interests. The belief in the ultimate success of the entire democratic schemata is based on the assumption that men prefer the safe and placid joys of peace to the spirited risks of war: an assumption which is refuted hourly, in spite of the fact that all the accredited mouthpieces dub the one the "lofty" and the other the "degrading." The reason the Government has thought it necessary to augment its ordinary great powers by the infinitely greater powers which accrue to it under socialism is for its own sake and not for the sake of those who will momentarily benefit by its action. The present socialistic conditions will last as long as the Government needs them. Should the politicians under popular pressure seek to perpetuate them beyond that period they will be faced by the opposition of the only persons who really count; those of initiative who, released from, or tired of the sport of the war, will be setting about their own individual business again.

p. 354
p. 218
p. 145
Altruism is egoism at the second and tenth rate, adopted because of one's inability to make headway in the best. If men do not feel themselves possessed of the power to make themselves respected on account of

their skill in getting what they want they compound in a purely egoistic bargain and become Moral. The voices of authority echo one to another all the world round with the cry of "Believe, believe." They mean, "Leave decision, leave it, leave it to us." Saviours, in concrete fact actually spoil the landscape for those whom they believe they serve.

Raise any issue which touches upon the fundamentals of the word-games, as distinguished from moves made within them, and the authorities encompass themselves about with the label "sacred," as promptly as a threatened city would hasten to ensure the integrity of its walls. Wisdom lies in choosing the kind of test which one may calculate one's preparations and increase of strength has fitted one, for it is the probabilities of success which make the joys or woes of the contest. p. 218
p. 235

The exhilaration of fighting which is an elemental need thus recedes from many men's grasp—necessary though it is: which explains why such men will fight for sides while they refuse to fight for themselves. Those who can least afford to spare attention from their own development are the very ones who are devoting the bulk of their energy to the purposes of others, for the simple reason that they are more attractive. After a while, relying on a little trick of words, they will even claim the alien order as their own. It is their own, of course, for just so much as it is—that is a sense of being in touch, however remotely, with the dominant. when the Sword is challenged, Promises are futile: they flee to the refuge of the future, and the Sword ultimately is absolute: it is blade against blade. There is lacking p. 235
p. 237
p. 243
p. 258

a High Gardener; hence the ushering of the Gods into the game. Since the game is earth-made we must all play in it; since only the Chosen may prosper, we all elect to choose ourselves and create our Gods to prove the authenticity of our Choice. All our Gods we create on one principle: we create them in our own image, and give them proportions to match our own; then "culture" sits in judgment and gives to the largest God the palm.

p. 260
p. 261
p. 291

The earlier human dodge of overcoming sub-human enemies by hurling weapons at them from a distance was an effort to protect themselves from the damage which results from an intimate trial of strength. Later, when men found their enemies among themselves, the more intelligent of them sought to overcome their feebler fellows without the trouble of a trial by strength, and invented "culture," whose essential function it was to furnish a super-gardener, who by his mysteriously intimate communications should persuade these that they are Weeds in the interests of those—His Elect. The Gods always play the gardener, making a bid for earth-room for their chosen by demanding that the non-chosen shall fall back to give them place. Culture says, "Thus far and no farther." Asked why, she replies, "Because you 'ought,'" or, "You 'ought' not"—the only effective opposition to the "we can" and "we can't" of individuals. The confusion has arisen out of an assumption that ultimate authority lies in words; that every difference can be settled amicably if only it is argued earnestly enough; that courts of arbitration are final; that the legislature is the fount of power.

p. 137
p. 112
p. 237

Moral and legal forces are part of the machinery

whereby those who think property "good" try to make us "respect" our neighbour's property: whereas the fit and feasible thing is for each of us to respect our own. The "poor" are submitting to a degree of governing which would never have been attempted had it not been glozed over by the fact that it was done *with their consent.* Those who can least afford to spare attention from their own development are the very ones who are devoting the bulk of their energy to the purposes of others, for the simple reason that they are more attractive. After a while, relying on a little trick of words, they will even claim the alien order as their own. It is their own, of course, for just so much as it is—that is a sense of being in touch, however remotely, with the dominant.

The fact to be borne in mind is that whether one "should" or "should not," the strong natures never do. The powerful allow "respect for others' interests" to remain the exclusive foible of the weak. There will always be those who are born tools, those who to relieve themselves of the burden of being responsible for themselves are more than willing to become not merely the appendages and tools of others but the tools of any instrument which should yield itself to their service. Some men are cuffed while others do the cuffing. The really queer and odd factor concerned in the morals clustered about theft is that the propertyless take so readily to them. p. 26
p. 51
p. 176
p. 140

Not all the "poor" however are thus pathetically and bemusedly silly. They are not all putty made for the moulder's hand, ready to be shaped by the p. 140
p. 141
p. 118
p. 113
p. 119

"statesmanship" of the perfect statesman. What the intelligent "poor" in their present perilous position are set to solve is the "calculation as to consequences." When the assumption that we all obey is shattered, the sense of responsibility for self-defence returns. They have either to be prepared to tug at the bundle of power and possessions or take what is given them—if anything is given them—and be thankful. Civil War would furnish a springing board for the "poor" to open up new "lines" of "order."

p. 226
p. 41

To kill is the first necessity of living. This fear of personal violence which we all have, and which is in no need of augmentation, has been sedulously worked upon in the interests of humanitarian democracy. Yet it is clear that all power in the long run is tested by its possessor's willingness and ability to risk encountering personal violence. All initiatory action belongs essentially to the spirit of fight, and is full of risks because it rouses antagonisms: a fact which the humanitarian, egalitarian, peace-loving fraternal spirit of democracy plays upon when in its systentatised attempt to eliminate exceptional power in the spirit of fight it tries to put force into the moral cry, "There is no precedent." Those who call out for freedom desire, not freedom, but property, and property is won and held only in virtue of the possession of power.

p. 77
p. 133
p. 297
p. 338

The power of self-appropriation and of self-defence will always dictate the terms in virtue of which property is held: will always decide what is "just." Apart from this power of the owner to work his will upon objects, "property" is not property: it is mere substance—part of the objective world, whatever we will to name it. Property is that which, being a non-initiatory body, can offer no self-defence, and becomes, automatically, the possession of those who can best defend it. "Being free" is a matter of possession of power, therefore: why then has the "cause of freedom" resolved itself into an onslaught—into endlessly reproachful tirades—against the iniquities of the possessors of power?

Authority is like opportunity: not something given and fixed, but adjusting itself from moment to moment. The very dash and daring and picturesqueness of the aggressive may actually give birth to an interest in which the non-combatants will find themselves involved by sheer fascination: to such an extent even it may be that to be permitted to share in the general risk of the fight will appear a high privilege. A great aggressor will find he can always count on this. The conquerors have been the well-beloved. The world should be moulded to my desire if I could so mould it: failing in that, I am not to imagine that there is to be no world at all: others more powerful than I will see to that. A willingness to risk one's life to the uttermost is as regular a feature with men above a certain modicum of soul-power, as eyes are usual features in the head. Risk is as necessary as water and bread. Not because a man does not value his life, but because his life has imperative needs which he is at pains to satisfy, and of these the excitement of risk is one. All growing life-forms are aggressive: "aggressive" is what growing means. Each fights for its own place, and to enlarge it, and enlarging it is growth.

p. 215
p. 277
p. 281
p. 265
p. 272

372

p. 228
p. 175

The artificialities of civilisations are not despicable because a sword may one day shatter all their delicate and subtle tracery; they are to be despised only when they fail in that which they set out to accomplish, *i.e.*, to provide satisfactions equal to or greater than those which they might have attained by a more natural, *i.e.*, a more frankly egoistic application of ability would have furnished. There will always be classes, and the power of initiation which a man has will always be the index to the class to which he belongs. The "competence" of individuals varies: varies to an enormous extent: and it follows, therefore, that what each individual can, in subsequent bargains, "justly" demand (justly, *i.e.*, with due regard to the individual's powers effectively to back up his demand), varies equally. That is why the equality argument never cuts any deeper than sound.

p. 179
p. 111
p. 28
p. 339

The crucial test of competence is not what men can force others to disburse, but what each has the power to set about producing for himself. The basis of all concessions, whether from men, governments, or nature itself rests on the power to compel them. Those who *can* govern, *i.e.* forward their own interest to the detriment of those who let them, *will* govern. What can entitle save power—competence?

p. 216
p. 197
p. 197
p. 321
p. 139
p. 40
p. 242

It is not the positive qualities of the great which ensure their instalment in office, but the negative quality of those who permit them there. The law is irrelevant as regards the rich who could have no sane motive in coming by possessions in the prohibited ways. That there are no laws against rent, interest, and profits, or against speculating for profit proves that by instinct the law has kept clear of any attempt to put a term to the obtaining of the lavish rewards which fall to the superiorly "unequal." Individuals may settle and arrange matters among themselves only within limits: by verbal or written means. Violence remains the prerogative of the State. Such is the basis of civilisation, and it explains what civilisation is the expression of: *i.e.*, enforcement by violent compulsion of ways of settlement among a governed people who have been deprived of any power of gainsaying such external settlement by a previous deprival of arms. The big thieves regard prison as outworks of their various enterprises: the houses of correction which a kindly state for some unaccountable reason supplies them with gratuitously. Universal brotherhood is mainly subscribed to by people very capable of giving the salutary cut to the simple brother foolish enough to assume that they mean it. Polite society being held together by an assumption that promises will be kept, the bounder can exploit it by utilising the assumption while failing to accord it respect. A society calls itself polite when violence is not included in its methods of reproof, and the bounder can therefore go far without hurting his skin.

Might even in these deluding times still forms nine parts of most laws. A law is a command accompanied by a threat, in case of refusal, to use all or any of the forces of compulsion which it is known or assumed are at the disposal of the framers. The stronger the State the more "liberty" it can allow: it need not shatter the first tiny little fist that shakes itself against it. Speech, press, assembly, love, all are "free" when they have

p. 293
p. 319
p. 341
p. 341
p. 322

power enough behind them to foot the bill when the consequences fall due. Though civilisation depends upon Justice, Justice depends upon gunpowder, and civilisation therefore depends upon gunpowder ultimately.

p. 76
p. 196
p. 134
p. 196

For it is obvious that the whole of "life" is based on a system of "stealing": that is a forcible laying hold of required commodities without permission. If the "eyes of God" have looked with favour on anything it has been upon the sporting instinct of good losers as well as good winners, and these same eyes have been always ready to frown on those who claimed to be equal with all men. Properly is "one's own," and driven from one owner it finds another as inevitably as water seeks its level. And an owner is a master—one who does with what he possesses according to his own nature. To maintain a fair field and no favour in order to clinch the matter: to be satisfied to let the best man win in ungrudging recognition of "inequality": these are the best traditions of virile peoples, and furnish the evidence that worth is shown not merely in the possession [of] a high degree of power, but also in intelligence which is capable of recognising it even at its own expense.

p. 111
p. 127

A man's "liberty" is always at his elbow: always as much of it as he has of "power." It is not the opportunities that are lacking but the power to accept them.

p. 307
p. 325
p. 243
p. 41

"Right" always, as the hymn says, wins the day: that is, Might wins it, and having won it, is automatically invested with its new title of Right. "Rights" shrivel to the dimensions of their virtual merits: to their might. Might is invoked to vindicate its offspring. Veiled though it is, the nature of the instruments which the penal code utilises are of the Sword: of Might: manacles, the bludgeon, the lash, the gallows. Authority shattered, the only right is might— right to what one can get, that is: one's just dues.

All directed forces are the outcome of the spiritual: that is, animated by the living spirit. A gun, an airship, all the material appurtenances of war are aggressive evidence that spirit has been previously at work. The army of the veriest tyrant is all composed of the workings of mastering *spirit*. Might is spirit: there is no doubt of that.

p. 311
p. 293

An egoistic explanation will always be confined to the very limited few who find their major interest in observing their fellows; and this for quite valid egoistic reasons. Power is the first requisite no matter what the "want." The necessity for power can never be laid aside, if there be any wants left: aggressive wants or peaceful wants. One's just due is what one can obtain if one chooses to put the particular issue to a test of trial by strength. The "free" and the "powerful" are one. When one has the power to encompass a certain end, one is "free" to do it: not before. To be free means no more than that—to be powerful in any particular direction specified. It is its possession which makes masters. The self-provisioning of weapons of offence and defence which will compare with those of their present masters is the first concern of the propertyless who now depend upon "employment" by others as a means of livelihood.

p. 251
p. 110
p. 111
p. 174
p. 312
p. 208
p. 142

p. 235
p. 232
p. 234
p. 234

The exhilaration of fighting which is an elemental need thus recedes from many men's grasp—necessary though it is: which explains why such men will fight for sides while they refuse to fight for themselves. None of the objections made against war in times of peace have the force it was calculated they would have in keeping the desires of the people weaned from war when an opportunity presents itself to wage a good one. A fight is merely putting to the test activities of any kind. Like a test in any other sphere it is of the nature of an examination, and its object is to ascertain status, by trial of strength. It is the pivot upon which turns the balance of what is elementarily just and exact. In peace we muster the strength which in war we put to the best show possible. To remain too long at peace is dulling and disappointing for ability as it would be for a young singer or violinist to practise scales and exercises interminably, without the hope of one day putting their powers of strength to receive the verdict of the world.

p. 283
p. 136

The "problems" of the world—which are no problems—will be solved by the "down-and-outs" themselves: by a self-assertion which will scatter their present all too apparent anarchism. All properties are as fluid to the acquiring as air is: they know only one authority: the will which can command them; and the means which can command them can be as readily sought and found in the individual will, as can the force which primarily conceives them as desirable.

p. 273
p. 137

The world falls to him who can take it, if instinctive action can tell us anything. Whatever method serves best to the getting and holding is best.

Quite possibly a life joyously, richly, alluringly lived, p. 266
is the fullest and finest gift to his fellows a great genius p. 308
can give. It is so easy to bruise the joyousness out of p. 254
life in crushing life's essences to distil Art. Out of an
audience of ten thousand there will be five men who
are chuckling under their breath at the spectacle: the
five who stand for more than the remaining thousands.
The track to anything we definitely want, we scent;
and though we might not be able to advance rapidly
along it, we should not be misled very far in a contrary
direction.

Sources

Glossary

bona fide (French, p. 199, 354): in good faith.

bouleversement (French, p. 213): overturning.

bourgeoisie (French, p. 36): wealthy and powerful.

de rigueur (French, p. 332): strictly required.

dramatis personæ (Latin, p. 211): main character.

en bloc (French, p. 231). all together.

en train (French, p. 79): carried by force

esprit de corps (French, p. 236): enthusiasm for membership

ex cathedra (Latin, p. 55): spoken with authority.

faute de mieux (French, p. 287): lacking an alternative.

French leave (English, p. 30, 31): to depart without approval.

henid (German, p. 75): "unconceptual feelings" (Weininger).

in Excelsis (Latin, p. 223): to the highest degree.

niaiseries (French, p. 335): foolish talk.

noblesse oblige (French, p. 125, 332): the obligations of nobility.

pace (Latin, p. 55): peaceful disagreement.

pari passu (French, p. 52): progressing equally.

pas du tout, messieurs (French, p. 118): not at all, sirs.

point d'appui (French, p. 236): location of assembly before a battle.

quid pro quo (Latin, p. 42): favor for favor.

réchauffé (French, p. 125): left over food or ideas.

sans cérémonie (French, p. 138): without ceremony.

tant pis (French, p. 320): too bad.

Tria autem sunt quae nos tentant, caro, mundus, diabolus (Latin, p. 329): Three things tempt us: the flesh, the world, and the devil.

A Brave and Beautiful Spirit: Dora Marsden (1882 – 1960)
by Dr. Les Garner
New edition, foreword, index, illustrations.
486 pages, ISBN 978-1944651145

Dora Marsden Bibliography
by Trevor Blake
Thousands of entries on Marsden, Joyce, Pound, etc.
318 pages, ISBN 978-1944651176

Der Geist
by Trevor Blake and Kevin I. Slaughter (editors)
The journal of egoism as published between 1845 and 1945.
200+ pages, ISSN 2639-5339

Confessions of a Failed Egoist
by Trevor Blake
Explications, ruminations and fulminations.
140 pages, ISBN 978-0988553651

These and related title available from the publisher...

UnionOfEgoists.com

Index

385

388

Lightning Source UK Ltd.
Milton Keynes UK
UKHW020640170321
380507UK00013B/1042